More Praise for *Even the Daybreak: 35 Years of Salmon Poetry*

This book is a marvellous testimony to what a small but passionate publishing house can achieve. Ironically, their strength lies in their size and the fact that they have managed to retain control of their destiny without compromising on their belief in poetry and their championing of writers who would otherwise not have been heard.

MATTHEW GEDEN, *Southword*

At her Cliffs of Moher base, Jessie Lendennie works in collaboration with Salmon's visionary book designer, Siobhán Hutson, who has designed fabulous covers over the years. So many poets have had the benefit of Salmon Poetry's care and attention that the index of poets represented in this anthology runs to almost three pages, aside from the extensive bibliography and biographical notes.

PADDY KEHOE, *RTE*

This beautifully produced collection is a joy to read. If you enjoy poetry, it will be a lovely book to add to your collection. If you are an occasional reader, it will give you the chance to discover new poets from among this huge breadth of writers.

SALLY VINCE, *The Clare Herald*

... I got up toward the breaking of the day
to take my bearings from that broken dream,
but all the streetlamp gave me was a room
much like the one I slept in as a boy,
except the buses didn't run all night
and there weren't any ships braying upriver.
Out where the planets were was dark as ever
for all my lack of motive to look out
and wonder anymore. Whatever they said
was there I took for granted, what was not
was not, and what a man could do I did
about the things I had some say about.
Anything much else was in the mind of God,
even the daybreak, what there was of it.

from "Manchild"
by MICHAEL HEFFERNAN

Even The Daybreak
35 Years of Salmon Poetry

Edited by
JESSIE LENDENNIE

salmonpoetry
*Celebrating 35 Years
of Literary Publishing*

SALMON POETRY

Editor: Jessie Lendennie
Book Production & Design: Siobhán Hutson

First published in February 2016 by Salmon Poetry Ltd.
Reprinted in October 2016 by Salmon Poetry Ltd.
Cliffs of Moher, County Clare, Ireland
Website: www.salmonpoetry.com
Email: info@salmonpoetry.com

ISBN 978-1-910669-40-2

COVER PHOTOGRAPHY: *Jessie Lendennie*
COVER DESIGN, TYPESETTING & LAYOUT: *Siobhán Hutson*
PRINTED IN IRELAND BY *Sprint Print, Dublin*

Salmon Poetry gratefully acknowledges the support of
The Arts Council / An Chomhairle Ealaoín, Culture Ireland & Clare County Council

for Eve Catherine Hutson Jeanotte

Contents

New Poems from Salmon Poets 1985-2016

(Poets are listed under the year they first published a collection with Salmon)

Introduction by the Editor

So, I was thinking about how hard it is to keep a reader's attention focused on what you'd like them to know, and how maybe it's me who has the short attention span; who feels like everything has to pack a punch. Poetry gets its punches in, for sure, but it's getting through the first layer of notions that makes the challenge. I've been writing pieces that I call poetry for as long as I can remember; which makes me one of those people prone to abstraction and easily obsessed with the worth of ideas and precise words.

Even the Daybreak represents 35 years of my life that wouldn't exist without poetry. Well, I would have existed somewhere, I guess. Let's say that it's 35 years that wouldn't have any meaning to me without poetry; without poets.

I'd like to say that I can look back critically, without nostalgia, but that's not possible. Talking to some of the poets Salmon has published in the early years is like dropping though time and bringing everything with you. In the same way, say, as reading Walt Whitman's 'Crossing Brooklyn Ferry' and know that you're listening to him right next to you; watching the Manhattan skyline. In other words, timelessness; essential in poetry.

In the late 1970s I worked for The Poetry Society in a lovely old Georgian at 21 Earls Court Square, London. This was a chaotic time in British poetry, basically the classic revolution/innovation vs. establishment battle. The 'spoken word' or 'concrete' poets, lead by Bob Cobbing were set on shaking the lead out of the British Arts Council bureaucrats, and you can imagine what fun that was. Crazy evenings with spoken word exponents, mixed with sedate middle class gatherings. Well, you can read about all that in Peter Barry's *Poetry Wars: British Poetry of the 1970s and the Battle of Earls Court* (Salt, 2006). When I arrived, the battle was calming, with poets like Ian Robinson and his little magazine *Oasis*, easing the pressure; smoothing some jagged edges.

In the 1970s Irish poetry was also moving into new territory. There were few literary presses in the early 1970s. Liam Miller's Dolmen, established in 1951, had a well-deserved reputation for excellence. Michael Smith and Trevor Joyce's New Writers' Press was very active. Peter Fallon's Gallery

Press was starting out. However, it took the womens' movement, and a broader view of what literature could accomplish to reflect the changes that were taking place in Irish society. Dermot Bolger's Raven Arts Press, established in 1977, initially published broadsheets of local Finglas poets. This was a great step in moving poetry out of its academic and historic restrictions. Arlen House, founded by Catherine Rose, focused on writing by women, as did Attic Press, founded by Roisin Conroy and Mary Moran in 1978. The Writers' Co-Operative, founded by Fred Johnston, Neil Jordan and Peter Sheridan, published fiction by new Irish writers. Beaver Row Press, started as a co-operative in the early 1980s. Its principal founder, Glenda Cimino, published initial poetry collections by Paula Meehan, Anne Le Marquand Hartigan and Brendan Kennelly.

That was all happening in Dublin (Arlen House started in Galway, but moved to Dublin). The rest of the country had plenty of poets and writers, but not a lot of outlets for their work. Wexford had *The Gorey Detail* and there were a scattering of excellent others. I can't go into detail here, so let me just move on to Galway, 1981. That summer, my then husband, Michael Allen, and I came over from London to live "a more creative life". Within a few weeks, we saw an ad for a writing workshop in *Façade*, a magazine from University College, Galway (now, NUIG, of course). How could we not go along? The workshop, based in the Ladies' Club at UCG, was loosely connected with the English Department and Tom Kilroy's classes. We soon moved away from any academic definitions, and within a short time, produced a pamphlet of poems and short fiction (of course, as one does). Initially *Poetry Galway*, with a focus on writers in the West of Ireland, after a couple of issues, it became *The Salmon International Literary Journal*. Nothing, if not ambitious! As novelist Patrick Sheeran, then Professor of English at University College, Galway (now NUIG), wrote in his guest editorial for our first issue: "... In a paradox typical of our time, the workshop is both at the centre and the periphery of literary activity in Galway. Meetings in the Ladies' Club of UCG on Saturday mornings is a sufficient indication of peripheral status. The making of poems and stories, their mutual encouragement of one another's work, that very difficult openness to all-comers, all testify to their being at the creative centre..."

Thinking of that time, Des Kenny of Kennys Bookshop & Art Gallery, Galway wrote to me:

"There is a memory, somewhat hazy and, therefore, probably romanticised, of the shop door opening one Summer morning and a young Lady sailed in wearing a flowing colourful cloak somewhat reminiscent of an Adrienne Monnier or a Sylvia Beach. In her hands she had what looked like a small pile of badly printed pages which with an air of pride and dignity she presented to my mother, Maureen Kenny. The mother graciously accepted the offer, priced the leaflets and placed them on the counter. The ceremony, for ceremony it was, was imbued with a tremendous sense of joy and dignity. Salmon Poetry had come into being and these leaflets were its first fruits. Over the next 35 years, Salmon Poetry was to become the platform on which the young poets of the West of Ireland and further afield, giving voice to such, now internationally known, poets as Rita Ann Higgins, Mary O'Malley, Anne Kennedy, Moya Cannon and Patricia Burke Brogan. This comprehensive anthology brings these 35 years back to life allowing the reader to relive the extraordinary poetic energy and creativity that it engendered since that halcyon day in 1981. It is a journey well worth taking."

Another early, and most welcome, supporter was poet Eavan Boland. She reviewed *The Salmon* journal in *The Irish Times* in the mid-1980s and commented later: "Salmon Publishing is one of the most innovative, perceptive and important publishing houses in the UK and Ireland. It has fostered and supported the work of new writers and has established them in the public consciousness."

Fintan O'Toole wrote: "In recent years, Salmon Publishing has become unquestionably the most important publisher of poetry in Ireland. The publishing of poetry has always been a venture which requires courage, dedication and imagination, since it is very seldom a straightforward commercial enterprise. With very few exceptions, poetry books are unlikely ever to be bestsellers. Yet anyone with an interest in the arts knows that poetry has an influence on many more immediately popular forms. The voices that are given expression in poetry go on to re-echo through fiction, theatre and even popular music, and this has been even more obviously the case in recent years in Ireland. In this sense, Salmon has been an essential seed-bed, not alone for Irish poetry, but also for a much wider spread of artistic activity. No one else in Ireland in the last few years has been as prepared as Salmon to publish previously unknown poets. Salmon has not merely accommodated new voices, it has actively sought them out. And the general cultural significance of this work has been made immeasurably more important by Salmon's innovation in discovering and publishing the work of so many women. Poetry has been arguably the most important mode of expression for a new generation of Irish women writers, and Salmon has been the most important channel of that expression. In this light, though it has itself been a small and quiet enterprise, Salmon's work in recent years has been of large and loud importance. Salmon has done Galway, Irish poetry and Irish women proud, demonstrating the great significance of forces that might have seemed to be outside the mainstream. It is important to Irish culture as a whole that that spirit should not only survive but grow and blossom."

This was great support, indeed, and it became even more so when Ireland had its own version of the Poetry Wars in the 1990s (more about that in my memoir!).

Over the years, it has been hard to keep going. In 1991, after 10 years of *The Salmon* journal, I had to stop publication for lack of funds. The Arts Council has given support since the early days, when the wonderful Laurence Cassidy was Literature Officer, but there are times when you have to sit and wonder if it's all worth it. To me, it's still about the poetry, and so we go on. I say 'we' because Salmon would not go on without Siobhán Hutson, who has worked with me for the better part of 25 years. Her beautiful book design, and production skills, are second to none. We share the load and I would be lost without her.

Several others have worked with us for varying times, notably poet Jean Kavanagh, novelist Elizabeth Reapy, and our super-intern Katie O'Brien. Elizabeth and Katie worked hard on this anthology, for which we are extremely grateful. We also want to thank Anne Kennedy, Barry Carr, Tim Jeanotte, Maureen Clancy, Brenda Dermody, Nancy Thompson, Edna Faye Kiel, Jacqui Hersey, Daire Skuce, Barbara Brown and Catherine Doyle.

My thanks to the original members of the Galway Writing Workshop, particularly Mary Dempsey, Mike Watts, Mike Reidy, and Trish Fitzpatrick.

Very special thanks to Michael (M.G.) Allen who was there at the beginning. Neither one of us would have done it without the other.

And for their essential support over the years: Tess Gallagher, Dermot Bolger, Eavan Boland, Fintan O'Toole, Des Kenny and the Kenny family, Adrienne Rich, Carol Ann Duffy, Ray Bradbury, David Hill, Victor Luftig, Patricia Monaghan, Jerah Chadwick, Sheila O'Hagan, Ted McNulty, Joan & Joe McBreen, Joseph Woods, Jeremy Addis & Books Ireland, Seamus Hosey, Thomas Dillon Redshaw, and all our brilliant poets.

The first section of *Even the Daybreak: 35 Years of Salmon Poetry* is a selection, including Irish language poems, from *The Salmon* journal. The second section contains new poems from poets who have published collections with us. Where a new poem wasn't available a poem from a previous Salmon collection is included. The poems are arranged chronologically according to the year of the poet's first book. Most of these poets have published more than one collection with us.

So, here's to Poetry, and the next 35 years!

JESSIE LENDENNIE
Cliffs of Moher & Ennistymon, Co Clare
October 2016

THE
SALMON

Poems from
THE SALMON INTERNATIONAL
LITERARY JOURNAL, 1981-1991

(Issue 1 — 1981)

JESSIE LENDENNIE

Misunderstandings

i.

With practiced fingers
the musician plays.
Behind his back
the listener sits —
aloof and watching —
seeing imprints,
fallen notes
upon the floor.

ii.

You and I
in fading pattern
weave our thoughts
with one expression;
phrase our silence
into meaning
only this to keep
our distance.

iii.

Days that find me
waiting here:
light and shadow
interspaced. Blue
and white,
clouds and doubt;
a stormy day's
misunderstanding.
From a weak sky
endless rain.

(Issue 1 — 1981)

M.G. ALLEN

New Ireland

You do not understand the steps of time.
Fearful of its faltering, you decry
our white new homes — the bones
of a long starved land at last revealed.

Each corner of the twisted road is hammered
flat, the stone walls where the forge blew red
and smelt of leather and of iron
are pushed aside, lie cold.

No imprint remains. Cattle nose for grass
through abandoned rooms, brambles
and blackthorn barricade the lanes
which tied the scattered homes.

We build, like conquerors, upon our own remains
giving no thought to the names of fields
or rocks. But this is our only certainty:
time here is slow, well understood.

It has draped around us, like an old woman's
shawl. We know each knot, the rising
and falling of each stitch. We follow well
the unbreaking, secret ways of thread.

A ruin is a ruin, from the famine
or the fifties' grants. When the fire
is not lit, the damp thatch sags and falls.
Time drips its salt upon the stones.

If you had lived on here among
these small flames, watched the families
flake away like skin, you would bless
these first new homes, naked and white.

Time will weather them
from innocence. The red west wind
will colour them, the untired land
will swallow them up, at last.

21

(Issue 2 — 1981)

TIMOTHY ALLEN

Snow

Excitement wells deep within
on looking through the cold window
at white flakes dancing on the wind.

I open the door wide and gaze
at the iron-grey sky and the wild falling snow.

The snow remains, clutching
tightly to the frozen earth and rocks.

Every way I turn, the cold whiteness
is all about me.

(Issue 2 — 1981)

MIKE WATTS

Peaceful the waves
As low as the east
The tide of the evening
Laps its retreat
Warm is the sky
As orange glows red
A blanket of velvet
Draws overhead
Softly the breeze
Stirs over the sand
The slap of salt water
Caressing the land

(Issue 3 — 1982)

MICHÉAL Ó CONGHAILE

Creimeadh

Péire seaclaí
mórthairnithe chíocha
scaoilthe scartha
ag rás na mblianta
á streachailt.

An dá mhórchíoch seo
rite tar éis a mblite
athscaoilte h'éis a mbrúcht athlíontái.

D'fhí aois agus siaraois
ag cur brí i mdaoine
a dhiúl lena mgcunnshaol iad
faoi smurach pislíní
gur mhair.

Anois i gcuimse reicne
de shiar gan staon
táid ag siarchrapadh
tirm
        seargtha
ag sealú.

(Issue 5 — Autumn1982)

GER REIDY

Daisy Chain Dream

Thistles rustle; in the ruts of the tractor wheels
Wool from unshorn sheep dangles from barbed wire
Cows intoxicated with grass doze in the midsummer's heat
Briars grow through the windows of the Morris Minor
While nettles investigate the engine
In the village they are dipping the sheep
An annual ritual with oriental gaiety
In Wood Quay they discovered the Vikings
A gladiator was found in Pompeii
In Mayo they'll discover a bachelor saving hay

(Issue 6 — Spring 1983)

GERALD DAWE

Responsibilities

(For Brian Friel)

The child turns in a cot
and stars increase what hold
they have over the infirm
and forgotten whose time
this is, near enough to dawn,
when back-rooms are washed
with light and down along
the Esplanade the sea booms
around the shining rocks.

It's like I haunt this
dormitory town of parks
and one-way streets,
of evangelical picnics
and children screeching
through days on the beach,
for there in the rented
redbrick holiday homes
families keep the faith,

and, for all I know,
those who lie awake
reading the Old Testament
dream of tomorrow's excursion
and pray for the sun.

(Issue 6 — Spring 1983)

MICHAEL EGAN

Letter to Roseanne

Lately I've been reading Emily
Dickinson. Her unruly presence rippling
behind the pages, slanting the sense,
reminds me somehow of you—

what a siege of contraries in you both.
Self-exiled to chintz and muslin, to filed
receipts for cakes laced with spice,
and one exotic outpost,

the garden, she caroused with sultry tulips
and strolled arm in arm with death
and madness. 'Like St. Jerome, a writer
should work in his cell'.

Perhaps she was the nun of Amherst,
its secret abbess. But you're the girl
who shot the nuns, zeroing in on blue
habits, on silver crosses,

watching the blood desert them, disloyal
to the end. Anorexic, beer in hand,
like Reb cavalry you'd turn-up unexpected,
wild with gothic highways,

weary of nights in the tank. When sheriffs
tore up your license, you rode with redclay
farmers on truckbeds or local buses,
or tracked the snow with your dogs.

You always loved loud weather, the tips
of stately trees swaying in windstorms.
But once I saw you sitting beside a woodstove,
grading student papers,

as if in lace and whalebone. Constrained
by the Old South, by white steeples
and brimstone mammies, you still wrote
'decorum's the fourth denial,

a refusal of light, a hoarding of blood.'
Lately I've been wondering how you are,
what towns you've stormed, hill and tidewater,
what waterfronts you walk,

the old shapeshifter, laughing in her beer.
And I've often wondered why, for you,
for me, a plank in reason broke,
and we dropped down, and down. . .

(Issue 7 — Summer 1983)

THOMAS McCARTHY

Ballot Box

Der Fallon took the black box in his arms
and stepped outside. The light of that morning
I remember well, and the little farms,
the smell of sealing wax on everything.
Even blackbirds were confidential in
trees: they moved when we moved, without alarm.

I had a day from school to help take notes
and Der had a restoration of pride —
the duties of Election Day made fate
seem kinder, brought power back to his side,
as he walked the lanes to the polling-booth:
box carrier and reaper of somnolent votes.

CIARAN O'DRISCOLL

Man with Macaw

This man with a multicoloured bird on his shoulder
often got on the underground at Burnt Oak.
The multicoloured bird would sometimes shed
feathers that schoolchildren grabbed as he sat
mute and trusting on the man's shoulder,
just a little apprehensive, you'd know that
from watching the not-quite-still claws.
Not so much as a squawk from this
serene and multicoloured bird
on the shoulder of a serene-looking
man who wore shabby clothes. They seemed
to lend serenity to one another.
Often he smiled back at smiles,
talked in a matter-of-fact way about
moulting and birdseed, and civilly answered questions.
Always for me his arrival in the carriage
was like the first time I ever saw him,
unobtrusive but slightly wonderful –
Man with Macaw, serene
man and multicoloured bird, children
watching for the fall of a dazzling feather.
Often because the tube went no further
we got off at Colindale and waited
for the next one to take us to Burnt Oak:
so ordinary it seemed then, a man
standing on the platform with a macaw on his shoulder
that stern faces softened and dry tongues
found a couple of friendly words.

(Issue 7 — Summer 1983)

MATTHEW SWEENEY

Lili Marlene

He sits at a table in artificial light
drawing circles on a page. A record
plays behind him, painting the air
the colour of old cleaned-up wars.

He thinks of the new strategies
that leave no room for blue fictions
only facts, such as radiation
and cockroaches who'll inherit the earth.

And stopped cars with their skeletons
hotel-suites, galleries, wine-cellars
music such as this — all of them
if they want. They possibly know.

The song begins again: words
about barracks, a corner light
and a girl who waits there at night.
He recalls a chemistry lesson —
how a tear makes a perfect meniscus.

LOUIS DE PAOR

Cluain

Mo lámh greamaithe i bhfolt na mná
airím do ghlao
ó thaobh eile an iarnróid chugam
is torann na mbuataisí
ar leacacha loma ag druidim leat,
is airím arís pléascadh na bpiléar
ag roiseadh an aeir go hard
os cionn tathaint gargach na traenach,
urchar ar urchar ina bhuille oird
ag daingniú na dtáirní tré mo chosa
go dtránn an traen as amharc orm
carráiste ar charráiste folamh,
go slogtar do ghuth
sa tost tórach ina diaidh
is seasann sí fós os mo chomhair
ag lúbadh focal
le clagarnach slabhraí ar chaola mo ghéaga,
a súil mhiotalach dírithe
ar chlár ró-leathan m'éadain,
méar léi casta go múirneach
ar an dtruicear.

JOHN F. DEANE

Last Days of Donatien Alphonse François, Marquis de Sade

Eventually, then, it has come to this
quiet; all that frenzy of flesh, the rare
extravaganzas of the brain, and all
those words: an old crabbed gentleman,
haughty, morose,
sipping his herbal tea
in the hospice for the insane;
he walks, burdened
with his chill courtesy, circling
perfect flower-borders of the lawns, ward
of the ministry of the interior.

'You will lay me out on a neat
four-poster bed, as if
I had found life a starched design;
now I fear
only death's semblance; watch
this body for any twitch of flesh, frisson
of thought; after two days
nail down my coffin as you will; scatter
acorns on my grave, and let my name
fade from the truckling minds of men.'

(Issue 10 — Summer 1984)

FRED JOHNSTON

My Father at Ain-El-Hadjar

My father at Ain-el-Hadjar
would have been, for a time, amazed;
he would have lazed passionately
beneath the sun

his back dug into a poppy-field.
He would have watched the train—
hands resting upon the barrier—
as if it should not be there

passing from mountains into desert
coming from nowhere. The buckled old
Arabs would have been old faces from
familiar days, their dark eyes the

eyes of fisherman relatives
at Portavogie. Life would make him
look quietly, but lack strangeness;
this would amaze him most of all.

The closed church with mosqued steeple
could be along his Sunday stroll,
back lanes near Castlereagh, the red
Sahara clay no less solemn—his people—

than the unwaving wall-grass, the
Methodist's piety written on the closed
doors. Here he would open the collar
of his shirt, relax.

He would call his son up from dreaming
of books he'd never have time enough to write:
frown into the crazy desert, clear his throat.
'Now, son, about your life. Let's have the facts.'

(Issue 11 — Autumn 1984)

ROISIN (ROZ) COWMAN

Peanuts

The way it was, for us children
during the forties,
in those narrow market-towns,
cow-spattered, curtain-twitching,
tinker-crazed on fair days,
and we picking our way through forests
of drunken giants' legs...

it should have turned out better
for Charlie Brown and Snoopy,
roller-skating, top-spinning,
in backyard prairies of bungalows,
down the broad sidewalks of A

MARK ROPER

Holly

for Joe

Branches flailed the sky,
Berries tight-stung like an abacus
To count away the winter
As you carried down the tree
Through a dead snow-shuttered land.
Later as we drank tea by the fire
I remembered the fresh white of the cut trunk,
The green bark's bitter scent.
I couldn't keep my eyes from a small shoot
Placed in a jar; its shot of berries
And glinting scalloped leaves a taproot
To a deep unnameable joy.

(Issue 14 — Spring 1986)

CAROL RUMENS

Presentation To An Art-Director

They've had 25 of your years:
That's why they've opened the board-room
to the trolleys of red and white Spanish,

to the crisps trodden into pale carpet,
the segments of quiche, and the peanuts,
and the gift you hope isn't a watch.

That's why they've garnished the lunch-hour
with well-chosen words from the bosses,
carnations in button-holes, wilting,

and the chatter and posing and noise
of a crowd mostly half your age.
Some of them dug out a photo

of you when you first arrived.
They pasted it onto a card.
Now everyone jostles to glimpse

the boy at the drawing-board, dreamy
but stern in his Van Dyke beard.
His expression suggests that he's seen you,

but is firmly disowning you
as you lay him aside, with your glass,
and, smiling, turn to the crowd...

(Issue 15 — Summer 1986)

GREG DELANTY

The Alien

I'm back again scrutinizing the Milky Way
    of your ultrasound, scanning the dark
        matter, the nothingness, that now the heads say
    is chockablock with quarks & squarks,
gravitons & gravitini, photons & photinos. Our sprout,

who art there inside the spacecraft
    of your ma, the time capsule of this printout,
        hurling & whirling towards us, it's all daft
    on this earth. Our alien who art in the heavens,
our Martian, our little green man, we're anxious

to make contact, to ask questions
    about the heavendom you hail from, to discuss
        the whole shebang of the beginning & end,
    the pre-big bang untime before you forget the why
and lie of thy first place. And, our friend,

to say Welcome, that we mean no harm, we'd die
    for you even, that we pray you're not here
        to subdue us, that we'd put away
    our ray guns, missiles, attitude and share
our world with you, little big head, if only you stay.

(Issue 15 — Summer 1986)

NOEL MONAHAN

The Bishop's Gallop

Why did you return
To avenge your swineherd years
Crossing hedge and lichen bog and fen
A stonemad countryside
Where unkempt women manned the earth
Made love in lazy-beds.

Was it to spoil sport
To uproot woods of sacred timber
Planting clergy in fields and gripe
Shamrocking, exorcising
Reducing gods to God
Foddering out sacraments
Smearing, sickling druids' oats
Assisted by habit making monks
Nuns knotted in vows up to their thighs.

Who gave you the reins
The easy gallop everywhere
The heartwood silence of the woodland priest
Felled in lowered darkness
Groping at the grave of change

The grass snakes were prudent
Took an early boat to England,
Missed the sharp dogma
On the whetstone crosses
The scars of heaven and hell
An infirmity we nurse since the orchard.

'Twas an easy gallop
A short race with a long result
Over a raw baby on golden straw
Frosty star years ago.

(Issue 15 — Summer 1986)

GERARD SMYTH

Corca Baiscinn

for James Liddy

None can leave and none may enter
the stone circle pitched like the ruins of empire.
And who is left to listen to rainfall
on the fresh tar at evening
on a road disappearing over the edge of cliffs?

Nothing equals the desolation
of the house where mist does not stop at the threshold.
The holy wells run dry —
drop by drop the thirst of those who've drunk
from them is multiplied.

Flowers of the Burren are balletic
in the penumbra of dusk.
Land of dark skies, land of too much light,
of bleached rock, karst meadow —
a bed for the hermit

who comes to rest, to hear the old music
of wind in the crevice.
The stump of the cross, the castle that crumbles
shall rise again
in the child's book of colours.

(Issue 16 —Winter 1986 — 5th Anniversary Issue)

EAVAN BOLAND

The Women

This is the hour I love: the in-between,
neither here-nor-there hour of evening.
The air is tea-coloured in the garden.
The briar rose is spilled crêpe-de-chine.

This is the time I do my work best,
going up the stairs in two minds,
in two worlds, carrying cloth or glass,
leaving something behind, bringing
something with me I should have left behind.

The hour of change, of metamorphosis,
of shape-shifting instabilities.
My time of sixth sense and second sight
when in the words I choose, the lines I write,
they rise like visions and appear to me:

women of work, of leisure, of the night,
in stove-coloured silks, in lace, in nothing,
with crewel needles, with books, with wide open legs

who fled the hot breath of the god pursuing,
who ran from the split hoof and the thick lips
and fell and grieved and healed into myth,

into me in the evening at my desk
testing the water with a sweet quartet,
the physical force of a dissonance —

the fission of music into syllabic heat —
and getting sick of it and standing up
and going downstairs in the last brightness

into a landscape without emphasis,
light, linear, precisely planned,
a hemisphere of tiered, aired cotton,

a hot terrain of linen from the iron,
folded in and over, stacked high,
neatened flat, stoving heat and white.

EVA BOURKE

The Alder

I come to the rescue of the alder
that grows at the back of the garden.
The old weatherer of storms,
host of pebble-grey spiders and their spun-yard
fabrications, their mock suns,
of enamelled beetle and countless
miniature armadillos,
of chaffinch and thrush,
is dangerously ill.
For three summers and winters
it deceived me with rich glossy foliage,
but now I've got wise
to its pernicious Siamese cousin,
the common creeping helix, the ivy
to spread out its own top-
heavy evergreen crown.

With sharp blade and clippers
I tear into the parasite,
lop off serpentine growths,
pull limb from limb,
lift varicose knots
to lay bare to the daylight the damage:
wild crop of deadwood,
corrugated bark, powdered with sawdust,
a trunk wrinkled like an elephant's leg
and desiccated by thousands of hairfine roots.
I cut and snip down the hanger-on,
the sap-sucker growing strong
on the alder, how it is everywhere,
this colonialist, holding the tree
in a wrestler's grip

with its bearded tendrils,
how it clings and chokes to put out
its waxen ink-coloured berries.

Why go to the trouble, I ask myself,
perhaps it's too late. Should I take the saw
and make room for fresh wood?
But I can't harm the alder
giving shade in farmyards,
hoisting its white flags over country roads,
holding out saucerfuls or violet-black fruit
all for the birds.
I think of the fragrance of the alderflower
on late spring days, of its yellowish wood
"pleasantly grained and very suitable
for carvings",
its lip-reddening juices,
its sudorific teas and wines and dishes —
Sambucus nigra, famous all the way
from here to Siberia.

I'll go on with this liberation.
A green mountain grows below me
as I climb, loosening tangles,
opening clenched fists,
unravelling this networks stranglehold.
And the alder thanks me,
so I imagine,
it straightens and breathes,
shaking its branches.
Its leaves rustle as green light strikes
the stem for the first time in years
with full force
driving the roots deeper into the ground
where the water is purer.

(Issue 16 —Winter 1986 — 5th Anniversary Issue)

RITA ANN HIGGINS

Men With Tired Hair

On a bank holiday Monday in Galway,
you can see old men
sitting on window sills in Prospect Hill

Time is not a factor here,
only images pleasing and displeasing
to the men with tired hair.

Despite this easiness with life,
there is a waiting, a look out
in anticipation of something.

The looking up and down continues.
The awaited stimulus always comes.

Day it's a young woman.
Streets it's a fire.
Years it's news of a tragedy in far off Dublin.

NUALA ARCHER

The Lost Glove Is Happy

Is it in the terminal I left
the brown, rabbit-fur-lined gloves
made in Taiwan? Gloves
I've worn in Ireland.
Gloves that kept my fingers
warm walking the bitter cold
coastline of Bull Island
with Howth and her necklace
of lights in the background.
Gloves lost now between Stillwater,
Oklahoma and Lubbock, Texas
on the way to see my mother.

'Come,' she said. 'I'm in
the midst of desolation. Come.
Take Southwest Airlines, past
Love Field. I'll be waiting
for you. I'll be waiting.'

And in the mall, when I got
to Lubbock, arrived to embrace
my mother in desolation, she had
me strip, try on outfit
after outfit — sweaters, trousers,
skirts, shirts, shorts, slips
and blouses — to see like
Mary, Mary, quite contrary,
how does your garden, my garden,
grow? She in her mid-fifties
and me at the cliff-edge of
twenty-nine. My mother had me
fly to Lubbock and on the way
I lost my rabbit-

fur-lined gloves. When I got
there, when I arrived, when
I reached desolation, my mother
alone, in the middle of crazy
cottonfields, I reached her,
I travelled to her,
to desolation, and in desolation
we were as lost as any
two mismatched gloves and
for a few moments we relaxed, lost
and strangely happy,
in the Lubbock Mall, without
labels, stripped to our bones.

(Issue 17 — Summer 1987)

PATRICK COTTER

No Surrender

As assuredly as our dreams will be peaceful
(you rolling as a giant penny down a hill
of fragrant orange trees, I as a swimming-
needle backstroking through a paisley sea
of silken twists and folds) the first flames
of evening will come whirring (musically
almost and like a bandleader's baton)
through our bedroom window,
asserting on us their exotic and highbred
origins: Cocktail de Molotov: Cocktail
de Moleneaux: de Molloy. Delightedly
we will bathe in their expressive warmth,
allowing the fire to lick and curl about
our most intimate parts. We will listen
intently to their messages, their theses,
their raison d'etre:
— We're here because you shouldn't be!
— Ulster is two nations, we one you another.
And then we will die, content that we have
shared in a cultural exchange of the most complex
and civilized kind.

(Issue 17 — Summer 1987)

HUGH O'DONNELL

Inarticulate

In Curragh Chase my throat is burning
with an April flu while the tea time sun
warms my back and shoulders. I am standing

halfway down a pathway by a stream
charmed by birdsong and, where it overflows,
a pan of water frying. I close my eyes

and dip my fingers in, let the chill
of water smack them cold. I want to drown
my ear in melodies that prisoners cannot hear

for I am cut off by words from what I know
I love. As I walk away with my cool shadow
for company, the lisp of fluent water grows

fainter until it mingles with the breeze;
this is the language in which to love —
beyond imperative, close to the bone!

(Issue 19 – Autumn 1988)

SARA BERKELEY

Less Than A Hundred Hours

I have put on a warm skin
I have come in
From the garden, where a pallor is caught
On every thorn.
You know it's you I see at evening
Before the light goes.

The secret alters with the hours
Sleep slows the colours
But in the morning, waking from some warm place
It flowers timidly against the covers
Pale on the pillow where six hours of sleep
Damp down easily to a drawing of breath.
You know it's you I see at evening
When the light goes.

It is less than a hundred hours
And the secret fits so close I have almost grown to it,
Something I have touched a lot,
I know its shape by every light
Its colours deepen as the day arches
Towards noon,
Dragging its heavy form
By night it has become
Hot and damp in the palm
And now it is less than a hundred hours
Until you come.
You know it is you I see at evening
Before the light goes.

(Issue 19 — Autumn 1988)

PAT BORAN

Have You Left Mountmellick For Ever?

Old yellow hut at the end of the garden,
jet sprays aerosol foam on the sky:
Have you left Mountmellick for ever?

The convent has me drunk on wine
uniforms. Maguires' dog snaps a trap
of teeth through their gaudy fence.

Have you left Mountmellick for ever?
The Christmas tree is still up — in April —
just a naked spear. I expect to see

the shrunken head of Christmas
or you continually zebra-crossing to make
the boys in leather jackets grit their teeth,

stamp their cigarette butts out and cry,
gulping back years of lust and tears:
Have you left Mountemellick for ever?

(Issue 19 — Autumn 1988)

MOYA CANNON

Thirst on Ceann Boirne

No other ground or floor
is as kind to the human step
as the rain-cut flags
of these white hills.

Porous as skin,
limestone resounds sea-deep, time-deep
yet, in places, rain-water has pocked it, worn it thin
as a fish's fin.

From funnels and clefts
ferns arch their soft heads.

A headland full of water,
dry as bone,
with only thirst as a diviner,
thirst of the inscrutable fern
and the human thirst
that beats upon a rock.

GLENDA CIMINO

Arthur and Marilyn

(People wondered what she saw in him.
People thought they knew what he saw in her.)

'With all her radiance she was surrounded by
a darkness that perplexed me.'

Arthur Miller, *Timebends*

He saw her light,
but was drawn to her darkness
the same darkness he felt inside himself.
For a while he loved her,
saw her as she saw herself,
even as she wished to be:

a serious person, an artist,
unifier of fragmented selves.

In the end he could not give enough:
To listen endlessly, to hold her
every night against the darkness
til she fell asleep, to exorcise the ghosts
of her troubled dreams, to be her bulwark
of strength to snuggle into, to take

responsibility for her life, to be
the person *she* wanted to be;

Perhaps to fill the endless unfillable lovehunger
of the abandoned child, to heal
the psychic bruises of the abused child
beneath the beauty
Perhaps in the end just to repeat for her
the old and painful pattern: separation, loss.

But maybe this isn't their story at all.
Maybe it is my story; or maybe it is yours.

(Issue 19 — Autumn 1988)

ROZ COWMAN

The Goose Herd

The first angels must have been
like this, intolerant, haughty,
slightly clumsy, their wings
more beautiful than themselves,

and not respectful to the godhead
but watching, chins lifted,
hearing false notes with
spiritual ears.

There would have been no mutiny,
but a remembering of wild
blood at the equinox,
a stir of stony wings

against dark cloud, taking
the last light with them,
leaving the godhead resentful
because it missed their noisy blasphemies,

cursing them, and naming as Hell
their destiny . . . a wild, lonely place
of sudden laughs, wailings, grey
down clouding the sight like ash.

(Issue 19 — Autumn 1988)

ANNE KENNEDY

Cairo

Rain straifes our city bus.
Beside me, a lady with tinted glasses remarks
she has no umbrella,
she lost it months ago in Paddington Station,
that cave of bears.
No doubt some station master's daughter
is sporting it through London's seamless streets
or knowing how they clean the trains
it lays still furled in a corner of the luggage rack.
She can see it laying there:
(she'd give anything to have it back).

'Oh, I've had other umbrellas,
a green one once with a broken spine
that I couldn't lose in a fit,
but this umbrella was special
because it doubled as a third leg.
I need that, you see, a disguised walking stick
and the handle, a carved bird.

Ah, but one takes one's comforts
in the ordinary little courtesies.
Just today a lovely man gave me a lift
when I asked directions
to a furniture showroom out the road,
'Hop-in,' he said and I was young again,
I was twenty and life was full of adventure.
I've bought myself a little house, you see,
and I want to furnish it.
Today was a very lucky day for me,
asking directions,
but nowhere in the world have I met people
who know so little about where they are —
the men are desperate but the women far worse.

Is it because they live under their
husband's protection?
Women do that, you know, they follow money,
they do, you know, they really do.
Myself, I'm a tough old bird, a wanderer, solo.
Did you know the French are building
a tunnel under Cairo?
Must be bread and butter in it —
The women here wouldn't even know
where Egypt is.'

The fierce low sun bulleting in
the scumbled bus
lights up her purple-tinted glasses.
I am hurtling beneath baking city streets;
I see Cairo.

(Issue 19 — Autumn 1988)

FIONA PITT-KETHLEY

Prostitution

My *Sky Ray Lolly* was a hit, they said —
few thousand sales, five hundred quid for me.
My *Private Parts* will do as well, it seems.

Chatto's my pimp. My cut is 5 per cent
(well in arrears). Clause after clause decrees
I earn less still and part's kept back for years.

I'm published now, so spin-offs come my way —
performances — I'm paid from fifty to
a hundred pounds for every one-night stand.
Some Scrooges think that I should do it for free,

I also tout my work around the place.
My clientele is small but most select —
George wanted twenty for the BBC,
Karl's had a lot of it at thirty quid,
Hugo and Blake have settled for a few.

It all adds up . . .

It's time to tell the world about my 'job'.
Last year I made about two thousand net.
This year if I am lucky, I'll make three —
too much for dole, less than a cleaner's wage.

I've taken off my clothes for many men,
but never felt as naked then as now.

I'm 33 and can't afford my rent
the smallest bedsit on my salary.
I live with Mum. Our house is stinking damp
and almost everything we own is old —
no, not antique — just knackered secondhand.

What should I do, what chances do I have?
Arvon — the poets' pools? (Yes, we all try.)
The odds are twenty thousand though, to one.

The under-thirties Gregory Awards?
(Twenty two women out of 144.)
I was turned down for one of those six times.
Anthony Thwaite seems guilty on that score —
since Chatto took me up at least — he rang
my editor to say it wasn't his fault.

The Cholmondley and the Hawthornden? They're both
awards where no submissions can be made.
Some men sit round a table, I am told.
Perhaps I'm wrong, perhaps I'm being unjust —
I wonder if they give them to their friends.

Of course, the Arts Council does grants . . . just three.
But '87 was Caribbean Year,
so every applicant had to be black.

One option I have left's to turn to prose.
(Nobody books me to adjudicate:
nobody wants me to anthologise.)

Fiction, I hear, can raise some decent cash —
a brief synopsis brings a good advance.
Half a collection wouldn't raise a p.

Novels have twice the pages, far more words
so editors can write between the lines
to justify their jobs.

I do a lot to earn my five per cent.
My brothel's tucked away in Bedford Square.
Bad pay does not breed loyalty.

I deal with piles of letters from my fans —
most need replies. A stamp and envelope
wipe out the price I'm paid for one book's sale.

I get more letters from my editors,
sudden requests of the peremptory kind —

query on query, meetings, calls on calls —
300 words on why I did the book,
a new CV, a photo or a form.
And everything is needed by return.

'Gifted and strikingly original'
my whorehouse/sweatshop dubbed me in one blurb
'Gifted and strikingly original'
does not bring in a greater flow of cash.
Even their typists get a better screw.

(Issue 19 — Autumn 1988)

KNUTE SKINNER

A Small Construction Site
in County Monaghan

Two men stand at a small construction site,
one middle aged, bald, lighting a pipe,
one young, in a green jacket, holding a shovel.
From time to time the young man lifts the shovel
as if to do something with it, and with himself,
but the older man, a man in a blue sweater,
is taking time with his pipe.

He has cleaned it and filled it, then tamped it several times,
and he has spent any number of matches,
but the pipe won't burn — or else it stops from neglect
as the man resumes what looks like a monologue,
a stream of words on a palpably serious subject.
And all this time the young man fidgets.
He shifts the shovel from one hand to the other.
He pushes it into a small mound of cement
only to pull it back and then shoulder it.
He is a good if a somewhat impatient listener,
and clearly he knows his place.

The bald man, now, has succeeded with the pipe,
and heavy smoke comes spurting from his mouth.
He places a cloth cap squarely on his head
and turns aside to contemplate their business,
a house in a halfway stage of reconstruction.
It's time, he knows, to stand and look at the wall
where a new window waits to be bricked in.
It's one thing to do what the young man now does —
pour sups of water onto the hill of cement,
then quickly, skilfully, fold them in with the shovel —
but the real challenge lies in assessing the window

and the open space along the sides of the timber.
It can't be, and it won't be, done in a hurry.
The space must adjust itself to his measuring eyes,
and some of the bricks will have to be reshaped.
He taps the end of one such brick with a hammer,
cutting it down to just the size that's needed,
working with such absorbing concentration
that his pipe burns out.

In time, when he has the brick just as he wants it,
he ascends a short ladder and stands on a scaffold.
The young man hands him a half bucket of cement,
and the man on the scaffold sets the bucket down.
He transfers the pipe from his mouth to his pants pocket.
He pulls up the sleeves of his old blue sweater.
Then he trowels cement onto a mortarboard.
He turns to the work at hand, so intent he appears
at that moment to be part of the work itself,
a part of something comprising himself and the wall.
The young man stands, a spectator, at a short distance.
He knows how to mix cement,
he is learning patience.

(Issue 20 — Spring 1989)

MICHAEL D. HIGGINS

The Master

There once was an old Master who was
very cold
Each morning outside his school
He'd line them up
Shine your shoes children
Be erect
Shine your shoes or you will
gather faggots from ditches
For the School, for the Parish, for
Jesus and the Civil Service
Shine your shoes.

Inside the school awaiting the
Inspector
He'd stand little girls on desks
And lash their calves
Until weals showed and the
tears came
Know your verbs or you're going
nowhere, he'd shout
You'll be gathering faggots from
ditches
For the School, for the Parish, for
Jesus, learn your verbs.

At evening going home
The villagers would avoid his gaze
Catching their eye the Master might
not
They always froze
For he was a cold man.
It was rumoured that even rabbits
caught in his gaze
would sit
as caught in a light
and wait to die.

At four his wife would say
The Master's home
Children finish your tea
Blessing himself he would eat
He was a religious man
But would not speak.
His Wife
Begetter of their children
would occasionally whisper to
the children
The Master's thinking.

In his room he would sink to his
knees and pray
Oh Jesus I've done all this for you
I've brought order
I've brought discipline
For the School, for the Parish and
for you Jesus
Send me a sign.

And thus it was that one evening
in a blue haze
To his room a lady came.

My Son asked me to come, she said
For he was afraid of you Himself
And he told me to tell you
For Mothers must always bring the
messages

That he said it all on the Mount
Love everybody
But above all,
Love yourself.

The Master jumped from his knees
And tearing off his clothes
laughed and ran from the room
I've had a sign he told his wife
I've had a sign.

Running into the street the
villagers heard the Master's
cries
I've had a sign
I've had a sign.

He ran to the edge of a wood
And they found him
Embracing a tree.

At first they were timid
They were all his pupils at one time
But the braver threw a blanket
over him

Saying
Yes, Master, of course Master,
You've had a sign

They brought him to hospital
Where all he would say was
I've had a vision.

At first the villagers simply said
'Imagine the Master of all people'
And then
'It could happen to any of us'

They visited him in hospital
and they brought him books
which he never read
Saying simply
I've had a vision

And after a while the villagers were
happy
They've allowed him to arrange the
flowers on the altar
Isn't that nice some said
but in the hospital the Master
knelt before the Tabernacle
and said
I've had a vision.

His wife and children came
And he smiled at them and said
I'll tell you a secret
Love everybody, but particularly
love yourself.
That was my vision
His son would sometimes say
Fuck your vision
Stop this nonsense
And they'd let you out.

But the Master would only smile
and say

No my Son
Love everybody
But particularly love yourself
It was my vision
And his son wept
And the villagers concluded
That the Master was mad.

(Issue 20 — Spring 1989)

JOAN McBREEN

This Moon, These Stars

Something is changing.
There is a September stillness in the garden.

We have woken in this bed for years.
You have followed me into my poems,
my dreams, my past, to places I scarcely
know of myself.

I called one evening
from our back doorstep. "Look," I said,
"look at this moon." We stood there
in silence, not touching, not knowing
what to say.

We have been together many days, many nights.
These stars have come out
over us again and again.

Here is the life we are living,
not on a windswept beach, not in vast
city streets, not in a strange country
but here, where we have chosen to be.

I look at myself in the glass, at the woman
I am.

I think of our days, our years running on
into each other.

What will we say,
what will we know.
Separate, together,
will we find the right way, the dream
neither of us can explain.

I pull the living room curtains together.
The garden is around us,
still above us are the stars,
light and indestructible.

(Issue 20 — Spring 1989)

PAUL GENEGA

Dog

The light, my friend,
I see you standing
in a light so bright
and white it's painful.
In the distance, water
winks like a dizzy
old flirt, but here
on the soft sand
of a dune, you seem
somehow to solidify —
lean-limbed, released,
sniffing the wind of
eternity. And almost
grinning, you hold
that pose, proud,
totally assumed.
Until moved by what-
ever it is moves you,
you sprint down
the slope and run,
run and run. Run,
dark speck making
for the ocean, over
the next crest and
nowhere to be found.

(Issue 20 — Spring 1989)

ÉILIS NÍ DHUIBHNE

The Consolation of Fairytales

In the byre with seven windows
where I grapple with a mounting heap of dung
throwing one prong out to see two more roll in
I am at home.

In the stable with seven doors
through which the steeds I try to bridle
run
I am at peace.

On the white mare's back, fleeing
the ogre through a lake of pitch
and a blazing wood

there is hope for me.

And on the wing of the white swan
Flying over the waves to the Eastern World
I am free.

(Issue 20 — Spring 1989)

KATHLEEN O'DRISCOLL

Green Welcome — Fáilte Glas

Sing to us.
Dance to us.
Jump to us.
We have paid our money.
Your traditional music is wonderful.
Your bread is very bad.
What do you mean you feel
It is now time to play rock music?
Everyone knows there is only
Traditional music here.
Your glasses of Guinness are wonderful.
The Irish do not work hard.
What do you mean your countryside
is under-populated?
Your barren landscape is wonderful.
Your roads destroy our cars.
What do you mean you wish
They would plant more fast growing fir trees?
Only deciduous forests
Are native to this environment.
Why do you say it is cold
Having no woods for shelter?
We have all studied ecology.
We find your bare mountains wonderful.
Your showers do not work.
What do you mean you wish
The land was all sown and harvested?
The harbours all full of ships?
The warehouses full of grain?
Your ignorant people should know
That our enlightened élite
Need a haven from the progress

Which has made our money for us.
Your air is really wonderful.
Your must preserve it for us.
Your climate is so wet.
Why do you wear thin shoes?
Your gaelic language is wonderful.
Your people speak too much.
Sing to us.
Dance to us.
Jump to us.
Our leisure is your bread and butter.
Your ancient culture is wonderful.
Your bread is very bad.

(Issue 20 — Spring 1989)

MARY O'MALLEY

Aftermath

Lines from a marriage

Last night I looked at you,
A stark man in this grey country
Of short days and long nightfalls.
I watched you and marvelled
That you should still be here.
I had not seen you much
In the storms of these past years.

Time and God and bureaucrats
Have pared us both down
To some of our essentials
With deft little secateurs,
Or blunt edgeless implements
Such as are sought in murder hunts.

Each inflicted its own specialised pain
As it peeled back, gouged
Or merely hacked away
To reach and reveal a deeper layer.
Here a terracotta shard
Of smashed solicitude,
There a flint of fear.

Perhaps even a purple thread,
Last remnant of some glorious bolt
Of desire. Such delvings and exhumations
Seldom yield the unbroken
Though sometimes beautiful tokens
Are taken out of their darkness
To be exposed
To the light in museums.

They have left me with furrows
And ridges that no coyness
Can rechristen laughter lines.
Yet you are still here
And I watching
Wondered if I would ever know
This defined and distant man
That I have lived beside
As I knew the boy the instant
The air shifted between us
Moments after we met.

(Issue 20 — Spring 1989)

BREDA SULLIVAN

All Souls Night

Last thing my mother did
on All Souls Night
fill the white enamel basin
with water gushing cold from the tap
place it on the kitchen table
turn out the light.

Wandering spirits, paroled for the night,
cooled burning tongues
in cold tap water.
Wakeful in my bedroom overhead
I heard the water hiss
saw the steam rise.

(Issue 23 — Spring 1990)

DERMOT BOLGER

Owen

There are childhood jungles
    Of potato stalks,
Cropped ghosts of gardens
    That I have lost,
Where you belong
    Beside a rooted fork
Weeding leadened beds
    Until after dusk,
Coaxing a damp bonfire
    And breathing in
The reek of green leaves
    And of paraffin.

A dog barking under apple boughs
    Scatters chicks in the hen-run
Where you seek out a treasure trove
    Of warm eggs hidden in straw.
A kitchen door is framed in light
    As the evening dissolves
In a chorus of rural accents.
    The scent of baking wafts
Across your hard-won lebensraum
    To this floodlit balcony
Where I wait for news of you,
    My favourite uncle.

How you would love this night,
    A cold nocturnal breeze,
The creaking limbs of sycamore
    Softened by amber light.
I start a cigarette for you,
    Inhale as slowly as I can,
When its light has burnt out
    Your life will have gone.
Every bulb in the apartment
    Stakes out the telephone
That squats like some sniper
    Awaiting a final summons.

Because now you are corralled
        Between hospital sheets,
Hands snatching at blankets
        Frantically trying to rise.
I know that I am dying
        And I don't want to.
What can you say to somebody
        Who realises the truth?
Uncle, there may be a garden
        Where leaves are never burnt
Like the lining on your lung
        After radiation treatment,

Or there may just be emptiness:
        All I know is that an hour ago
When you lay semi-comatose,
        Your ringed eyes burst open
With a saturating blueness
        As you whispered names of women
That have long been in the grave.
        Then you fought your way back
To the blurred circle of faces
        Who came to share your vigil,
While down the polished corridor
        A pay phone dreamt of coins.

Soon it will be spring
        In the gardens of Finglas,
Lilac and cherry blossom
        Will bloom in your absence.
Another child will run
        Home from the chip shop,
Moist beads of vinegar
        Perfuming his jacket,
His eyes already turned
        Towards Amsterdam or Paris,
Beyond that suburban terrace
        Your country hands bought

With money orders sent
        From an English car plant,
Rhubarb and cabbage sown
        Before reboarding the boat
In expectation of a time
        When you would finally return.

How could you have known
        The cycle would start again?
The final night we drank
        Your skin was drawn tight,
As if already the skull
        Was straining to come forth.

Your features floated back
        When my love's mouth sought mine,
Your scared eyes warning me
        That there is such little time.
That night her lips seemed to taste
        Of all she was or would become,
The mature woman of a new century,
        A dissolving alabaster skeleton,
Back to that knuckled blue embryo,
        Veins luminous in the womb,
With her unformed face upturned
        To engulf my ageing tongue.

Those who planted gardens
        Believed in the future,
Those who built cities
        Had faith in tomorrow.
Fewer neighbours will lean
        Over walls this spring,
Fewer drinkers will argue
        Across that pub table,
Fewer children will be left
        To plant shrubs in your place,
The lilac will wither
        Unplucked on the branch.

Above me a late jet
        Winks one bloodshot eye,
An aisle of young faces
        In a doctored newsreel.
I try to cup the hot butt.
        The cigarette is finished.
Worms of ash scatter
        Down onto the car park.
The telephone is throbbing,
        I step through the door,
It takes me a life time
        To lift the receiver.

(Issue 23 — Spring 1990)

JERAH CHADWICK

Storm Watch

Lichen scaling rock and weathered wood,
young gulls at the tideline
where the sea grates
the shore to gravel, shreds of mist
on the headland — all shades of grey,
the incantatory local colour.

For months I've watched
this beach, the storms
thinning and draining from the horizon
or spreading overhead,
mirrored in surf. And the wind,
relayed by whitecaps, grasses,
as if its violence required
witness, words like the cries of gulls
that flock the updrafts, plaintive

and extolling. Now breezes drive
the water's sheen from slate
to steel. Arguing the tideline,
gulls flap and settle
like the breakers beyond them
trying their wings on the headland rocks.

(Issue 23 — Spring 1990)

PATRICK CHAPMAN

Why I Want to Eat a Dog

Two men meet each other in the sand.
I am one, a wreck behind me,
A can that smells of petrol in my hand.
I ask the other man: is the oasis far?
He doesn't know, and drops down dead.

Days or maybe weeks have passed
Since I have tasted more than air;
I eat him and move on.

An hour after he is bone,
I feel his brain make thoughts inside my own.
He is taking on my body as I walk,
But by the time I fall asleep, he's gone.

Next day, the sky makes matchwood of my skin;
I throw away the petrol can in fear.

That evening I can see the dunes throw shapes.
They dance themselves into a pack of giant dogs.
I want to eat a cocker spaniel, but they disappear.

(Issue 23 — Spring 1990)

R. T. SMITH

Pip

Sea-sparrow and cabin boy,
black Pip from Alabama dances
his Nantucket jig on the Pequod's
calm deck, while the salts
clap hands or reef the shrouds
to the hornpipe's tune and their
mascot's goatskin tambourine.
Later, Pip will pour the master's

grog and lie curled as
a whelk's cell, harbored
under the gunwhales and sucking
a stolen lime. He loves
to scrawl his crude scrimshaw
and call to the gulls, but
water and whales are his bane.
His nightmare is Leviathan's

oil flaming the horizon,
while St. Elmo's ghostly fire
glows in the halyards, but
tonight he is bedazzled by
the rising moon and Starbuck's
talk of Bibles. This child
whose kin crossed the Atlantic's
savannahs shackled in the hold

can write no words or name,
so signed the ship's book with
Christ's cross, the dogwood
mast. His sweet voice and
dervish whirls are enough to

save him in Ahab's wild eyes.
He is no slave nor orphan,
no lost pilgrim after hard

penance upon the waves. Reel
and aire are his scripture,
but his last jig will be
a longboat's pitch, the dirge
of a great fish sounding while
the harpoon's line uncoils
and sings. He will breathe
brine and the sea's green, till

a sturdy current shunts
the dice of his white bones
back to Africa, where no
chains or God-mad captains
rule, where water is sweet and
orchids grow in glory, where
sparrows sing forever and
the moon-hued whale never goes.

(Issue 23 — Spring 1990)

BERTHA ROGERS

To a Lost Friend at Strawberry Festival Time

In the Brooklyn Museum
feathered baskets lay trapped
in sealed cases. Quail and hummingbird
fringes stir, Pacific shells clack
songs nearly audible through the glass.

When the Trickster came disguised,
came looking for California,
the Shaman grew confused, he forgot
his name; his tribe neglected
to clothe themselves
with the feathers of escaping birds.

By the summer of 1968
one old Pomo woman remembers
some shards of language;
a few others grind
acorns into mush, coil
blackroot sedge and rushes
into intricate baskets.

Passionate young men, lazing
over the fenders
of broken-down cars, laugh
from their eyes; they point
fingers at passing pretty girls
who stuff strawberries
as if they were kisses
at their mouths.

Tribal elders cluster
near the edge
of the reservation;
their masked faces unsettle
the upland air. In the valley
the Russian River winds;
the rattlesnake turns
in the vineyard.

Stooping through
the sweathouse door, we hear
voices reach for fragments
of chants. We two white women,
holding our daughters
like offerings, watch
self-conscious braves stumble
to the Singing Sticks.

Then, suddenly, you were lost;
and I, gone in another direction,
our heart-words swallowed
by air, by time, by civilization.

I read the newspapers,
O, my friend, I looked for you
On the lists of Jonestown dead
– you, your flower daughter,
Snow White to my Rose Red child,
children born to hungry-hearted mothers.

I imagine you enticed
by the charlatan, dying in the heat;
or safe in the suburbs,
matron to a well-suited husband.
I see you, wish you walking wild
over the California hills,
your spirit flying above your head,
your feathers lifting in the wind.

(Issue 26/27 —Winter 1991)

ROSITA BOLAND

Mr Larkin

You seem to have said it all, you bastard.
Although writers have coined new words and expressions
That have entered easily into the English language,
Many of your poems have sunk in whole
So that to think of ambulances or high windows
Is to feel whole poems shiver and reverberate;
To feel that this is life faced up to dispassionately
And to have chuckled at it quietly
Without flinching at the bleakness of its reality.

You have pinned down something real and living
Within the frame and structure of your poems,
And they are not butterflies with gorgeous wings
They are dark-coloured moths
With strange antennae that reach out and out
Which I sometimes run from
But always return to,
Lifting the underside of those paper wings
And turning the pages of your calm, grim verse.

I feel I could add nothing but superfluities,
Yet that's what you'd have hated most –
To be set up as some type of guru
So I blunder on,
Often sobered by what you say
Yet immensely exhilarated by the manner
Of your saying it
And so – I blunder on.

salmonpoetry

New Poems from Salmon Poets

with collections published between 1985-2016

(Poets are listed under the year they first published a collection with Salmon)

1985

EVA BOURKE

Berlin Nocturama

The nights are getting colder but the young men
beneath our windows have to stay
on their post till the small hours.

They have come here from Africa:
Eritrea, Zambia, the Republic of Congo,
Cameroon,

we can hardly imagine how, or what
they might have seen
before they left to cross deserts

continents and seas —
in rusting containers, in boat wrecks,
strapped to the underside of trucks —

and were washed up on some
unfriendly northern shore.
They chat quietly

or listen to music on their phones,
they smoke, they wait.
They are masters of waiting.

In summer they stash their merchandise
under tree roots. *Something beautiful for you?*
they say, when we pass.

Now in December they keep it hidden
beneath parked vans.
They ask in a whisper *Everything good?*

blessing us with their smiles.
They wear beautiful colours, sky blue,
bamboo green, corn yellow, soil red,

the colours of their countries
on a colonial African map
for children.

At night you hardly see them
in their dark winter jackets
in the weak glow of the gas lamps

but their dreamy faces light up
when we pass by them,
guardians of our door,

the fireflies of their cigarettes
dance around them
going on and off.

They shelter beneath the descending
wing of the dark,
share it with a lone clubber

or a Roma bottle collector who pushes
his clinking hand cart
along the street.

When they leave
they take the night with them.

1986

MICHAEL EGAN

Letter to my Daughter

Elusive as North Atlantic winds
and as wilful, you foraged the water's edge,
a landbird at sea along the shoreline,
a barometer Gretel in wax and wane

with the sun. Mornings you scoured the dunes,
clearing nests in the thistles, curling
in some sandman's morning-after rest,
in lumbering sleep, uneasy as surf;

and nights, floating free,
you circled the boardwalk comedy, the bible-thumpers
and bikers, or met with friends, and talked
until talk was a trouble, too,

and moved on, free of grounding, as if
the flesh had gradually melted to spirit
under the hands grappling your wrists,
the nameless untyings of your swimsuit,

the sprite in her own Tempest, in hand
to hand combat with nothingness.
If air is all we are, its lulls
are deaths. The spirit knows itself,

and self-contained, may flash with a fire
that sets us free, from net and tether,
the alarm slumbering mornings, the fondlings
we cling to, and finally, even from death.

RITA ANN HIGGINS

Looking out from the Fog

He was an awful liar.
He said they took out his tubercular gland
and hung it on a tree to dry.
No one else said things like that,
it gave us a laugh at the wall.
We were the last of the
leaners-and-blamers-gang.

Gussie owned the tubercular gland story,
and all stinking liver, big small
and middlin' sized tape-worm
in the intestine stories.
He could weave us a lonely streak
with his war and loss stories,
that would make us nearly cry.
And we were big men.
Well some of us were big
most of us were shrinking,
from getting a taste of nothin' these days.

The amount of times he got thrown down
a well and left for dead in his stories
was not funny but we laughed
as we leaned and blamed.
Gussie was a spitter
as well as a leaner and blamer.

He used to say, cross yourself thrice
if you see a suitcase bobbing in the canal.
Like, when were we going to see a suitcase
bobbing in the canal?
He had a whole charm bracelet of weather stories.
He didn't like fog, any other weather
the body can beat he'd say.

But the fog mangles the lungs
like a net curtain jiving with wasps.
He had a thing about lungs.
Wasps he could take or leave.

With fog you don't know who your enemy is.
You don't know where he's been
before he went in.
Is he just a man of fog
or a man looking out from the fog,
or is he a spectre from the suitcase
bobbing in the canal?
With most stories we'd laugh,
with this one we didn't.

1987

CIARAN O'DRISCOLL

The Copper Mines of Peru

A sullen-faced youngster
is getting into his father's car.
He's had a bad childhood.
I had a bad childhood too
but I got over it. Look at me,
I'm going through the cycles
of eternal recurrence.
Unlike my father did on me,
I never laid a hand on him
and yet what his eyes are saying
every time I look at him
is that I have failed him,
that I embarrass him,
that my very existence
was the cause of his bad childhood
What he needs is a good funt
but you can't get away with that
nowadays. I'm driving him to school
but he doesn't want to be driven to school –
above all, he doesn't want *me*
to drive him to school,
and if he *must* be driven to school,
it should be in a Merc or a Beamer.
But what he really really wants
is to have his own Merc or Beamer
and drive himself to school.
Would he be happy with that?
No, there'd be something else
biting him. Some day one of his pals
would descend to school in a helicopter.
Then he'd want a fucking helicopter.
And would that take the perpetual sulk
off his face? Would he get a life then?
You can be certain he wouldn't,

because I'd buy him a shit helicopter
having mortgaged the house to pay for it
and sold my wife into slavery
and sent his younger brother and sister
to work in the copper mines of Peru.
While other fathers would buy his classmates
brand new classy twin-jet-engined helicopters,
his would only be second hand
with a single piston engine
and not one of the girls in the school
would ask him for a lift.
And if I tried to reason with him:
'Son, you can take it from me...'
'Oh Jesus, not that again,' he'd say.
'Let me talk, you little fucker,' I'd say
and he'd throw his eyes to heaven,
heaving a petulant sigh.
'You can take it from me,' I'd say,
'that if a girl likes you, *really* likes you
she won't care if your helicopter
is shit. It's you, not your helicopter,
she'll want – your personality.'
'Tell that to the Marines,' he'd say.
'Anyway, I don't have a personality.
I had a bad childhood – remember?'
And this is how it would finish:
we'd settle down in our sleeping bags
in the cabin of the shit helicopter
parked on a flat rock
on the top of a mountain.
'I miss Mom and Billy and Frida,' I'd say.
'So do I,' he'd say.
'Fuck you and your teenage angst.'
'Fuck you and your shit helicopter.'

'Night, Son.'
'Night, Dad.'

1988

FRED JOHNSTON

Procedure

It will be like this, a fusion in bright light of flesh and steel
Blue smocks that never tie up properly, one's backside hanging
Out like a prank; the quick jabbing nicks and scrapes, days in limbo —

Hung up between knowing and not, it's no place to be
Try reading a book while they pass sentence somewhere
And then go for tea; try to imagine love in such a storm

Better to know, pedestrian opinions say; but it isn't —
You've seen your father strain between morphine sleep
And bone-scouring fire, it comes to you in technicolor, frame

By frame. Better, you say, to hop a 'plane, outrun the thing
Commit unfathomable sin, kill an old enemy. Go beyond ordinary
Law, go down in flames. But you'll do the everyday and pay

A bill here and there, sooner or later pretend nothing happened;
Keep up the scribble, keep shtum, wash the windows —
They may stamp your visa in the end, may yet wave you through.

JESSIE LENDENNIE

Alien

for Eve

There are space aliens
in the trees in my back yard
only there aren't any trees
just mud and rocky holes
made by stone-mad dogs
looking for dog-gold
and once I went out at 3am
and a dissolving star told me
that I had only one lifetime left
and I thought of meeting you
in another country
and you laughing, and saying
that my middle name Aliene
was alien in disguise
and I thought of all the trees
I'd never live in
and I thought of years spent
digging for stars
watching their alien sparkle
drift through the holes in the sky

CLARINDA HARRISS

November Moon

At dark dinnertime yesterday
you dragged me from my desk
where I was trying to cipher some sense
out of the muddle and mess of things

to an east window where the moon
had got snagged in black branches
like a huge balloon, a bulging bag of light.

All last night I thrashed and flailed
drowning in cares and nightmares
till you hooked me under my arms
and pulled me to a west window where

the moon, still enormous, was about to sink
into dawn-gray trees, and I understood
the bed was a berth, the house a hundred
year-old ship rocking on the swells

of the wide wet world as it flowed
around the sun, and I slept
till the sun was halfway overhead.

KNUTE SKINNER

Let's Say

Let's say you're at an open doorway
and standing upon its threshold.
Through the open door you can see
that another door, at the far side of a room,
also stands open.
It's not your house, but you enter.

Let's say that everything looks familiar
but not quite right.
The mirror positioned above a mantel
has cloudy corners.
A bare bulb overhead
hangs at an awkward angle.

An abrupt cloudburst spatters
upon a window.
It desists but heavy drops
depend from the sash
until drop by drop by drop
they gather along the sill.

You're cold, you would like to light a fire,
but the sticks beside the stove
are not your sticks.
Is there anyone there to light one?
You can step through the second door
or you can go back through the first.

There are those somewhere else, perhaps,
who depend on you,
and others somewhere else, perhaps,
upon whom you depend.
Let's say that the rest of your life, perhaps,
hangs in the balance.

1989

ROZ COWMAN

Dream of the Red Chamber

Red tides have filled
the estuary; dykes
are down; the land
of the two canals
is gone.

Old hill, if I tread
stepping-stones of black
bungalows back to the first
threshold, the dream
of a red room,

will you accept
my journey as a rite
of passage, and absorb me

as the hare mother absorbs
her foetus children
into her blood

when spring is stillborn,
and late frosts
salt the earth?

from *The Goose Herd*

PAUL GENEGA

Flung from Pegasus

he dreams only of flight,
wings beating weather,
white mane flaming snow
as he drums the moon
like ewe skin, glissades
distant stars, then storms
the gods' own mount.

Bellerophon wakes
between sheets on the earth,
wakes in prayer
to grey-eyed Pallas
who holds the father thunderbolt,
sets the birds on course —
give back the golden bridle
and I'll never again fall.

But the gods spurn last night's
hero as he spurns mortal men.
Alone, he builds stone temples,
shrines to his own might.
The stables are black,
dawn-edged like Olympus.
Inside he takes vengeance
gelding the only thing he's loved.

ANNE KENNEDY

The Dog Kubla Dreams My Life

I acquired you, old companion,
on impulse from Palo Alto pound
to satisfy an adolescent
urge for someone all my own.

You crouched shivering on the back
seat of my black '48 Chevy, shedding
fair hair, your obsidian toe-
nails slipping on slick upholstery.

Transported into the redwoods
you tore off down the old highway,
a gold whipcord,
lured back with a bit of steak.

In the cabin bathroom, your corner
stake-out made ferny wastes our outdoor
toilet, as you snarled comic guarding
your own ceramic reservoir.

Tamed with coos and coaxings
inta a loyalty hard-won,
I called you *Kubla*
after that nervy invader.

In an attic in Berkeley, you shredded
the socks of my first lover, pawed
ravelled strands beside my rumpled bed,
then patrolled the narrow stairs.

Pacing the pine floor-boards, those wolfish
toes tip-tapped a sentry song. Nobody's guide
dog, you wore no harness, roamed at will.
You could be gone for days prowling

lanes and harbour wastelands or snoozing
contented in some student's kitchen.
They called *Kubla* on Telegraph Avenue,
you glinted sidelong.

When I moved to L.A I entrusted you to a friend
until I settled in where dogs were welcome.
He said you got lost, wandered off, followed
some family back up to the redwoods.

He claimed I had made you too friendly.
Years later I heard you were killed
the week I left,
running towards a woman
calling *Kubla* from the kerb.

from *The Dog Kubla Dreams My Life*

CLAIRR O'CONNOR

Terror

I've been circling the House of Terror
for weeks. I clatter out of the apartment,
down the caged lift, in that one piece
of fine metal that Stalin missed.
Out the front door on my Smile scooter,
pushing and free-rolling my way onwards
along Andrassy, its broad boulevard
making me, if only for a minute
queen of momentum.
I put my foot down, almost
overshooting, when I reach
number sixty. The uniformed security
guard is gasping between puffs
on his cigarette as he talks to an
old woman who, visit over, cries into
her handkerchief. She talks in a soft
American accent—but she was born
in Budapest, fled after the failure
of '56. On the outside walls of the museum
are black and white photos in oval
frames of the long since dead.
Her husband's arthritic hands
film her in front of half a dozen
photos of old friends
as she tells their stories
in Hungarian. From an ancient
string bag she offers Vim,
Tide, tooth powder, Eucryl,
then a pair of red-velvet
high heels—as if the Dead
can be helped by this
postponed largesse.
She is weary now.
The security guard crushes his cigarette
into the hand-held ashtray.
I push myself off
take a right down Csengery,
circle towards home.

JO SLADE

Five Fables

Each time the baby leapt in her belly, the string broke
and she'd tie it again.
She was remembering a child in the next village
how the girl turned a knot of rope, round and round
making a complex puzzle.

Each time the monk hit the wood, the sound of his axe
travelled inside the walls of the monastery.
Locked in a jam jar in his pocket he kept a bee —
he was remembering how easy it is to enter the forest
and find honey.

Each time the shopkeeper swept out his shop, mice scurried
beneath the floor boards.
He could feel them, but he couldn't catch them.
He was remembering how long it takes a man to mine gold
how he can spend a whole life panning
for nothing.

Each time the hairdresser wrapped her head in a towel
her skin darkened, her eyes flashed like two coals.
She could see her sister in the mirror and hear women whisper
huddled in a corner of the souk.
She sat in the chair spellbound.
She was remembering the distance she'd travelled —
how glass holds a truth.

Each time a storm entered the lighthouse, bones of the dead
appeared on the cliff.
The keeper carves them into fish that swim in the depths.
Out in the ocean oars are eternally rowing.
The keeper is silent. He's remembering the last wind that struck
how a boat of migrants broke on its rock
and no one but death to find them.

1990

SAM BURNSIDE

The Salt Box

We were just chatting—
you know, the way people do—
when I asked,
where's home?
Well, she replied,
I love Quigley's Point
that's the place I always return to—
the hills behind, the water in front,
the road running between
taking us away
bringing us back
back
to the house
to our house
to our home
to memories
to presences
my father and his father—
all those generations
tending to it.
But, I feel at home in other places:
places like Hampstead;
I love, best of all, that place
(it's in a painting by Constable),
Hampstead Heath, and a house called
The Salt Box, with Branch Hill Pond
beyond, a shimmer, rising off it
like you'd find on the Foyle
when seen from our door-step
early on a cool May morning.
Yes.
These are the places:
places, people,
homes of the heart, really—

Branch Hill Pond
and the Foyle
The Salt Box
and Quigley's Point
and most of all
all these men and women
who make the real
who give them life.

First published in *Salmon: A Journey in Poetry 1981-2007*

MOYA CANNON

Songs last the longest...

my mother, who could not sing, told me.
As a young woman, she helped garner
the last grains of Tyrone Irish.
A teetotaller, her job
was to carry the whiskey bottle
which uncorked memory -
the old people remembered scraps of songs
when they remembered nothing else.

And today I heard a recorded lullaby
sung by a woman long dead
in Kulkhssl, a language also dead.

No one understands the words
or knows what the singer might have sung
to an infant who could be a grandparent today
walking, haltingly, in the shade,
down a street in South Africa.

Did she sing about stars, or rain,
or tall grass, or blue flowers,
or small boats on a quick, brown river
or antelopes in a mountain valley
or a dark spirit who might snatch away
a little child.

Whatever promises or prayers
the song's words held
in that forever lost language
the mystery remains
that any infant on this hurried earth
could still understand the lullaby's intent.

Through its rhythms and syllables
love pours still
like milk
through a round sieve.

MICHAEL D. HIGGINS

The Inter

for Alice-Mary

Watching you preparing for the Inter,
My daughter,
I see in the chaos of your room
A bird
Scratching its nest into shape
And, through your door,
As between branches broken
With violence,
Come my words
That startle.

What value
My distraction
From your task?
Yours was the work of shaping,
Making your own order
In the chaos of others' demands.

Oh, I would that I had come
With a whisper,
Edged one twig towards where you saw it.
But I am burdened with
A catalogue
Of prefabricated designs,
Ugly, efficient and guaranteed
To do the job.

When I come again
I will bring silence,
But know,
Even in its noise,
It was love that informed
My bad choice.

Move your twigs
Into the pattern that suits
Your moment
And, not from a distance
I hope
I will look and wonder
At whatever shape
Upon which my love
Rests.

First published in *The Betrayal*

HUGH O'DONNELL

Between One Breath and Another

With the second hand bookshop behind me
I crossed from shadow, bent down and picked up
the sunny side of the street and as quickly
set it down in a rural village sleepy with low morale
where residents waken to a coronet blaring
and women sashaying towards the crossroads
so that the sergeant is compelled to raise his voice...

At which point the spoilsport intervenes, removing
half a street to the consternation of the locals,
(quite unaware of the sleight of hand), and easing it
back into its home place, realigning cars, reassuring
those who had almost stumbled, the upheaval felt
as no more than a frisson in the air or a brush
with a patch of stellar dust on the merry-go-round.

                                            Strand Street, Cape Town

MARY O'DONNELL

Air

In those summers, jets appeared on high,
a miracle of faraway drone,

the definite line of travel. Locked in the sweet green
of Monaghan and summer daisies,

mother explained to my upturned face
the fathomable heights of moving in spheres

where gods and angels hovered carelessly.
Who were they who leap-frogged the globe,

to reappear in some distant place?
Like peasants struck mute by an eclipse,

we pointed and marvelled. Now I play
noughts and crosses with sky-lines.

Summer and winter bring daily crossings.
Jets take off or land close enough to mark

lights, windows, a tail fin. I see what those
passengers see. Wet verdure of land,

dark, trafficked roads, the fungus-like cities
munching Wicklow, Kildare.

And when helicopters slash the sky,
and teams of fighters crack through cloud,

there is no mystery. Travellers, that is all —
visitors, restless for refuge, asylum.

MARY O'MALLEY

The Bite

After living alone so long, the negotiations
Houses and where to live, China, the Balkans
What made the Irish take pennies from heaven
The smaller matter of roads, waterpipes frozen
We agree or give up easily on who's responsible
But my accounting skills which run
To a sick stomach and the shakes cause you alarm.
Just as one round ends another starts —
Cromwell, the role of the Catholic Church, trees
Decisions reversed by the cold light of experience
Why bills are kept in the wastepaper basket.
Can you think of a better place? In conscience.

This morning, punch drunk after the late night
Disagreement I walk downstairs
You are watching tennis for breakfast
Smiling over your toast, innocent as only a man
After a good sleep can look. Your cheek is smooth.
Watching you, I know why Sylvia bit Ted Hughes.

MARK ROPER

Milkweed

for Carole Herrle

They'd cling to my fingers but not be caught.
Up in the air almost before your envelope was opened,
the seedheads — as if possessed of motive power.

Magic Milkweed you'd written. You must have known
how they'd lift and drift through the room, sunlight
silvering their silk. If you meant a blessing, I was blessed.

I thought of rich runnels of milk sprung from rock
at a god's command; of Vermeer's Cook, from a jug
never-empty to a bowl never-filled her steady pour;

of the milkweed these seedheads would give rise to,
sap and nectar to sustain the miles of butterflies
making their way Mexico to Canada to Mexico;

of that lava tunnel, the vicious, fire-spiked walls
and the blind crabs so small and white
in the spotlit pool, their one home on earth.

As they went their own way I could almost hear
the seedheads' hunger, their itch for increase.
They wouldn't be caught. They wanted the earth.

EITHNE STRONG

Fifty Years On

You were right you know,
I got him wrong.
He was none, you said,
of the things I saw in him.

You'll remember my poem: I called it
'Twenty-five'—his age—it's in
the 'Early' section. Yes you were
right: after fifty years I've met him again.

No 'pale wistful boy'
no 'naked soul' in the eyes.
One of the practised diplomats,
the clever stare requisite.

No 'searching, seeking humanity'.
He had slimed through
all the sticky channels
to that post of seal and style.

As 'lonely searcher
under the wetness of mists
blown from shore mountains'
I fancifully saw him

It strikes me now
his shakes, pouchy eyes,
liverish yellow, testify
to saturation of another sort.

Of course I was romantic then:
there were sheep and goats.
I'm still shortsighted—always
those saddling spectacles, but
a thing or two I see more clearly
and lately I walk a bit better—
my two sheep hooves, two goat.

from *Spatial Nosing*

118

1991

HEATHER BRETT

Colours of Peace

The Irish winter arrives breathless,
gasping out short intense storms,
a deluge, reluctant frost.

Somehow the season offers itself again, intact
and joyous; firelight reflections flicker, challenged only
by sprinkled stars

or excited innocence in a small child's eye.
As always, December carries a scent of crushed pine,
memories and sorrow thick as incense

at a Christmas Eve funeral.
Pale blue shirt to lay you out in,
tinge of vacancy on once sallow skin.

But, rituals are important; layers of straw
that form a strata of coping; to stay.
Bandaged and re-bandaging of wounds.

I place the two poinsettia; my Christmas stars,
one in the wild flameleaf of crimson,
the other a quiet ivory, radiant and luminous.

MARY DORCEY

Writer at Work

Beginning once more after long absence, you have
forgotten all of it; even the common rituals of
evocation. How to listen, how to idle, how in
darkness to strike a bargain with the dead. So
you rehearse in order, ancient rites of passage
to still sense, make welcome. First light the lamp,

Set a fire for heat. As in an old, disused house, to
air the soul; throw all the windows wide. Then,
silence laid, and white page, words in vigil, sit and
let the ghosts come in. Gingerly at first, fleeting,
from the corner of an eye, a glimpse is caught or
scent, a sudden breeze, casts a footstep on the

Stairs, a tremor or a sigh. Flame drifts on glass.
Slowly they gain force, the shadows murmurous.
Every voice is known to you, each breath resonant.
Only you have altered after all. They take their places
one by one, the last to leave is the first returned.
Each draws another under the lintel, a necklace of

Pearl, strung in the order of their loss. Do not question,
nor reproach as they congregate. Accept the only
consolation they can offer; their memories of you,
invulnerable to time. Take what you can see and hear,
abandon touch, breath on skin. No power of longing
can restore this earthly gift. Do not be afraid then —

Stay; let them cluster at the hearth, about your table.
Grave or whimsical, out of their element, do not ask of
them what they did not ask to lose: weight, coherence.
Sit hear them out. They have come all this way only to
render an account. As the light grows cold, stay. Do not
turn your back on their entreaty; their clamorous hunger.

ANNE LE MARQUAND HARTIGAN

Branches

1

Words are always with me
they lie in myself   but the energy
comes from the heart   or

is it the body?   Around the lungs
in the breath – in the gasp, the gulp down
that aching place that broods passion?
Raw, flesh, blood.   Guts.

The cat walks across the table,
the sun slides in on the polished wood.
The trees toss their shadows over
my page making their winter dance,
bare and shining tips raised to the skies.

2

Now we go into the bare bleached world
Winter, so simple, empty. The wind uses the space
between the branches to whistle it's tunes.

Forget Christmas, that hurdy-gurdy is gone.
Now we stand on the cliff looking over
the edge of the future. We have to compose
life again. Take it on. Just simply, work.

3

We do
We really do –
Have so little time
This life swings by
Seems there is ages

Don't you believe it
It's gone in a flash,
Before you've cleaned up the dog shit
Before you've parked the car
Before you've kissed your lover

Oh so quick – dear little death
Opens his wide wide eyes
And looks – my darlings

Straight at You.

JOHN KAVANAGH

Star Child

for Monika Wikman

House hushed and light killed
the others sleeping soundly,
she slips into the inked California night
across the ponderosa needled garden

spidering to the tree house
on familiar toe hold and branch stump,
bony fingers rounding dangled rope
for final, white knuckled heave.

There, she secretly lays, tawny curls pillowed
and propped, under calligraphied canvas,
tracing the powdered river of Milky Way,
a skilled child's eye threading oceans
of splash and twinkle, into constellation and cluster

bearings taken by the Dipper's tilted nod
to high hovering Polaris,
then her own sign of Leo.

In leaf-rustled, beyond midnight quiet,
legs penduluming over the doorway's edge,
neck craned to the outer heavens
she searches out Sirius, the Pleiades,
— sits locked on to Orion's three pearled smile

rocking to its siren song beckoning her
from earth-bound exile.
Osiris calling his lost Isis home.

NOEL MONAHAN

Honey Bees

The hive is empty, waxen walls of honeycomb
Crumble. I miss the murmur of the honey bees
Flying from flower to flower. The purple and white clover
Has stopped growing, bees lose their way home.
No longer the bee-music, mandala and waggle dance
On the floor of the hive, giving bee-line directions
To the wild-flowered hills, purple heather bogs.
When stars are bee-eyes
                              In the hive tonight,
The bees dream of white-faced flowers
On May bushes and no one left to smear honey
On the white bride's lips, on the doors and lintels ...
And love, as true as daylight, continues to speak to the bees
And night, as still as a full-moon hive in winter
Makes promises of honey to heal the sting.

TOM MORGAN

Mullanfad

I do not see myself
carried the long street
of a town or village,
past grocer and baker,
the jaundiced face of a publican,
under flags and bunting
of any denomination.
After the furnace has eaten
plain wood and handles,
I would be put in an urn
and my ashes scattered
on a dead day
over my hardest making;
the septic tank, its strong smell
under concrete lids
to keep bacteria in,
cloying Summer air
as a handful of poets —
no masks supplied —
read poem after poem
under sycamore and ash,
not looking for rhyme or rhythm,
for that will be my will:
the big sea-captain first,
maps and territories next,
and "look at the stars" third.
I was confined in the urn
but now I am mobile,
waiting for wind to blow me
past this wasteful energy
up mountain paths and fields
craving the sky.

First published in *Salmon: A Journey in Poetry 1981-2007*

DESMOND O'GRADY

Olga Rudge Pound

on her one hundred and first birthday
13th April 1895 USA — 15th March 1996, Venice, Italy

Your vine of life fruits full again this year
and vintages your best to share with us.
We'll taste and feast on your ripe memories
of past times and lives lived as time's guest.

At first light your birthday will dawn and shine
all day for you. All your love will radiate
response in kind. The stitch in time of your
first decade saved your tenth decade to knot.

In childhood we gather life's images
round us: places, people, those things that catch
our attention, please or displease all, as
they may do thereafter when they repeat.

In youth's dreams of adventures in new ways
of life we dare to broaden our horizon.
We work in happy hope through hurt and heal
to shape life in profession, vocation.

To live our love of life defeats mere death.
All live, all die one way or another.
What we make that outshines our mortality —
children, lives for others, art — examples.

Human history effects all life in peace,
through war. What we make well helps growth improve.
All love helps heart and soul survive through strife,
inspires each joyful flight of peaces's dove.

The peak of life, when real, rejects all masks,
stands clear as truth. It may revive oldtime
values to live the age process with strength,
enliven each day's order with fantasy.

Aging matures, mellows our stress from struggle
and those who order time to live life well
find joy in age, comfort in nature's law.
Age's serenity transcends all that is mortal.

Physical passion spent, the mind follows
its own commitment. Now age resists,
declares its right to decisive seniority.
Our time flows on until our life drains out.

Keep an interest in the parts you've played,
your last act will demand, reward example.
Your last part played, exit with composure.
Those who applaud will follow example.

First published in *Salmon: A Journey in Poetry 1981-2007*

RICHARD TILLINGHAST

I Tuned Up Seán's Guitar

for Thomas Lynch

I tuned up Seán's guitar,
        gone unharmonious in the weather,
and gave it an airing
        on the flagged forecourt outside Lynch's house,
the wind whipping steady off the North
    Atlantic three fields from where
  Clare drops off cliffs into the sea.

Soon I had it ringing
        with songs of my own country,
muddy rivers, green mountains, deep declivities
    dark as a dungeon and damp as the dew,
griefs and enmities that almost outlasted memory.

I shot a man in Reno, I sang,
        just to watch him die.
                I had no fiddle to liven it.

The foal's whiteness was something not of this world.
Not till tomorrow would she feel
    on her coat, that was new as anything,
  what we call rain.
Camilla licked the foal's sylvan
    leaf-like ears
as I sang out those dire things
  that happened *ten years ago on a cold dark night.*

Even the black crow left off cawing
    when he heard about the long black veil and the
night wind that moans
        and the living who cry over gravestones
    way back in the hills.

What business did I have
        singing into her still-damp ears
ballads of murder and horseback journeys,
    duels and scaffolds
            from a country she had never heard of?

It was some comfort to know
she and I shared no common tongue.

1992

NUALA ARCHER

Swing Low Cuyahoga

Slowly, on a riveted, refraction-red swing-

bridge spanning Osage articulations, a wake

aiaiaiaiaiaiaiiaiaiaiaiaiaaiaiaiaiiaiaiaiaiaiiaiaiaiai

of seagulls, eee-k-e! k-e-yee-k!, startles citizens

& the barge, passing between my toes, tugging the Cuyahoga's

longings & inconstant, cleft

dreams. Vagrants, outwitting the slammer, cleave

cardboard & cartoons into a shelter-proof-spill—

in view of the Cuyahoga's

oxbows—medusa scrolls a-swing

with migrating ducks, river-rat addicts, citizens

caught in a chrysalis' salt wake. . . .

A prayer pollens my lips. . . . Near the ravine's wake

& erosion walls, incendiary tears hammer Cleveland,

nick the roses rambling a socketed trailer. Citizens

crumb clouds, steal stow-away bubble-wrap from ship spillage,

quicken over Cleveland's diamond—a merciless swinger

at bat. Cuyahoga

bends—(a hair-pin-kink)—near the Columbus-Franklin
intersection, then swings

its metallic currents against blue herons & that Clevelander

"named"—The Girl In Blue—with 90¢ & a riderless ticket—buried
by Willoughby citizens,

a train's lamp on her grave. "Blessings on your skull & ill-age

Unknown Girl In Blue: this burial song's indigo spill-

way & green dust are for you who are not unlike the Cuyahoga—

O Unknown Citizen—

O Girl In Blue—O Keeper of the Keys—waking

against that assuming shape that double-shades Cleveland

with weather that forks her flesh & bones swinging

an unquiet heart, winging

hallucinations—spillage

of immigrant dreams. O Queen Cleveland!—

wrapped in the Cuyahoga's

squeeze—rapping your rockbirds, wracking your wake's

fusion of sulfur & nervy Lazarus-citizens—"

Swing low Cuyahoga—

carry home Cleveland's ache

of soul-citizens & song-spill.

VICKI CROWLEY

First Irish Spring

For my mother, May Xuereb

Everytime I hear a cuckoo sing
I think of you
And how you ran into the house,
Cheeks ablaze, and cried,
"The cuckoo sang for me."
Everytime I see the daffodils unfurl
I think of you
And how you stood
Reciting Wordsworth in your stout voice.

Everytime I see the Gentian violets appear
I think of you
And how you crooned "How sweet, how sweet"
Until I thought my heart would break.
That is why I embraced you in the supermarket
Beside the rows of razor blades, by the cashier's till.
For there you stood alien and tanned
In this land of muted tones.

Everytime I think of Spring
I see you amongst the daffodils
And cuckoos sing unceasingly.
With violets in your buttonhole
You laugh like a child,
Our roles reversed
In the joy of your discoveries.

TED McNULTY

The Cave — Stephen's Green

Haze of old gold
autumn sun
makes a shadowpark
and he is the boy
who after school
went to the zoo
in the Bronx
with a bag of currant buns
to make friends
with the bears,

a huddle of them
waiting by the cave
for the buns to fly over
they'd catch in the air.

Today the same
scent of cold
in city centre air
as he lingers
under the scarlets
of a maple
in the Green,

a man thinking
of his winter
wishing it was as easy
as finding a cave
on the island
of rock and bramble
in the pond.

from *On the Block* (1995)

SHEILA O'HAGAN

September The Fourth

At four am today my lover died
He didn't reach for me or call my name
Dreaming he would waken by my side
But turned his face and shuddered as some shame
Or haunting shook him and his mouth gave cry
To a portentous and unearthly pain.

Between darkness and dawn that cry of pain
And nothing warm has reached me since it died
Some ethos of cold starlight I can't name
Possessed my love while he lay by my side
Something strange, inhuman, born of shame
He had not said goodbye, called out or cried.

Some ghost or spirit left his mouth that cried
Out and he'd gone from me, had gone in pain
Into an alien world yet as he died
He drew my spirit to him, gave her my name
Something possessed him as he left my side
His face was turned away as though in shame.

I took his absent face and murmured shame
To that which claimed him, for my love had cried
As though some shady trafficking in pain
Some curse or Judas kiss by which he died
Unknowingly in another's name
Had come to term as he lay down beside

The one he loved. Perhaps lying by his side
Fearful in sleep, I had called up that shame
And he, my love, unknowingly had cried
Out in redemption for another's pain,
As though a chosen victim. My love died
Because some cursed spirit took his name.

For he was loved and honoured in his name
And I, as I lay sleeping by his side
Guarding his innocence, knew of no shame.
On the stark cusp of dark and dawn he cried
Aloud so strange my heart burned cold with pain.
Not one warm thought has reached me since he died.

Still I call his name. All hope has died.
My unspent love's my pain. I have not cried.
Such is winter's shame, all's bare outside.

First published in *Salmon: A Journey in Poetry 1981-2007*

OLAF TYARANSEN

Portrait

Finally the first two pages were written
after months of never trying.
This was going to be huge, daring,
ambitious, controversial, award-winning,
and really just the beginning.
This would make him a household name
in households worth naming.
This would make Her proud
and Them jealous.

Awakening from his dreams,
fresh from the plunge,
he pushes back the chair,
smiling contentedly.
Two pages, not bad for a…
well, not bad anyway.
Two pages — two drinks,
sounds about right.
He'd toast his future success
in the very bar where he had
fashioned his masterpiece
through the art of conversation.

Two drinks.
Two more.
Too many.
Two pages.
Two weeks.
Too busy.
Two months.
Two years.
Two kids.
Two jobs.
Two decades.

To do.
To do...

Years later, on a rare day off
work and drink and the rest,
he found the two pages
yellowing away
under a stack of old reviews
that he'd written for the money.
Ink faded, the idea jaded.

Two pages
Too little
Too late.

1993

ANGELA GREENE

Visitor — Colden Valley

at Arvon Foundation, Lumb Bank

Stepped into what seemed a May-soft, water-lit place
that reaching out, included me in its parade
of beech-green and birch-silver along innocent,
wet banks above the skitter of the bright beck's
downrush. So safe.

       Drawn by the hill's craggy face
in sunlight, the millstack elegant in high
jet beading; not until I'd crossed the bridge
and stood, did they explode their fire inside my skull.
the women gave out.
       Of his millyard's looms
which wove nothing but black silk to clothe
the cleft hearts of the widows; how work-raw children,
on this track, went into the wind their cries had become.
How stone and ground were shut over crushed
and stunted lives.

       Suddenly I am caught in it:
the brute misery rooted in this valley; compelled
to touch, to risk the burden of the stone's
brooding silence: part of how the world knows
its grief and pain filtering through us, is what
cries in the dark, disturb dreams.

from *Silence and the Blue Night*

BREDA SULLIVAN

Widow

i.m. Basil

you left me
on the brink
of winter

the signs were there
i refused
to read them

i heard you creak
a tree
weary in wind

your blue eyes dimmed
your voice faded
to a whisper

nurses
in arabesque
about your bed

at the window
the first
red leaf

ii

in the coffee shop
i watch a couple
he carries the tray
she chooses a window table

they drink our tea
share our scone
while my hot chocolate
grows slowly cold

iii

it was easier in the old days
a black diamond stitched
to the sleeve of my coat
and all would know
i am bereaved fragile
like a parcel stamped
handle with care

iv

christmas morning
three year old lauren
refuses to leave your grave
don't go wait for yaya
he has to come up
he has to come
home for christmas

v

on the bus from galway
i look at my watch
know about now
you put on your jacket
look for your cap
search pockets for car keys
when the bus stops
you will be there
waiting for me
then i remember…

vi

in sleep
you are warm
beside me
ready for love
i snuggle close
waken
to cold sheets
nobody

vii

unable to empty your wardrobe
fill a bag with your clothes

i bring them one by one
week by week
to the charity shop
i sit on the bed and hug
the brown aran jumper
i knit you that winter
replace it on the shelf

viii

I switch off the engine
sit in the car
reluctant to open
the locked back door
enter the empty kitchen
turn on the light

ix

all i can do for you now
fill a pot with compost
make a hollow in the centre
for another red begonia
place it on your grave
with all the other pots
all i can do for you now

x

i want to sit in the passenger seat
a map on my lap you beside me
at the wheel your favourite place
and off we go destination
god knows where

xi

from my home
i walk to the bridge
a distance
less than half a mile

the tullaghan flows to

        the inny
        the shannon
        the ocean

1994

PATRICIA BURKE BROGAN

Beyond

Beyond my window
three spiders weave veils of silver.
Three trapeze artists
swing from clustered woodbine,
their mysterious tapestries
glisten in fractured sunlight.

Beyond my hall door
one human
pushes three dustbins
to the roadside.
Three plastic monsters,
their blood-red jaws
gristle with offal.

Beyond my gateway
three trucks,
haloed in fumes,
hoist the monsters,
unload and masticate.

Beyond my window
one feather floats
through clustered woodbine,
its silver-white filaments
transport me
to that other world
of angels and archangels.

MICHAEL HEFFERNAN

Mystique

In Banagher in County Offaly,
I watched the landscape turning drearier
than it had been in Galway or Mayo
across the Shannon broadening toward the sea
past Clonmacnoise, where Vikings often chased
the monks up the round tower and Rory O'Conor,
last of the high kings before the Normans came,
had lodged himself amongst the ruins
as a breath that scoured the ground beneath the winds
that ages later on whispered and cooed
while Pope John Paul II bowed to say Mass.
I could do no more about it, no I could not.
So I drove east up the hill and on beyond
into the countryside on the plateau
toward a tavern with a phone box where I called
my sister up, in Tempe, Arizona,
to tell her where I was and how it was
where I had come to, God knows why or how.
She had to have been surprised to hear from me
where she was standing out beside the pool.
I cannot remember what she said to me.
My fantasy attended me till I had come
to Brendan's broken chapel with the faces
gazing down from their portal in Eternity,
if not quite to it, if that's where they were.
I don't know what to make of this myself
twenty years later. How I found myself
in Ireland then was nowhere near the way
I go there now or ever will again.
It's nothing about the times that we are in
or have been all the while for fifty years
since when that limousine turned onto Elm
and took us with it into where we are.

CATHERINE PHIL MacCARTHY

In the Studio, Marie Bashkirtseff, 1881

She surrendered her carmine cloak
for nest, or cage—Academy Julian—
and here she is with companions
crowded in, to that congested
attic on the fifth floor
off Boulevard des Cappucines,

slate-blue apron, ankle-length dress,
fair hair or dark, plainly rolled back,
a few in hat, or lace bonnet. They stand
canvas at easel, or chair, make-do
with knife and mixing board.
Before all eyes, poses a young boy.

Far right, a skeleton observes the room.
On higher walls are nudes, cast aside.
The *atélier* clock tells Paris Mean Time.
Daughters of wealth, of noble birth
and foreign tongue, paint from eight
to five with those on the bread-line

famished at night. She reads
La Dame aux Camélias and promises
to take the cure. 'I cough a deal
and breathe with difficulty.'
Before sleep, and each morning she wakes
figures on the canvas taunt her eyes.

ÁINE MILLER

Kavanagh's Kingdom

The bicycles go by in twos and threes —
Sally's and Michael's among them —
Out from Dundalk on an autumn evening.
The air is giddy, the breeze beside itself
Lifting her skirt, wisping under her cloche hat.
Music is drifting through hedgerows,
The wheels spin a new story.

They are flying, away on out from her
Father's wrath, in a race she has promised
To lose. They will fall together soon
In the lap of a Monaghan ditch, sinking
Heart high in parsley lace, vetch, wild garlic,
Her back against stone that carries
The ghost of the sun. These were my parents

Shadowless then in Kavanagh's kingdom.
The story goes on. He plies her with chocolates
And love, till a soft centre held to his lips,
She catches his whiskey breath, the flush
On his sandpaper cheek. His box of chocs sent
Sailing must startle some drowsy ass
Or that lonesome poet rueing his solitude.

First published in *From Inniskeen to Parnassus* (2004), a collection of Ireland's best-loved Poets and Artists paying tribute to Patrick Kavanagh.

ROBIN SKELTON

The Names

(Rannaigecht Mór)

Air me your favourite name,
one you would give to a stone
you felt had a pulse of flame
untamed by the known, alone

there on the earth at your feet,
or tell me the name you'd give
to the first child that you meet
in the street where lovers live,

or the one you long to write
on vellum to see it shine
with elegance and delight
bright as the sacred sign

on gospels in bishops' courts,
or tell me the name you share
with nothing in human thoughts,
but with water, earth, fire, air.

from *Samhain*

EAMONN WALL

Independence Day

In yellow oilskins on an orange bollard
a child shifts, hand-to-hand, a 99 in time
to Sharon Shannon's accordion playing
on the main stage. It's the Volvo Yacht
Race, the rain has started, the yellow girl
on the orange bollard is the Kurt Cobain
of the 99 in the manner many consider
Sharon Shannon to be the Jimi Hendrix
of the button accordion, old folk fogies,
I would guess, distraught at such crank
comparison.

            She has managed to keep
time and eat, the unnamed girl I should
add, not the great musician on the big
black stage, sacrificing neither flake
nor ice cream. A moment's quiet at tune's
end releases to air cawk of gulls, cling
and clang of tethered yachts. I maneuver
a slow turn toward my wet companion
though I can't find a phrase ripe enough
to tease. We begin to wind our way
toward home, stepping to one side to allow
cheerleaders pass. It's yellow oilskins
Independence Day in Galway, I say, even
hordes of Americans gather here to play.
Hark! A rake of diplomats bused in today
all Ballsbridged, North Faced, not so gay
who stand before us, cold, wet, in some
disarray, another bolt of water washed in
from Galway Bay. It never rains in South-
ern California I remind the cultural attaché
who busily wipes her smartphone down.
An old pop song we liked back in the day:
We sang along to wipe our Irish blues away.

1995

THEO DORGAN

Waystation

A lone cottage, the wind clattering an unhinged door.
Damp-reek, vetch and bindweed climbing to empty windows,
scabbed lichened plaster, peeling; rust-red corrugated
threatening to take flight — nothing unusual here,
common sight in this tumbled landscape of rocky bog,
of windshorn blackthorn stubbornly rooted on ditches,
scant grass, the glint of oil and water on shabby fields.

A brother and sister lived here. Neither had married.
They kept to themselves but were friendly in company.
Sometimes he'd take a drink but was never offensive;
at a wake or a christening sometimes she might sing.
All this I learned from an old man who had stopped to chat.
The tale and its variations, I'm hearing it since
I embarked on this long course through empty parishes,

unpeopled countryside, lanes closing in on silence.
I was being measured as we sat there smoking, the man
turning me over in his mind. There was more, I knew.
"Two things we always noticed," he said eventually,
his eye on a pair of ragged crows battling the wind,
"There was a light left on in that kitchen all night long,
and the half-door to the cowshed was never kept shut.

Nothing was ever said, see, but we loved them for it" —
I startled, it was not a word I had expected —
"a desperate boy breaking out and striking for home
would see light, slide by, find the door open to shelter
from rain and cold. Bread and milk, dry straw and an old coat."
He stood and stretched. "Good people," he said, "I admired
    them."
A pause. "Men came from all over to their funerals."

JOAN McBREEN

April in Rusheenduff

These nights in April
stars gleam over the ocean.

Morning after rain, yellow gorse
thickens, smothers in the ditch
wild cherry, hawthorn and frog-spawn.

Yet in the undergrowth,
among snarls of weeds
and rough stones,
garlands of mountain creeper
weave their black roots.

The senses are not visionary
and we ask neither more nor less
of this earth in whose measure
we are fixed.

BARBARA PARKINSON

Where the Plane Dropped Me Off

I am dreaming here now
Under the shade of the stately Sequoia
Five years and one full moon later
Able only to think about the things
I left behind

My orchid
Did it die I wonder
The purple one I bought that evening
I wanted to be decadent with wine and orchids
The night I saw no scar

And the fiddle
Out of place on the wall
Now part of a system
That knows nothing of me
How can it ever again
Rise the air with music and
Meet me with a smile

That part of my ghost
I no longer stay for
The part that never saved me
My green chair
Does it still stand sentinel
Watching for those birds of prey
Who scavenge in the lowest of places

No moon offers a going away outfit
There is no prescription for that the doctor says
No procession in the sun's suicide
Only bats eager in their flight
Place the odds on how my heart works

No longer the snake eye
In all that I fought for
No longer Cinderella
In this house of cards always on call
To the silence
That weathered our story
Where no one ever witnessed the glory

When the dawn cracks
And my leaving is loaded
Who is going to pull the trigger
When those scavenging beaks
Pick my key from the lock

JANET SHEPPERSON

It Was Already Crumbling Before
The Sixties

Their wedding photo. 1950.
Curls cluster round her powdered face,
her dark eyes glitter, shy, defiant,
a cheap brooch clutches her shiny collar;
you can almost smell her borrowed scent,

and him in his good suit standing there,
scrubbed up and Brylcreemed, hand over hers
holding the knife that cuts the cake
in all its carefully layered whiteness,
for generations, perhaps forever.

Sixteen and nineteen — how can they know
they're both the last of a dying breed?
Sixteen means *filling Mammy's shoes*.
Nineteen means *a steady job,*
about enough to marry on.

Beyond their power to imagine
the bleeping, pulsing, speeded-up
digital flashing bubbling flood
where their children's children sink or swim —
teenagers, an alien species,

courting by text and e-mail, spending
fortunes on downloads, nights online
layering their self images,
a shaggy herd, like musk oxen
stranded on a vast ice floe,

grim in a circle, horns pointing outwards.
Between them and the old, tame life
is a heaving, seasick-making ocean

strewn with mangled floating relics,
souvenirs from a lost world —

rags that were once white tablecloths,
drowned words that were invitations,
splinters for their discarded selves
to clutch at, while horizons lurch
and soft winds mutter about *home*.

JANICE FITZPATRICK SIMMONS

The routes of loss are varied

there is one, it seems to me
a narrow mountain track with roiling
grey clouds full of fears and rushing wind.
I must turn my back on that; stay indoors,
light a fire against the cold,
sit thinking of what might-have-beens;
hope that *this too will pass*.

The routes of loss are varied
it seems to me, there is one as dark
as lough water — a wild sky scatters its light
mine eyes dazzle.
And for an instant, I fathom the depths,
then darkness again. The wind dries my tears.
I steady myself. The day has cleared. I face
south and west; lake water still,
mirrored and myriad trees reflected on the surface
a glass of lemonade in my hand at a small table
where sun warms my bones. All of it,
all of it for love. I raise my glass,
fill myself with its sharp sweetness.

JAMES SIMMONS

Janice

My love, my softy, my brown swan,
swimming now in the brimming rier
of my affections. Will you swim on
forever and forever.

My love, my freckled gardener
busy with balm and briony,
Americanly kind and conscious
of the limitations of irony ...

supportive to a fault, hurt
by local abrasiveness, our wit,
the winding up and putting down,
brilliance that has no heart in it.

I grow less Irish every year
with kindly love to lean upon.
Our home and garden is my nation,
my freckled gardener, my swan.

JEAN VALENTINE

Tonight I Can Write . . .

after Pablo Neruda

Tonight I can write the lightest lines.

Write, for example, 'The evening is warm
and the white mist holds our houses close.'

The little evening wind walks in the field grass
and hums into her own chest.

Tonight I can write the lightest lines.
I love him, and I think he loves me too.

He first came to me on an evening like this one
and held me in his arms.

He kissed me again and again then,
under the motherly bending down stars.

He loves me, and I think I love him too.
how could one not love his calm eyes, as blue as the earth.

Tonight I can write the lightest lines.
To think that I did not know him, that now I am
    beginning to know him.

To feel the warm lamplight: soon it will warm his brown arm.
'And the verse falls to the soul like dew to the pasture . . .'

from *The Under Voice*

SABINE WICHERT

'A Strip of Pavement Over an Abyss'

Step aside and you fall —
schoolgirls conforming in rebellion
with whatever latest fashion
adults disapprove.

A north-easterly gale is blowing, straight from
the Pole it seems, whipping clouds over a milky-
blue sky, bending the branches of trees, troubling
the house-martins with its permanent uplift.

Flitting like small birds from day to night:
the schizophrenia of getting it right:
as you grown up there is little choice but
to consume what the market offers.

At night you defy the fashion,
eat, drink, put your feet up; guilty
with hangover in the morning, or the
added weight you promise virtue.

Consume therefore you are: glamorous
clothes which may not fit and gorgeous mouth-
watering food-advertisements
compete for your life.

The abyss is never quite defined
and the pavement stays narrow:
they tell you not to look down, but
up and ahead, not to bother your head.

Once you do, vertigo
sets in, difficult to
resist the pull, not to
stumble, not to fall.

First published in *Salmon: A Journey in Poetry 1981-2007*

1996

RORY BRENNAN

Self Portraits

It is the cheapest way to find a sitter:
Prop up a mirror on the nearest table.
Stare. No one can stare back better
Or as long. Perhaps no one else is able

To refute the other witness in the case,
The evidence not traced in any spindly line
But in the cobwebbed window of the face.
Let doctors probe to find a vital sign:

Great works linger forever in their prime
Though they siphon terror out of eyes
That leave us shattered after a long climb
Up centuries or the stairs of galleries,

Like Piranesi's prison. Framed in a cage
Whose bars reach up above, around, below,
The portraitist glares at his own damned visage,
Then dons, like a cocked hat, a crumpled halo.

PATRICK CHAPMAN

The Key

Shackled he waits by the tank
for Bess to bring him the kiss.

In his heart he has guarded
a promise unspoken.

Should the moment come
when there is nothing on her tongue,

he will take it even so, that kiss,
without complaint, comprehending

what has passed between them,
the weight of her emptiness.

He will urge the men
to lose no further time,

to drop him inverted
like a saint but not a martyr.

As they draw the crimson velvet
he will smile upon her

desolate refraction through the glass
and let the water in; and know

that he is not to be awoken
by her tapping on a tabletop.

1997

MÍCHEÁL FANNING

Croagh Patrick Ascent

for Michael Gibbons, Jeremy Grange and M. Symmons Roberts

For two hours we ascended
through cloud and fog,
"small steps," scratched on the quartz
stones and well-demarcated path.

The cloud did not lift,
lost in a labyrinth of mist—
the soul-land of Crom Dubh,
Celt in the outer ramparts.

We had talked of Assad in Damascus
and mostly of Patrick,
the English priest who wrote stumbling Latin
in a colony of a hundred different kingdoms.

We reached Candida Casa, the white
church on the summit. The wind threw
us over and over, crawled close together,
we crouched on Leaba Phádraig.

Here, Patrick fasted and prayed where
the storms of wind blow now unabated round Candida
Casa. He prayed in earnest as Moses did on
Mt. Sinai in this station of changing devotions.

"Life is so strange now, tasteless and colourless."
Perhaps, the anchorite Patrick will save us four,
feed us with faith and communion, reclaim
the love of God, feed us with faith, banish our devils.

There is so much more to say, larks sing with
the ordinary people of Connacht and Ulster

—Our Resurrection Body guaranteed—
mortal changed into immortal,
death is destroyed, victory complete.

We shall ascend Patrick's pagan mountain,
claim and climb the Cruach with sticks
again and again in this secular and punitive
world of fingal, racism and brutality.

Peace finally reigns here.
We view Clew Bay
where drumlin islands bask
in the tombolo-sheltered harbour.

from *The Separation of Grey Clouds*

BEN HOWARD

Inkwell

Think of it as the fount
to which our pens return,
we keepers of the pure,
unhindered common word.

I recall the novelty
of Disappearing Ink,
gone before we knew it.
And on my father's desk,

the bottle of Permanent Black
from which he filled his dark,
marbled fountain pen.
It was there I learned the word

indelible, its once-
and-for-all finality,
its solemn reassurance,
its hint of mortal woe.

Gone before we knew it,
the permanence of *longhand*,
that intimate conjunction
of hand, pen, and paper.

And yet we still return,
we keepers of the notion
that what we write by hand
might bear our signatures

and be indelible.
How beautiful the flow
of unencumbered ink
drying as I write.

RON HOUCHIN

If My Dead Friend Came Back Some Night

> *death of friends, or death*
> *Of every brilliant eye*
> *That made a catch in the breath—*
>
> W.B. Yeats, *The Tower*

If he came right up to the side of my bed
and jarred me awake with the memory
of his weight, speaking so much I could

not understand, would I think he wanted
to tell me of the Zero Point Field
or what's in the Akashic Record? Would

I hear references to unknown times, mistaking
them for images of blank boulders, still
cataracts, and caves of echoes hollow

as caskets? Or would I even know he's
there, would I go on dreaming
the museum where he lived and see

only the glint missing from some
scheme in his eye, like the black spot
left from a star missing in night sky?

JEAN O'BRIEN

The River's Dream

'Today for the first time
I hear the river in the trees'

E. Dickinson

I am the river's dream.
Lapped stream of lost words
eddying around stone stops
in the riverbed and limbo pools.
I glide and gloss through rills and runnels
where minnows swim in sunlit shallows
shoaling left and then right in silver flashes
of morse as they mouth warnings.

Blur of algae stirred by the rush of river water
clouding, nothing comes clear.
Further up, clay outcrops still hold
though shape-changing torrents
overwhelmed nearby fields seeking
other outlets they poured over ousted green grass
taking new forms. The flame belly
of the rare bird skimming over me.

I go thrumming over the weir, clattering
on the long drop into the maelstrom
foaming on the waterfall's stone apron
a broken river of light.
Blue of sky breaking over me
with splitter of raindrops swelling
the currents. When the wind lifts
and the day dries, I too ebb and drift
as the dream recedes and shrink
back to known gravel beds and shallows.

Now at last I hear Emily's river murmur
in the trees, as with the fall of leaves the trees
are in me and something grievous
is dreambound. The tender tips of willow
fingers sway like dowsers divining me
just out of reach. The muscled tongues
of eels speak momentarily with cursive
curls on the under-skin of my back, liquid
dreams of the becalmed Sargasso Sea,
but my thoughts are always coastal.

1998

LELAND BARDWELL

Moments

for Edward McLachlan

No moon slides over Harcourt Terrace.
The canal is black. The barracks
crouches on her left.
She sees the child. He holds his coat
across his chest. On his hands,
old socks blunt his fingers.
The handle of his fishing net
has snapped.

Sleep escapes the old woman
on her angry couch. Such images
assault, torment and tease
the sense of her.
Time rolls back on its silent wheels,
empties itself into moments.

How many guilts can one human endure.
One human in all the world, alone
one man or woman holding moments
of a child running, holding shut his coat
with socks on his hands.

from *The White Beach*

MARVIN BELL

Marine Recollections

A shell that held the ocean,
the alterations of sand, a planet moving in waves,
and no one but whose mind drifts

out to sea — the side-to-side rigor
of a jury-rigged clammer
coughing in the current past the buoys.

A time to be nowhere, to be unwatched,
nor missed,
nor flown by nor flown over nor stalked

by rising seas. Early in one's life
to have known the indolence
of the beachcomber raking the sand.

Some drowned who farmed the waters,
the catch crusty, the salt-scarred deck,
the prow leaping then hovering,

and I who wears his past on his sleeve,
puffing to stay abreast —
you don't go there without a lifejacket.

JERI McCORMICK

The Escort

He joins me in border territory
  where two Irelands stretch back-to-back,
    where a sheep field meets its fence,
      and woods sneak up in broad daylight.

He is a scent-seeking machine
  beneath the Queen Ann's lace
    amid rhythmic waves of goldenrod,
      his tail a shake of happiness on a day
        that knows its calendar, savors its July.

We choose the woods, the hound and I,
  circumventers of straggly growth,
    the pines directing us with low fingertips
    gentle on our shoulders, leading us
      mile by mile to the hidden lake.

We stand listening, and I do not think
  of *The Troubles* or weapons or the meaning
    of mounded dirt beneath the matted
      leaves. There we simply listen,
        and in the stillness a fox emerges,

explodes our heartbeats. I lose company
  to the chase that must be run, the race
    the fox must win; but the dog returns
      to lead me back, his tongue lowered,
        the miles grown longer, the road

returning at last, leading to the bend
  toward sheep, the first laced window —
    our rendezvous of hours ago.
      At his gate, my escort waits for me
        to choose my way, watches

with good brown eyes, sends me home
safe in this place of uncertain loyalties.

177

TOM O'MALLEY

Meath's Lost Railway

Where limestone bridges leap a gap
Between twin Meath fields
A railway track has disappeared.

Like stoats with arched backs
Hindlegs/forelegs at a gallop,
These bridges cross/re-cross rich pasture.

Where oaken sleepers lay in gravel
Chestnut horses frisk and start;
Cattle graze where a train ran.

With motte and bailey — castle,
Hill-fort, tumulous,
A railroad steams towards the prehistoric.

I ghost-ride a screeching train
Along fantasy's relaid tracks —
Get off at a vanished platform.

First published in *Salmon: A Journey in Poetry 1981-2007*

GWYN PARRY

Barclodiad y Gawres

We modern people
muster at the tomb entrance.
The guide provides
initial information
but nobody 'really' knows.

There are speculations
of 'important' people buried,
of alignments and rituals,
a place to gather.
The Shaman connecting
to the spirit world
twisting air and time
with fire, sound and stone.

Our time has come
and we are led in
to fumble about
in the blackness,
our hands grabbing
at air,
the rib of an animal
long dead.
As our minds open
we see the 'Apron Full of Stones'
rise from the ground.
The concrete protective dome
arcs over our soft heads.

Gradually, we wake up
to find spirals and zig-zags,
whirlpools, star charts,
serpents of old.
Two bodies were found

in the side chamber
but now there is only echo.

Under the redundant capstone
there runs sweat on stone,
long tears of morning dew
lit bright
by the crystal light
down the passageway.

As we modern folk
poke about in the dark
with our torches, cameras
and digital equipment,
one day
the old gods will return
and split this concrete dome
like an egg,
releasing these captive stones
with fire and smoke.

Once again,
embers will burn
yellow and orange,
rise up
to a star filled heaven.

NOTE: Barclodiad Y Gawres 'Apronfull of Stones'
is a megalithic tomb on the West coast of Anglesey.

ANN ZELL

Weathering

I hunch into the wind, remembering
the day we showed the children marvels.
How the sea shimmered green above shifting
tesserae of refracted light, and how
a sea anemone transformed itself
from a bruised nipple to an oriental
flower; mouth urgent as a baby's.

The strand is a scrubbed slate floor
littered with bone lengths of deep-sea wrack
still attached to their failed anchor stones.
Light comes and goes in waves across
a hammered pewter surface. You
are exchanging elements — becoming
driftwood, leached of all heaviness.

from *Weathering*

1999

LOUISE C. CALLAGHAN

Dreampaths of a Runaway

Toddler found one mile from home!

The child scaled the crossbar of his cot,
landing softly enough, not to waken a parent
in the sleeping house. He slipped out wearing
just his runners and his Batman-pyjamas.
Was it an adventure, some kind of quest,
who can guess—we will never know.

Nor why I, all those years ago, left home.
Setting off on the little two-wheeler,
pedalling fiercely down the back road
to Shanganagh, past the Monument
Marble Works towards the river. My sister
to the rescue, came to bring me back.
We must have played at the river,
raced our sticks in it, under the bridge—
running from one side to the other
to glimpse our little ships…

But no-one asked him why, neither
newspaper, nor radio reporter.
Had the student, the hero of their story
not seen him, not handed him in, I wonder
would he have kept on walking. Noticing
for the first time the blackbird's three-note
call, a fox on the lookout for him
along the Old Dublin Road. Or the hare
racing across a stubble field. And way over
far beyond Garryowen, the morning star.

JERAH CHADWICK

Sudden Landscapes

Unalaska

Winds from the north for three days
then from the south, blasting the snow, the clouds
roiling over ridges weathered
as boulders in surf.

Next day the hills are arrested
with mist. Lone peaks drift
in their auras of storm
like ballast to the diffused,
the indelible openness.

Illusion Islands, I've heard them called,
as accurate a term as any, remembering
lava flats from the ferry, black
expanses above the distant surface.
How as we neared they flew up,
not solid ground but seabirds,
thousand skimming and whirling.

WWII Ruins, Pyramid Valley

Wood crumbles as I climb,
each step sinking
into mosses grown back — all dry rot
and lichen scab, these stairs

to nowhere I thought, hiking
toward them and up
to this flat rise no different
than surrounding tundra.

No, different
because of the stairs,
the past they imply,
how in a few more seasons

the slope will absorb them.
Not this place exactly,
but the sense of it,
this sphagnum, wind-wracked

bracken and cheat grass
I scuff through
like any animal located
by where its kind have been.

from *Story Hunger*

JOSEPH ENZWEILER

The Wind

All my life I've been waiting here
and never knew till now, for the day
long ago in March the phone lines
held their breath, and doors
about to speak, hammers raised
in the strenuous sun that had no echoes,
when running children froze across the lawn
with their lives as thin as cups.

Each troubled car intent on evening,
faces blurred toward cruelty or truth,
the clocks and mirrors of their eyes,
when every destination stopped

the second you smiled at me
from the bus window. I stood there
on the pavement in a black roar of diesel
at four o'clock, a day like any day
until I was visible. Around me the mud
smelled cool with spring and sour straw
and the potholes shivered with rain.

We were fifteen that year, strangers
to ourselves. I must have smiled too,
waved and when you did. As the engine
wound up and pulled away, clouds
in the glass swept over you,
bright hurried countries of the sky,
faster till at last your very thoughts
were clouds to me, your face
a window to another day.

When I turned for home, my chest
caught the wind and I was gone,

reciting the shape of love
past the locust of trees through the gate,
feeling in your dark eyes
as my steps grew bigger
I'm as large now as my happiness.

I never saw the hammers fall and build
the world. I thought I could come back
and always find you there, your hand
in the green coat sleeve, not knowing
we are the wind itself.

That night at supper, my family
ate the same in their same chairs.
But for me the fish was beautiful
and sweet I opened with my fork.
They did not see. I never spoke to you
though my blood was curving to the sky.

This all was long ago.
But I sit outside many days with coffee
or look up from my tools.
These thoughts are holes where the wind blows.

from *A Curb in Eden* (1999)

GABRIEL FITZMAURICE

The Inspector Calls

The inspector calls, we all stand —
"Tá fáilte romhat", I take his hand,
He flaunts his Irish (mine is better)
Then turns to English. Like a debtor
I fawn upon him while he goes
Through the books, then strikes a pose
As he probes my class to find out if
I've been doing my job, and, by God!, he's stiff.

I've done my job, no thanks to him
And those in power who, on a whim,
Deprive us of the things we need
To teach our kids because their greed
Broke this country and now we
Are in debt for all eternity;
And still I come here, day by day,
To teach these kids to live and pray
But prayer is now frowned upon
By the commissars of education.

The inquisition over, it seems I've passed,
Myself and my faithful class,
He turns to Irish once again —
To me Irish is a friend
But to him it's a means to show
Just who here is in control.

He leaves my classroom, we all stand —
"Slán abhaile", I take his hand,
But I swear beneath my breath
It's men like him will be the death
Of all the things that I hold dear,
The republic of conscience we have here
In this classroom where I teach

And laugh and learn. By God! But each
Of these children deserve more
Than to be insulted by a bore
Who thinks that schooling is a way
To preserve the status quo. I pray
For these children and for all
Whose backs are lately to the wall
Crippled by austerity
That we can still stand proud and free
For freedom is that blessed state
That's born with us, that tyrants hate,
Who use schooling to control
What's innate in every soul.
By God! But they won't control me
For in my classroom I am free.

In my classroom I am free.

Tá fáilte romhat: (Irish) Welcome
Slán abhaile: (Irish) Goodbye

FRANK GOLDEN

Declension in April

I sit in the blue chair facing south,
rain on the circular field past Ballyhaine,
rifts of blue opened by the wind,
a taper of baling twine
from last year's sweet pea
caught in the current and blown
to where the tulips lie gusted in defeat.

I watch some footage of Auden
on a summer's day in Kirchstetten,
holding a canvas sack,
jaunting down a narrow grassy track,
tilting as though he might fall
starkly in the grooming apple grove.
He makes it to the picket gate
and to his white VW,
which he opens brilliantly,
then drives off in the summer heat,
dust raised along the dirt road veering north.

He is going somewhere for a reason
to buy a carton of milk or cigarettes
to meet an appointment with a doctor or nurse
to admire bodies on a tree-lined lake
to stop and look at a suicide's grave.

The wind slackens
before an onslaught of rain.
I'll not stir out today.
I'll clean the grate,
build a fire,
close down the damper,
return to the blue chair,
and watch the storming day
berate the windows.

'I was never bored,' he said to Parky once,
'fatigued, disconsolate, melancholy,
but never bored.
It never was a feature of my generation,
never.'

Between Eros and dust
between one Martini and the next
between poems and wars
sonority and authenticity
everything that happens
happens to persist.

He viewed it as failure
not to affirm the flame,
that burning desire
to celebrate being
in all its forms.

Another storm streams in
from beyond Black Head,
fire shadows rise and fall,
I stir the embers to a blaze
to a shatter burst of tongues,
and cast my eye to the storm-bent sycamores,
knowing the resisted life —
intricate in the darkness,
is everywhere to be seen.

JOHN HILDEBIDLE

A Stroll in the Cold Wind

In the night, a reassurance of rainfall
As I lay abed late, reading,
Not quite able to turn the corner into sleep.
In due time, the moon, slipping toward the half,
Resumes its dominion. Today a back and forth day,
Now spurts of rainfall, then sun slanting on the town
At the bay-edge. The dogs won't agree to join me,
But a lone magpie is on duty, and the horses
Look up from their lunch to snort welcome.
Back, warming, I spy a wagtail on the stone wall.
Ease, comfort, a home feeling.

GERALD HULL

Falling into Monaghan

for Margaret

'*No hospitality is dangerous because
of the suspicion of murder.*'
— Gerald of Wales

A spirit stung your heel between mists,
laminate hexed will: a Tara evening, morning
in Tyrone. Your family would pluck us back,
you three parts Eurydice. We turned from
Tudor Park to horses, the old railway.

And penetrated high ground. Aeolus loud
with harmonica, falling into Monaghan,
a Land of Cockaigne. Teasing hard at
Newbliss, Aughnacloy: street signs in
bars, their photos of seedsmen fresh
in our minds. The unknown over hills,
far away; switchbridges, lines awry.
Un-British, a giddy vertigo where cars
hobbled off, bicycles waved and colours
ran ill-defined.

Returning up a scabbed border by Drumfurrer
we smelt the dead, the cattle unburied.
People had emptied, dark holding down.

Then shock of reeling light spread copper
over backing plains. Our heads roared with gold;
translated into birds we fell to a drowning moon.
Countrymen's words gripped our clowning, on
through a hundred townlands.

Annaghmakerrig 1996

MÁIGHRÉAD MEDBH

Three Good Reasons to be a Vivienne Westwood Tartan Dress

*'It's quite incredible to think that we might
be able to save the world through fashion.'* —

Vivienne Westwood

When global warming worsifies,
Earth will shrink incredibly to
Size 4 or so, a billion souls
Tightly squeezed on a patch of ground
West of the water, the measure
Of a Hermès dip-dye silk scarf.
Off the shoulder will be good, but
Diamante with long train, no.

Vivacity takes the biscuit
In all famines. Red crayon lines
Vie with wrinkles and brighten eyes.
In the Nairobi slums she mixed
Effluence with style to make bags
Nifty enough to fill with nothing.
Never wear knickers with a skirt.
Ewer twill says so much about ewe.

JOHN MENAGHAN

Just Another Night in Donegal

Three A.M. and I'm down to three stations on the TV which once got seven and there's nothing on those so I decide to read even though my eyes are burning but I read one bit about two orphans obsessed by the spirit of death and decide to rest my eyes

only to wake four hours later and decide I should go to sleep so I lie back down across the bed sideways to stick the remote on one of the folding chairs I use for end tables in this under-furnished house I'm paying way too much for and end up kicking the other one and a glass full of water goes flying and lands with a crash

so I have to get up and clean up since that's the side of the bed I get up on and I don't want to step down tomorrow and find I have two wet feet full of jagged glass so I head for the kitchen half asleep and come back with the dustpan and some paper towels and by the time I'm done cleaning up I'm much too awake for my own good

but at last I lie down again and slip gradually back to sleep only to wake to the dull thump of the steam shovel at the not quite finished new house across the way then drift back slowly into slumber but the thumping keeps shoveling me out of sleep then dropping me back in again

until at a certain moment I see through closed curtains and a solid wall a group of children running and dancing about in a kind of ring or patch of light and find myself wondering are they the neighborhood kids who I barely know would I even recognize them if they were or are they faeries or what and is it sunlight or faery light

but before I can even decide they're gone as quick as they came not just the children but the whole deal well not the thumping but everything else and I lie there thinking what a weird little dream and it's noon before I wake up and wander through what's left of the day until just as I'm about to go out for the evening I happen to look across at that unfinished house only to see four men all dressed in black what are the chances of that lined up beside the picture window and looking my way

but it's only later that night alone in the ice-cold kitchen that I suddenly get this strange desire to call my parents 3000 miles away and tell them I'm fine strange not only because my parents are dead and buried but because I'm not o.k. I'm really not fine at all and what's maybe stranger still I can't for the life of me tell you why.

ANGELA PATTEN

The Writing Process

Mornings I lie in bed sipping coffee
letting my mind off its weekday leash
to go roaming like a multicolored mongrel
following its moist nose, snuffling
under lichen, mud-loam
the leaf-mulch of the past.

Sometimes there's nothing much to show
for all my rooting at the tuberous rhizome
of family relationships, worrying
the labyrinthine radicle of memory.

Sometimes a few small bones
to chew over later by the fireplace—
crosspatch, snoutfair, colossive.
An archaic adage—to be *moithered, flummoxed*
chuffed by a chance remark
gnawed down to the marrow—
her skin like bellows leather—
put to the pin of her collar—
he was forced to eat his words—

Sometimes my ears twitch, head lifts
as if at the tug of a choke-chain
remembering the moment each gob-stopper
was turfed up into the light.

R.T. SMITH

Cardinal Directions

In the body of a cardinal
who hops along the tamarack limbs,
cathedrals are collapsing. Whole
worlds are falling, exhausted
stars and dialects no one left
can translate. This crested finch,
red as the last cannas
wilting, is famished. He scavenges
in a dry season for pods,
cold grubs, any scrap to sharpen
his beak or hone his sight,
and also within me the tree
of bones is giving way
to gravity, the tree of nerves
surrendering, memory's tree
releasing its leaves, though my
eyes are still seeds looking
for fertile soil, and the one bird
heavy in my chest, the cardinal
heart, still has ambitions
to forage, to sing the litany
beyond language, and fly.

PETER VAN DE KAMP

A Dutch Uncle Advises His Older Self To Behave

Breathe in like a mountain:
Breathe out like a nun.
Hold your breath like a fountain:
Hold off death like your mum.
Fold your loves like a wheelchair;
Scold your nurse like a rum.
Wreathe a smirk through your nightmare:
Just pretend that it's fun.
Let your smile be your curtain,
Since your bastion's undone.
Bequeath no opinion:
Just fade out of time.
Never follow instructions—
And make sure not to rhyme.

GORDON WALMSLEY

Tree

Once upon a moment there was a tree
and the tree was a tree of dreams.
Strong and firm
it curved like a woman dreaming of flowers,
leaning against the breezes of summer or bending with them,
expanding into the the fullness of a day
or folding in with nocturnal rains,
never quite stiff
never quite straight.
And because they were pliant and could bend,
the flowers dreamed into a greater dream of butterflies,
leaves and of branches,
flourishing in the spirit of quiet adumbration.
And on one of the wings of one of the many butterflies
was a most amazing tree, strong and firm
and very nearly
straight.
And the tree on the wing sighed into the evening's mystery
and the butterfly trembled with delight.

Once upon a legend there was a country
that imagined itself as an eagle.
The eagle flew over rivers and sands,
over redwoods, sacred with the silence they have brought forth,
over cities, thrashing with dreams.
And when the day was near its end,
with the moon longing towards the horizon,
the eagle began to imagine
doves and larks and nightingales,
dreaming of how it would be to be able to sing like those birds,
much as a round stone might dream of the sun,
or a flurry of moths might dream of an ocean's currents,
rising and falling in a rhythm of days and of nights.

Once upon a time there was a hush.
And the hush gave birth to a dream.
The dream touched the wing of a butterfly.
It touched the wing of an eagle too.
From the deepest part of a silence
the dream of becoming was born, a mystery
so resonant with hope
you might think
she had been dipped
into the liquid substance of angels.

For she moves with an angel's swiftness
returning to a most amazing tree,
filling its branches with the dreams she enables,
filling its branches with the dreams she becomes.

2000

CATHERINE BYRON

Bare Forked Creatures

In their last days each of my parents became
an infant. Without speech.

                              Words failed
even my mother.

                    My father mouthed for one
last morning, inaudibly, then turned
to a sort of drowning semaphore, his hands
plucking his throat.

                    My mother set her jaw
against all solids. Jerked her head away
as if seeking the breast.

                    *

                    In their last days
my parents were back in nappies, back on their backs
and I was cleaning up between their legs.

Her sex, a liverish frill of labia.
His sex, a stub no bigger than an acorn.

Each child lay at last on a narrow bed.
I drew the white sheet up to her chin
                                   his chin.

I tucked them in.

JOHN UNRAU

Vespers

Rachmaninoff, Op. 37

The voices drifted away some time ago,
along with the bathwater.
No need though to rewind the old tape
with that sombre sweetness still
stirring across my throat and guts.

I've been stupefying myself again.
on a giant disquietude,
the undirected cravings
your music lures me to;

and though it's been a privilege
to join you in this vigil,
the cold enamel against my spine
tells me it's time to snuff the candles,
down these 17 last drops of wine,
and hoist myself back up and out
into the smaller world I left behind
an hour or so ago;
though not without a parting glance
at whatever stars happen to be moving
across the open skylight overhead.

First published in *Salmon: A Journey in Poetry 1981-2007*

MAURICE HARMON

Fr. Sean

Whenever he had to deal with sexual issues
Fr. Sean felt at a loss. In confession penitents talked
About bad thoughts, secret touching, French
Kissing, dirty books, adultery. When it came to advising
Them he was ill-equipped. Women wanted to know
How much they had to put up with. 'He wants me
To take all my clothes off, Father. I get cold.'
Men wanted to know how often they could do it.
'Would once a week be too much, Father, or twice?
Jesus, if she had her way I'd be sleeping on the sofa.
Do you blame me if I do a hand-job?'

Older priests were no help. Some chuckled, 'Ah, sure
What do we know about it?' The more people
Told him about sex the more inadequate he felt.
He was a dark figure in a dark box listening
To another dark figure telling him stories.
He began to ask questions, trying to get details,
Interrogated one woman closely until she cried,
'What's it to you?' and strode out of the box.

Unexpectedly, he met a woman who answered
Whatever queries he had. His ignorance
Seemed to delight her. She called him Seanie.
They walked and talked, kissed when they met,
Played tennis and there too he enjoyed
Her sense of fun and competition. He had the advantage
But she had skill, swept about the court, served
Craftily, angled her shots, varied the pace,
Laughed out loud when she missed a return.

She liked his thoughtfulness, he was completely natural,
His desire for her as unforced as leaves appearing on trees
Or drops of moisture clinging to branches. In all his loving

Consideration, as though years of training made it impossible
To overlook her needs and rights. Humour was part of it,
Enjoyment mixed with playfulness. When she lay
Under him she peddled the air. He would see her legs
Flashing past, hear her cries. He loved to see her
Above him, rising and descending as though moved by waves.

She filled his being; he wanted to be with her,
Any time, any place, to make love every day,
Every night — in bed, on the couch, the floor, the table,
To touch her anywhere, anytime, anyplace.
When he touched shoulder, back or face, her whole body
Came into his hands, head, shoulders, back, bum, thighs,
She was all of a piece, as alive as he was, when he bent
At the altar she smiled up at him, when he stood at the lectern
Her arms encircled him; he might see her lying beneath him,
Her hands on her breasts, nipples stiff and expectant.
He felt able to deal with others, was one with them,
Had gone down into the depths, risen to the heights.

She loved being with him even though she knew
It would have to end, if only to protect him
From gossip and reprimand. He was a good priest.
She observed his subdued grace at the altar,
When he stood at the lectern, handled chalice and paten,
Genuflected before the tabernacle and murmured the words
Of consecration. She saw the beauty and reverence of his hands,
Sometimes went to the altar to receive Communion,
Feel the quiet authority of his voice, 'Body
Of Christ, Body of Christ', to respond, 'Amen'
In shared belief, love and humility. She might linger
To see him greeting parishioners, shaking hands,
Exchanging greetings, occasionally with a note of concern.
Once joined the queue to take his hand, to hear
The quiet murmur, 'Bless you, child. Bless you',
Before she turned and walked away into the street.

JAMES LIDDY

What Does A Man in Love Have To Do?

A man in love: makes moan and labours to an understanding. A man in love has to take shelter in institutions conceived by history or philosophy. A man in love protests himself from the banality of love expressing itself (dosage).

In prayer for solace a man in love moves towards the temple. He trembles in guilt and hope because he has had a great experience. He wants to find out how he can give himself. Temple flowers are watered the candles are lit before the images.

What are the correct procedures? How are the safeguards for the beloved set? Divinity has discovered love first. Man has been handed it on a plate at a banquet. Perhaps what he feels has taken place before he was born. It is part of a retrospective exhibition.

But there are two temples. First on the moon in spraying light questions about love are debated basically its origins. Love is rehearsed and performed in a landscape that is like a nightclub. Participation is clarified. Do not make haste to the wedding. Clothes do not count. Wherever you are you may look on the beloved.

The other temple is the church where there is an altar for sacrifice. This is where we pray for each other whether lovers or not. For a moment we hold each other's souls. Sins are forgiven because at last something amounts to knowledge but sins are also forgiven because of attachment to specific people. The priesthood of lovers does not pass away.

Rules can be reversed they are similar for lovers and beloveds.

First published in *Salmon: A Journey in Poetry 1981-2007*

TOM SEXTON

Crossing the Prairies

for Sharyn

Driving west, we came this way fifty years
ago when we were young and invincible,
singing Johnny Horton's "North to Alaska"
as we drove deep into the star-crowded night
in a Volkswagen bus with four bald tires
and a spare with its sidewall cracked,
back on the road at dawn, running on caffeine.
Now we both bear fresh scars from a surgeon's
knife. Your heart no longer inviolate.
A long scar like a scimitar on my neck.
I watch your face when a voice on the radio
says, "my fields are beyond green with only
a little rot from rain, I'll harvest in a week."
On both sides of the road, the land is as flat
as a griddle. You could watch your dog run away
for a week as the old saw goes. We drink it in:
slight wind moving the grain, the endless sky,
wires sagging between poles, a red-tailed hawk.
"Beyond green," you say, "beyond green" and smile.

MICHÈLE VASSAL

Leaning on Anthracite Skies

I realise now, that the limitations were not yours
but mine. Whilst you were holding the earth
in cupped hands, the children faded into adults
the soft under-layer of laughter and padded dreams
seldom visible now, under their new exoskeleton.
I leaned on winter, on flayed trees licked to the bone by
a goat of a wind and, when the spun sugar of the almond
orchard infused the air with suggestions of marzipan
I wished for the Autan to heave from the South
for its spoor to singe the pale uncurling buds

and the animals came to us from the woods
and the woods took them back and I leaned on loss
on anthracite skies, to hollow out my days
whilst you were holding the earth in cupped hands.

2001

ERLING FRIIS-BAASTAD

Trilobite

Esse est percipi

Another era
is ending, yes,
but there are always
ages to come—

all that's needed
is one small
creature, some
designated observer,

to maintain
the watch, not
even a long watch,
a glimpse will do

to celebrate
and maintain
whatever it is
that's coming up,

to manifest an era
at least as real
as our own
might be.

NADYA AISENBERG

The Singer

The woman knows she is not a metaphor.
Not a willow, pliant, sad, leaning
toward water and her own reflection.
Nor is she the moon, cold distant
object of interperate desire. The self
may not know its own shape, whether
the sum of all the pointillist dots,
or the barely perceptible spaces between them.

She believes in the power of spirits,
magic, as in abduction, seduction,
the need to imagine the ugly as part
of the beautiful, for her hands to caress
the skin of all things. She remembers
how she kissed a Frog into a Prince,
handsome in green doublet and hose.

Can a self be chosen, inscribed,
the way a photographer fixes a subject
so there's no need to ask: Who am I today?

The woman remembers a moment,
a child tossing rhymes in the air,
learning, before she can write,
the incantation of words,
how they came from inside the body
to settle around her like birds,
some on her shoulders, some
pecking sounds from her hand,
how they'd return to sing
the longing she felt
as she sat on the steps
of the west-facing house
watching the sun sink the day.

from *Measures*

MARY O'DONOGHUE

The Eighties

Dolls 'tached. Sindy, Jana drowned. Six and seven.
Cat flat dead on a Massey. Burials. July's hot smother.
A pony trucked away. Playing didgeridoo through wavin.
Eight and nine, Two Tribes, war. A friend's older brothers,
always plotting their murders. Hazel woods. The lake.
Nettles dock-leaved. Calamine. Electric fence susurrus.
Seven Seas gloop on a spoon. Gypsum. Buck rake.
Ten. Statues crying blood. Liking the word brucellosis.
Jeyes' Fluid puke-thud on tiles. Talk about the feeks.
Eleven. Rhombus desk. Feet in the stove. Poodle socks.
MT-USA. Walking like an Egyptian. Padre Pio's mitten.
Supergran, Falcon Crest. Twelve. Ganders' wicked beaks.
Horse jumps. Chopped fingers sent from the Border Fox.
The telltale heart. The half-blind dog. Being bitten.

First published in *spoKe: a Poetry Annual* (2015)

LAURA LUNDGREN SMITH

Discourse and Distance

for Cathie

Our lives are stored
in wires,
but we whisper together
through telegraphing roots of trees
and the sharp teeth of
all the wild things.
Rains rolls our parley
in rivulets
and rushes,
drowning this distance,
absorbing this absence.
I will send you verse
in numeric semaphore,
coded in electricity
over miles unseen.
But the fox outside your fence
is the poem.
My graceless words in
graceful form.
You transmit your art,
pixelated and voltaic,
broken and torn,
through the lines.
But your image
is this storm:
silver
fulmination filling
my eyes.
How close we are,
yet far apart.

The moon will mutter
this ode to you.

For me,
you will paint the dark.

MARK GRANIER

Dead Zoo Blues

An astounding crate full of air.

— Seamus Heaney

Great Irish Elk, Giant Reindeer,

who else will air
you? Black-boned roof-raiser
aflame with antlers

and a bull-snorting absence
of Attenboroughs whispering in
the undergrowth, zooming out

for an aerial shot
of the herd spreading its dark
quickening water,
                        is it over

as we view you from under,
standing here on
the tiled floor, the tundra?

*

More inscrutable than the Sphinx:
the trophy-head of a rhino
bagged over a century ago
by a Colonel Spinks.

*

And here
my marginal, 12 year old self-
displacer, soft-eyed hoarder
of Wildlife magazines, haunter
of ditches and bogs.

DO NOT TOUCH

the rhino's tarry flesh
just yet —

wait for the rat kangaroo
and the parchment bats

to undo.

*

Here, touching what
he should not:
an elephant's cunt,
a wound
in an old coat.

*

How to fade
from a dazzling op-art zebra
into just that shade
of sepia.

*

Or here, this child who holds
to his hiding place among
the grown-up coats hung
in a glass wardrobe

*

while the Fin Whale's skeleton
                              suspended on wires, shipshape
as a longship, swims overheard.

*

Further, upstairs, along the galleries,
dust-coloured moths and butterflies

(ribbons from an antique war)
recall the killing jar,

though one or two
still flash

forget-me-not blue.

*

Creaking Victorian ark
whose hold is a maze
of mirrors — our faces

afloat over the glass
eyes of your great
and less great apes —

*

here is a space
reserved for all of us

antique as H.G. Wells'
leather-ivory-and-brass
armchair traveller

working the lever,
setting the dial, the date.

2002

MARY COLL

Moving Out

You said he loved you, and that you loved him,
as if that was all there was to say.
So I held my tongue all summer, until it got too heavy.
Then a week before you left I made my salad, without the olives,
Two days later I made my apple tart, without the cloves,
Your last night at home, after the car was packed, and the house was
finally quiet I added an extra quilt,
stuffing it in as if my life depended on it, or yours.
Sometimes that is all a mother can do,
Leave things out, or add things in,
hoping through a sequence of tiny gestures to tell the whole story.
One thing I never said is that neither of us
are ready for this goodbye,
though only one of us sees it now,
by the time the other figures it out, winter will have come,
at which point, an extra quilt will be essential.

THEODORE DEPPE

from The Little Colloquium By The Sea

In a former life I worked twenty years as a nurse
    and never saw anyone
        nail their exit so perfectly,

so last summer, when my father stopped breathing,
    I howled and laughed, both at once,
        a death so gentle:

ninety-one and living on his own
    terms till the end.
        And later, seated on a plane

across from a novelist I recognized
    from author photos,
        I watched his total concentration,

submerged in the creation of some world I hope
    to enter someday, fingers coming down
        on the keyboard almost all at once like

some sort of weather that can dash and lift
    and console and break us
        with a single word.

~

After a month of conferences, we arrived home
    in Ireland and my wife led me
        into the North Atlantic.

How could I know our hearts wouldn't stop
    when we entered those icy waters? We waded in,
        splashing cold onto our arms, then chests,

trying to get used to it before the plunge.
        Having survived that, I find myself
            swimming daily now, late into the fall,

preserving this space to somehow be with my father,
        though he would have been the first to laugh,
            and I'm not sure how I could have explained.

~

Our neighbour says I'll be able to swim all winter
        since I started in August, as long as I go in daily.
            Wasn't it his father who said he could lift

a three-year-old bull above his head if he started with a calf
        and followed through each day?
            Then first thing every morning

didn't he do just that? *And could he really lift the bull?*
        Oh, we'll never know, our neighbour says.
            My father strained his back and had to quit.

~

Father, each day I walk to the beach wearing your coat
        like another skin. I remember you asking,
            Where's Dougie? and we'd point

to your shoulders, *You're carrying him!* and you'd crane
        your head to the skies and say, *I don't see*
            anyone. Where's Dougie? and we'd shriek

with laughter. A game played all the way to the beach
        where you'd lower my brother to the sand
            and ask, *Where were you?* and he'd say

On your shoulders, and you'd look at both shoulders
        and say, *There's no one there. You're*
            on the beach! And the gentle dispute

between fathers and sons continues, *You're there,*
        You're not there, while the waves
            come in and withdraw.

ETHNA McKIERNAN

Nighttime on the Island

for Kate Stanley

And the foghorn a hollow tube
or maybe a calliope breathing its contralto
through the chambers of my inner ear.
And the wind traveling free
through the house, billowing
then slapping this curtain and the next,
blowing toasted bagel crumbs
from the moonlit maple table,
swaying heads of roses in their vases
as it passes. And the faint tick-tock
of the kitchen clock, and the laundry
on the line perfumed by lavender.
This is the hour of sleep on Martha's Vineyard,
the time when woods behind the house beckon
and thin before dreams begin.

PATRICIA MONAGHAN

The Butterfly Tattoo Effect

Does the flap of a butterfly's wings in Brazil set off a tornado in Texas?
— Edward Lorenz

Charlene was fifty when she got it:
one small butterfly, perched on
her right shoulder, bright blue
with stipples of pink. Everything
in her life seemed safe by then:
husband, children, house and dog.
She wanted to be a little dangerous.

When she left the Jade Dragon
she called her oldest friend, Maggie,
in Florida, with the news. A tattooed
gal at fifty, she bragged. I ain't down yet.

Maggie laughed that throaty laugh of hers.
An hour later on her way to work,
she stopped on a whim and bought
a gallon of red paint for her door.
That night, she didn't drive straight
home but stopped for a drink at an old
haunt from her more dangerous years.
No one she knew was there, so she talked
awhile to Flo, the bartender, told her about
feng shui and red doors, and oh yes, she
mentioned the tattoo just before she left.

It rested in Flo's mind all night as she
uncapped the beers and mixed the drinks.
She was warmer than usual, sassy and loud.
Things got wild. There was dancing.
A new woman stopped in and picked up
one of the regulars. Washing up past midnight,

Flo thought of her old friend Paula, who
lived in California. It was still early there.
Flo picked up the phone, right then,
and called. Somehow the subject of Charlene's
tattoo came up. Paula had been thinking
of getting one too. Why not? Life marks us all,
why can't we chose our scars just once?
They talked till late. The next day Paula
walked into a dealership and bought
the reddest car she saw. By nightfall she was
driving fast, towards the south. And the next morning

the world awoke to news of seismic
convulsions on every continent brought on by
the simultaneous shifting into high gear
of millions of women in sleek red cars.

from *Dancing with Chaos*

JUDE NUTTER

Field Notes: Watching the Crew of Atlantis Renovating the Hubble Telescope

What comforts me most is imagining
the calm and regular draw and blow of their breathing;
that they are floating, for a while,

> in exile and surviving
> because after weeks of drifting tethered
> to a machine that pulled in
> the room's ambient air, compressed it and vented
> off its nitrogen with such a quiet,
> relentless suck and surge, my mother
> had crossed into the homeland
> no one is equipped to travel through. Tethered

securely, and laden with tools
and equipment, the astronauts bury their arms,
elbow-deep, into the silver torso
of the telescope. Beneath them, across the Earth, night's
precise curve approaching and nothing
around them but the constant
wash of their own breathing. What I remember most

> about my mother's last breath was the way her eyes
> opened slightly—slim buttonholes
> in the body's fabric—and my father rising
> out of his chair and leaning over
> the bed's chrome railing to get as close
> to her as he could, to rest his forehead against hers
> and whisper *hello, Eileen*; and I found

> myself thinking about that white
> and half-wild pony in the pasture next door;
> the way, each morning, behind a single strand

of fence wire, it waited—a solid pale patience—
until my father trailed through the damp
nap of the lawn with his small offering;
the way it would lower its head, then,
to press against him, with such restraint,
the long, heavy treasure of its skull.
The thick plate of the forehead. Each nostril's
soft cuff. But it was over

already and that machine went on breathing
without her until I rocked its small red switch
into silence. There was the fixed curve
of my father's spine. There was the still weight
of his head against hers. Our first night on earth
without her. Wind in the hawthorn and the great
carnival wheel of stars. The astronauts

are repairing the gyros; they are fitting
the spectrograph and the wide-field cameras
that will allow us to gaze right onto
the cosmic frontier. And the undertaker unzipped the dark

bloom of his body bag. Later, the froth
of the first birds, and the lights of the fleet roped
three deep along the quay fraying
in a dawn that arrived like wood smoke and,
for a while, my father and I not knowing how
to be with each other. With their gentle

and deliberate gestures the two astronauts
appear almost tender, like lovers.
The visors of their helmets are golden
blisters of reflected light. It is impossible to gauge
the ferocity of thought inside them.

Winner of the 2013 Strokestown International Poetry Award

2003

DAVID CAVANAGH

Remembrance

Flip a card, then another. No match.
Then your brother flips two more,
your mom, your dad, two and two
until a pair of threes turns up.
But what really counts is how you lean
over those false starts. They're burned
onto the back of your eyes. You've got
the picture now of a jack, a queen,
the black eight over in the corner.
You will not forget your family's foul-ups.
You wait for the right card, perhaps a king,
maybe a five, then you picture its twin,
third row, second one in, and you're off
gathering pairs lickety-split, what a snap,
your private magic, as if it all makes
sense, all comes together, you feel a strange
new power swell, you're doing it for all,
and you look up, flushed, to see if this time
they look grateful, happy, or at least
impressed, until the table's bare.

PAUL PERRY

Leap Year Lake

at the asylum seekers support group meeting
where after three weeks the caring committee members
have still not come up with a name
for the party and have wrankled over the words
for its mission with painstaking deliberation

I think of it, leap year lake,
the joy in just saying it, the lake
we passed on our way to Moydow,
after an afternoon of poetry in Virginia,
a palm of water which was not there,
hidden like an innuendo, or an unspoken
thought, curled up into some arid underground fist,

assumed though that it would arrive,
like a rumour
or a slur, the kind you hear on Dublin street
about our guests, who are bored and crammed
and live under direct provision
which itself sounds like a sentence
to serve under

we are careful about what we say
in the constitution to the unnamed support
group for those who have arrived from other places
and may have names we can't pronounce and faces
we have not yet recognised

it's there as the politics and rhetoric
makes me dizzy an image of the lake arriving
like a black bead in a rosary of reds or blues
and the water, its water, the lake's,
leap year lake's water

is like a dark spell the sky has cast,
its own secret reflection,
a beautiful disappearance elected to arise
once every four years, but by whom,
or by what, a common syntax or better yet
a language perhaps
which suggests sustenance, breath, life, our wish
to return always to where we started from,
to be present always, even when we are not
or cannot be

with the rain, which has created a season of itself
and which punctuates the lake's return
leap year lake
go on imagine you are there
by its banks now
pushing your memories out
like a boat
not with a name, an agenda,
but with an exhalation and a mysterious plangent
grammar, nominated, seconded, at once unanimous.

from *The Drowning of the Saints*

2004

MARCK L. BEGGS

The New Communists

are not under your bed, in your closet,
or dropped to your roof by silent drones.
They wave flags as they crawl over your fence,
treating your property as theirs to roam.

They cannot see purple, cannot read signs.
Here in the land of the brave, anyone
is free to open up the boundaries
unless you were to enter their own homes.

They kill deer and call it a harvest,
mark their paths with trash and spent shotgun shells.
Their minds spin with excuses to enter
your land, to leave behind their bloody trail.

The new communists leave death in your woods,
then head off to church to learn what is good.

THOMAS KRAMPF

A Cup Half Full

Even when old
a parent will always view
a child grown old

As a child

Otherwise, edited by time
like a missing bed or the proverbial
airplane door

Suddenly blown open, over
a dark sea

A parent will always view
a child grown old, as
half a child —

GARY J. WHITEHEAD

Purgatory Chasm

Now I spelunk through time,
thinking my way between heaves
of doubt, feeling
in the dark for passages
and hints of diffuse illumination,
less sure than when, as a boy,
I slid head-first into that womb
of glacial confusion,
probing with a diminishing
beam slick seams and strange
formations—Corn Crib
and Coffin, Pulpit
and Fat Man's Misery.
The point then was to slink
as deep as I might, lose myself
in dead-ends and sharp enjambments
until, too tired to move,
penlight dead, I'd lie panting
and panicked in cool blindness
like a wounded mole.
Was this the purgatory
I'd been taught in school,
postmortem lay-over?
Sandwiched in granite,
I loved the not-knowing,
and I still do—the crawl forward,
word after word,
the glimmer on the rockface,
and, finally, the way out
and the white so bright
that my eyes, without
my wanting, must close.

ALAN JUDE MOORE

from Mayakovsky 1916

On the Green I was reading about Mayakovsky's Maria
     and the sun exploded into a thousand pieces
Heavenly ordnance
     His broken heart

On the street I came across countesses grieving
     for palatial hotels where they lost their reason
the natural order
     the best of starts

In Paris songbirds drown in liquor
     for hooded men the singing stops
Dumb waiters haul their cargo
     from the bottom to the top

Tomorrow the market crashes but that's OK
     The doorman weeps into 100 handkerchiefs
Night sticks, hooves and shields
     beat in sync

here and across courtyards of death
     anywhere really voices are raised
into the faces
     of the faceless

*

Still
　　　we stare out across Lubyanka
　　　　　　across the square and the stables
　　　at panting men in heavy coats
　　　　　　making eyes at traffic lights

who knows who to tip their hat to?

the fountains and flowerbeds are brimming with poets:

some rushed right in from the factory floor
some still digging up graves
making quick abandoned incantations

some crawling down broken from the lampposts
some out from under the tramway
or turning up under torn up flagstones

some lost beneath tin whistles and tunics
some formed from the air of anthems
and some from the small diameter
　　　　　　　　　　　　of red suns

bleeding
across your torso

2005

SIMMONS B. BUNTIN

Desert Cottontail

Hopper but not hare, bunny but not jack, shit-
eater but not jackalope (that giver

of shit, launcher of tumbleweeds): cottontail
you zig through my thoughts like you zag

through the keen mind of my dog, the bone-
white shih tzu tracing your evening trail

& your riotous tail & so we both know
you are also on the mind of the rattler

who seeks your fur-lined nest, the coyote
who plays the opportunist (& why not:

he too steals the prickly pear's ruby meat)
& also the owls—great horned & barn—

not to mention, of course, the cats:
the yard's fat tabby you'd think couldn't catch

a whiskered thing but look at that bloody haul
& also the margay & bobcat, ocelot & mountain

lion & if the rumors are true the jaguar,
whose name means skull-crusher—

so back then to the canines: let's admit my pup
cannot compete with kit fox or gray fox or Mexican

gray wolf & also my flavorful friend
you scamper through the mind of red-tailed hawk

& Harris' hawk, Cooper's hawk & American kestrel
(ambitious, to be sure) & below them

the badger & the bear, weasel & raccoon, striped
skunk & hooded skunk & after all that

I coax my dog back as you sprint from every
talon & claw into the ravenous night.

KEVIN HIGGINS

Inappropriate Comparisons

If I could be bothered, I'd compare you
to a television presenter rubbing Nutella
into Chris De Burgh's buttocks; say
that you are only slightly less likeable
than a twice defeated election candidate who enjoys
hanging around funeral parlours;
that your words are accurate and beautiful
as boiled eggs peeled and tossed out windows
at random passing cars; that your smile
is all the sugar you didn't take in your tea
during Lent; that you're almost as lovely
as the economist, who was wrong about everything,
giving his bald patch its daily sprinkle
of bulls' urine. But I'd rather not
acknowledge the ongoing tragedy
of your continued existence.

2006

PHILIP FRIED

Late in the Game

*In 1931, [Kurt] Gödel published results in formal logic that are considered
landmarks of 20th-century mathematics. Gödel demonstrated, in effect, that hopes
of reducing mathematics to an axiomatic system, as envisioned by mathematicians
and philosophers at the turn of the 20th century, were in vain.*

——Institute for Advanced Study, Princeton

In heaven's bleachers, it's the 7th-inning
Stretch. God and Gödel, standing side by side,
Cap on head, Bible and scorecard on seat,
Are gazing down at the green in America's soul.

Want a dog and a tall cold one? asks God.
Thanks, no, Gödel demurs, *I never indulge.
I am, I admit, sparing in what I eat.
But, as I was saying, the incompleteness theorem
"Knocked the legs out from under," is that the idiom?,
Russell and Whitehead's quest for an unbroken, logical
Basis for mathematics.*
                              Just what I did
To the snake, says God. *That slithery hissing devil,
That terrorist* . . .
                              *By the way, I proved you exist,
Ontologically, by using an ultrafilter,
Together with a modal plenitude principle.*
——*Awesome!*
                              *But I've discovered a logical flaw
In the Constitution, an inner contradiction
That could make a dictatorship legal.*
                                        You're a good citizen,
On earth as in heaven. Can't give you a Halo Dog?
——*It's in the section about executive power.
You see, Mr. God, or President?* . . .
                                        Just then,

The Seraphim finish their cover, to loud acclaim,
Of "God Bless America," the boisterous crowd
Of the blessed, re-seated, is stirring, and He is purring,
That's ok, kid, but let's get back to the game.

ROBERT GREACEN

Carnival at the River

The procession of ghosts shuffles by,
Faceless, bannerless, blobs in a landscape
Of dead trees, rotted flowers.
Gradually the blobs dissolve into people.
Father steps out in Edwardian style,
Links arms with mother in her flowered hat.
There's cousin Jim, his gun lusting for snipe.
Aunt Tillie's fox fur dangles at her neck.
Teachers pace by in funereal gowns.
Boys in uniform, bare-kneed, sulk past
As if they'd been cheated of a holiday.
Stewart pushes a 1930s Raleigh bike,
Willie McIlwaine drools over an oval ball.
I turn on my side and hope for easy sleep
Away from the images of childhood
But the procession sidles into dream.
I am walking beside grandfather.
He plucks his beard, tells me softly:
'We're going to the carnival.
We are gathering at the river'.
I feel cold, my guts tighten.
Father's father, take my arm!
Grandfather holds me, quotes Beckett:
'Je n'ai rien contre les cimetières.'
We laugh, walk arm-in-arm to the carnival,
The gathering at the river.

First published in *Robert Greacen: Selected & New Poems*, edited by
Jack W. Weaver (Salmon, 2006)

STEPHANIE McKENZIE

Jean Rhys's Granddaughters

for Mary Hanna

I did not want to be cast into other lands, wanted
the islands and mainland separate. I didn't want
archipelagos to connect.

True, at Marshall Falls, inland from the Essequibo,
I'd thought of Jamaica, Reach Falls, how beauty
is similar. And different.

And coming back, dredged churning of the muddy
water, warning on a sandy cove where we'd stopped
that I should not swim and suffer infection left
by parasites my body did not know, or cyanide
from hungry mines, or refuse and garbage,
I'd thought of Long Bay. Jamaica. How I might fling
myself haphazardly there.

I did not recall the beach at Ochi where you'd sat
hunkered in your dreams of childhood, a summer
as a little girl. Parents still alive.

On public transit from downtown Georgetown,
I hadn't thought of you until there you were in death,
and that island flooded me, connected. Somehow
the Caribbean was together again.

Nothing in the lesser or greater Antilles or secrets
lodged in Guyana's woods could make metaphors
serve this poem, whatever the remembrance
might be. Your death is as inconvenient as the history
that shaped you, the might of some inheritance.
Isles and families.

Tonight I've come to a garden restaurant not for food
but to hear crickets, re-create a meal we might
have shared. What sense can be made of this anyway,
the islands broken up like stones in fields the angry
might have smashed, taken with their brutal lot,
languages separate, as foreign as a good dose
of justice, women having taken the worst, even
if white and born to a palace?

You were rich, by all accounts, backra lady.
Yet the museum which houses this history
is rugged and a liar. Full of catheters
and sores.

Your ancestors crawled to the top with tents
from Lebanon's deserts.

2007

EMILY WALL

A Galaxy of Flowers

It happens sometimes, on June afternoons—we witness a butterfly
rising out of deep grass and light, moving with purpose. Is she a pilgrim
heading for some holy site? A petal to touch, a galaxy

of flowers to kneel in? Thousands before her, galaxies
of wings, have done the same. We stand on a disappearing glacier, watch butterfly
migrations following climate signs. We read about millions of pilgrims

damaging the holy sites with the weight of their bodies. So we pilgrim
ourselves into the stars, into the sea, needing to touch just one galaxy
of the untouched. Where does this old desire come from? To butterfly

galaxies into touchstones? And yet, if I could touch this one pilgrim's wings, I would.

MICHAEL S. BEGNAL

Homage to Séamus Ennis

What is revolutionary art?

Revolutionary art precedes the revolution,
the note in the pipes bent higher,
the bent notes trilled,
it doesn't know that it inspires revolution
just that it it goes somewhere nua
no matter how many times it has gone
and its drones and dord have preceded it

there is the possibility that it does
not observe time as Ennis does not always
but holds the dissonant note,
signatures whiskeyed at times
and it is good that they are so gilded

from his body the winding notes,
from whatever beings too—
bend these notes mo chara, bend
and drone, drone, for hours on end!
flurry the chanter! blow out yr elbow!

What is the revolution?

The performance of
that time is not linear or circular
but unpatterned,
but other times it is indeed in jig or reel time,
a performance
that alternates when
the artist feels, drawing on his/her years
of study and praxis, it is time to—

that the air, though, is the desirable mode,
the slow air, the bent notes, dissonant drones,
that it floats over chords of differing
elements, jarring and
holding the note in ever-new performance,
takes us now to a space úr, an expanse
newly informed
by the golden thread,
       stream,
            ocean of air

DAVE LORDAN

Someone Else's Turn

Three years after her classmate Danny, who also loved
dancing, dies in junior infants of cancer,
my daughter's in the back of our car after school,
and we're stalled at the lights, and we're all looking out
at the afternoon sky over the Wicklow Mountains.

Wow, says my wife, the driver, *see how those clouds
hang so low on The Sugarloaf, and the gold
of the sun right through them, like a crown
for the mountain? Isn't it striking, so rich and so colourful,
like you'd see in a gallery?*

Every year, says my eight-year-old daughter,
*when it's Danny's Anniversary, the clouds float down
from heaven with Danny floating down on them so he can see his friends
and family and say hi.*

Really?, say I out of curiosity, but also mild concern
... What else happens on Danny's Anniversary?

Oh, says she, *in the nighttime Danny jumps out of his grave
and dances in the moonlight
to his favourite music
like Michael Jackson
for a while
and when he finishes dancing the moon applauds
and so do the yews and so do the crows and the cows
and the toads and the ferns*

*and so do all the other dead people in the graveyard who've been
watching him dancing away....* And I say *Really? Why's that?*

—— *Cos it's someone else's turn the next night
and everyone has to get a clap and a hip-hip-hurrah
when it's their turn
you eejit.*

251

MÉLANIE FRANCÈS

Sierra Leone

You imagine blue roads in the dirty green leading to the village.
The faint screeches of tires that lead to a silence full of panic.
The cabins' roofs are distorted by the lens or the heat or the void
and soldiers in washed out uniforms, bogus soldiers, bogus rebels
of a bogus war inspect villagers with fingers glued to Kalashnikovs.
You imagine sick mockeries of heart shapes in the nearby trunks
made by rocket leftovers. You see soldiers looking for a mission,
possibly dazed with cocaine, soldiers that you can't understand,
their war like a snake swallowing its own tail to stave off hunger.
On one side are those who have nothing.
On the other are those who have nothing but are armed.
You see the soldiers and the impression gets blurred by normalcy
and press reports and the time to eat and practice human games.
I am astounded that I have to concentrate to care fully.
Sierra Leone. The name hovers over dinner time and television
and all the faces that are caught in distress in war photography.
These faces are the slap given to our millenium craze.
This is where my festivities snap: they fire and I am concentrating.

First published in *Salmon: A Journey in Poetry 1981-2007*

SEAMUS CASHMAN

for love is

for love is
quadruped
to the fall

1

I
rise
I lean over,
& across
& in between

then, I press on

2

Somewhere in there
is a seahorse spined
sensitive and mysterious
afloat above my thumb
and a child lost almost
in earnest contemplation
a gentle flower petalled
in excruciating thorn
absorbed and undisclosed.
Around and in-between,
the fluted tiles of a kitchen
floor or summerhouse
emerald across the universe
like some ceramic
encyclopaedic skin
shed by a lucky snake
just there on a horizon
disappeared

eyeballs burst
into what is not
even looking, and sigh
the egg fossilled in volcanic stone
beak beckoning mudplast
ectoplast — this last echo
millennia beneath skyblue
reflections raw   orange   blazoned
palms searching texture's mane
in wracklike mirror flame

now I'm ablaze too but cold.
Waiting too but spoiled
by the rays of a living sun
and towelled dry by your
fallow moon, shadowed, gone

3

Razor sharp on the first of April
this unconstructed I beckoned
did not, no no did not salute —

what is yet unknown
remains unknowable in
curious awareness of
no thing thang thong
no truth thought
broth forth except
this — saw it later
hanging on a wall
in some version of Tate
I now forget:
my pedlar, my revenge
and all the world stolen
by thieves hanging from walls
and dropping like spies

—O signature eyes!

4

Gingerbread man
woman and bird
flattened against your
imaginary wall
and aerated with stampings
of cake mould cut-outs
configuring in biscuit
reveals and sunlight
a convulsed threat
in silhouette writhing
passionate linkings,
hardening in
avian coils, and
sex with a kind of charm
in the eye and fear
in the vulva-less belly

Evening's translucent sky.
Lost. Love.
Loving in the world's silence.

Goodbye.

NOTE: Max Ernst died on 1 April 1976.

2008

J.P. DANCING BEAR

Only Human

I'd spent the night in a creaky old bookstore/house
listening to the Irish rain pelt the roof
and thought of the centuries of ghosts
wandering the wetlands, moaning the old
paths and trails, that might now be the new
motorway. How many times are they run through
in a night by a lorry or speeding coupe,
and what could it mean in their ancient minds?

*

I loaded the boot of my own ghostkiller
in a pre-dawn blue that made all of Ennistymon
look as though it had been submerged.
I left it that way, struggling to reveal
it's brighter colors. For an hour,
I was the only human,
and when I'd thought about it,
I hadn't seen anyone since the previous night.
I thought of an apocalypse and how I may
expect the dead to shamble across the road
but the downpour washes away everything
but the cattle grazing the lush fields.
Even in this dim light, the gorse flowers look
as though the sun exploded
and fell onto the earth.

*

No, this is the land of the living,
and all the suffering that goes with it,
and I, stranger that I am, racing past
it all, am merely a ghost,

that should have lingered a little longer.

SUSAN MILLAR DuMARS

Moon, Alone

Although she drags the heaving sea behind her
she feels reduced, a lozenge on the tongue
of God; a sugar circle melting bright.
A light dissolving — kind, and turning kinder

for kind is all she ever wished to be.
Not wild, bewitching, not an opal shine
alone and distant. Creatures howl with need
beneath what seems a milk-soft mystery.

But Sister Moon is no mystery.
She's just a girl alone in the dark.
The night has teeth. It bites and bites till Moon's
reduced — a smile without eyes to see.

She had a brother once — quite blonde, quite bright.
The sun fell down, so now there's only night.

LORNA SHAUGHNESSY

Always the Bridesmaid

At seven, draped head to toe in lace,
he peeps coyly from behind the veil.
Later, with moustache and small paunch
he poses again, slumped in an armchair,
whisky bottle on the floor, tiara askew;
the king who wanted to be a bride.

He writes to thank me for the poems,
says he especially liked the one about money —
the way money, like birds, constantly flits
from one place to the next. The card is Victoriana,
a mock-up of lace made with paper doylies
and photocopied in the palace.

PAUL ALLEN

One Too Many Mornings:
Unfinished Letter from West Virginia

1967: I felt your soul leave in a golden carriage
behind the chapel of our Methodist school
in the rain. Low branch of the tree,
you pushing me up to the clouds,
pulling me into you.
Our smell, your root note pure, your whine
a diminished, blessing the world
like our twilight Ian & Sylvia covers in the park.
My shirt stuck to my back.

2013: We've lived the days between lives—
distances, years, loves—good piled on good
to no avail, evil wrapped in chocolate.
What does any connection with the past mean
beyond flubbing time? Yesterday, we watched the Potomac
and Shenandoah join to form the Potomac,
Shenandoah losing her name,
her identity. Harper's Ferry, West Virginia,
where John Brown's dream broke into 313.9 million pieces.
Small, break-away state.
I shan't lie. I kind of wanted to know
whether we'd connect again and sing harmony
into the night's sky. You didn't know
I took my guitar but kept it hidden
beneath that pile of crap in the crew cab.
I didn't know whether we could bring the songs out of the 60s again.
But we were so full of *I*, you and I.
Your sentences, my sentences began with that rat pronoun,
chewing through the rope of *we*.
The rope broke: "Isn't it good," you said,
"That we can meet, and not think about sex?"
Some questions have only one answer.
Our parallel 4ths or 5ths would have been disaster,
I knew, our registers so altered by time and circumstance.
You could hear it in the *I, I, I*—unresolved melodies.
We're old. We watched the river turn gold.

CAROLINE LYNCH

The Match

I told the woodsman that hurleys are made of ash
and about the clash that is the cliché of all that.

By Salisbury Cathedral he explained the rules
of cricket — the enthusiastic inflection, lovely round

vowels bowled across the grass. The I picked up
a sliotar on a flick of air held like a hurley

and pucked the tight wad of nothing: high, long,
over the cathedral spire's great struts of Irish oak.

from *Lost in the Gaeltacht* (2008)

TYLER FARRELL

Beast and Mankind Dream of Costa Rica

Tico time blends animal kind and rainforest forever relaxed
drinks and feasting with jaguars late December equatorial morning.
Books and games with sun white faced monkeys on balconies all day
smelling grill grease, our meal at last slow dusk of fish and shrimp
hungry hands and light fixed a fall over large pacific rocks, wind—
sailors can view rich coast life, the gentle species of Central America.
Now, banana blight eradicated, coffee beans with ocean breeze
blown far off palm oil dangers shadowed by snakes, sinful
poisonous tall stick machetes and crocodiles under bridges.
Bicycles hide the shade from backs, long legs of jungle.
Dirt roads carved with workers used as mules for tourists
to zip line mountainsides strung by insect explorers. Chest
thumping optional. Immense leaves with small pools of dew.
We animals watch heavenward, water trees in the clouds.
Most days we are aroused by ghosts of saints, weather
wet from the heavens, sky dark — light instinct, small faith found
on basilica floor prayers to La Negrita. We, reverent, solemn
each of our bended knees round and whole, like the sphere.
Cartago's world runs miles past the farmers, industry
for Quepos fans us with the flame, the holy heart and
sweaty rebirth in heat Manuel Antonio Christmastime.
We hear howlers in the distance, under new moons.
We claim and believe as Toucans sit and listen quietly—
geckos geometric on the windows, lizards jump from stone patio
to thick brush. Soon, for the Feast of the Epiphany,
we will north Midwest home again without immense yellow sun,
blink my eyes with God and beasts in fever weeks to Milwaukee.
Negative nine grey degrees as I drive to the store—
milk has gone sour. Football fans stock up for the big game.
They rumble from the snow. I float with my cart. I am a dream
of a sloth asleep on shade branch tree, refusing to come down.

PATRICK HICKS

Klara's Son

I see where he got his steel-grey eyes,
that basilisk stare. He takes after you—
you, who placed warm lips against his skull,
you, who loved every atom in his heart.

But when your breasts filled up with cancer,
you worried about your boy, this art school
reject.

Klara, after you died, he toted your photo
to the trenches of France, to beer halls in Munich,
and then on to the capital of Hate.

Your image was next to him in 1945,
down in that concrete bunker
as mortars struck the ceiling
and dust was pounded loose.

And when he picked up an oiled pistol—
its steel mouth kissing
the underbelly of his chin—
he probably glanced over at you.

Klara, wherever you are now,
do you know that a curse sprang from your womb?

Tell me, one parent to another,
can you still love your boy,
after he slaughtered half of Europe?

PETE MULLINEAUX

Fair Way

How could he have missed the final easy putt?
Facing the TV reporters for the ritual post mortem
having played a flawless approach, a sensational
drive from the tee, a string of eagles and birdies
carded, placing him on the brink of a course record —
the seasoned golfer could only recall considering
a line of fire, trying to read for bias in the green,
when the grass appeared to ripple in his direction,
then grow exponentially like a speeded-up
wildlife film, as if suddenly remembering
it was a living thing; an earthquake-like shudder
that shook his club so violently his arm vibrated
and the hole appeared a million miles away,
the slight incline a mountain slope — benign clouds
overhead took on the shape of zeppelins, a flock
of starlings became a fighter squadron, it was all
he could do to hold his ground as the world
ripped to pieces before him.

The briefest of flashbacks —
a younger self cornered in the school yard;
but the clearer image came from earlier
in the hotel, chilled-out on the comfortable bed,
idly watching TV — the program had finished
and as the News came on, with the remote out
of reach some unaccountable lethargy stopped him
getting up to retrieve it, switch the channel —
a bombed-out building peppered with holes
filled the screen, some foreign dusty place —
then a child's face, a small boy holding a stick,
prodding a loose stone, staring at the camera.

PATRICK MORAN

Bulbs

It was (I dreamt) years from now.
My father had long since died, and memories
of him, so vivid once, were fading:
the man whose deft touch could rouse
a sluggish fire; whose fingers knew
the inner workings of clocks and watches;
but most, the inveterate sower of seed,
so indulgent he'd let stray lettuces
or spuds flourish in a drill of carrots;
who, even when stooped with age, could still wonder:
Where do all the weeds come out of?
This stubborn man whose gifts I didn't have,
whose paths I wouldn't follow.

So there I was, standing
on a neglected patch of ground,
not knowing why: Instinct? The lengthening
evenings? A bird's lingering notes?
And I didn't seem to know what to set:
Flowers? Shrubs? Organic vegetables?

I was just getting down to work,
turning scraws over with the spade,
when I came on them, snug as landmines: bulbs
he'd planted years before, still waiting there…

Innocent, helpless, strangely eloquent.

CECELIA McGOVERN

Dispersal

A membership card
with your signature falls
from the bag you borrowed,
unfolds on the words Organ Donor.
I retrieve it as though
it were a leprous thing

knowing I could never
want you less than whole
my just-grown daughter,
never share your fearsome
generosity with the body
this body nurtured;

reminded of predators who invade
the bone-temple of their prey
in search of the vitals;
the heap of coiled entrails
one early morning in the front garden
with not a scrap of feather or fur;

a sheep's heart with its lopped
arteries and veins in the school lab.,
the human heart mislaid
on a hospital shelf. Everything
that lives, at the mercy
of the forces of dispersal.

I turn to a photograph to find
the untransplantable,
the essence of you, warm
myself in the steady flame
of your eyes.

from *Polishing the Evidence* (2008)

TODD SWIFT

Promise

She asked me not to die,
Not something I can do.
Caesar Antony once stood to try
To tie together an unravelling

When kneeling would have worked
Just as well, or better; that Dante
Was guided into trouble by Virgil
To see buffeted souls suffering:

A few former enemies;
Too much pain to write but he did.
Two brothers with their wings,
Curie's rays. Prisoners swelling, ice

To break impostor bars to flood
Peace or blood, whatever the good
Calls for in its need. The done, undone,
Sly envisioned or raw invisible,

Threaded needles start with a squint
To spy a thin thing — spit on the finger
Can wheedle the argument through plying.
Child, I won't die easily, for you.

ULICK O'CONNOR

Heron

He is perfect
From head to claw
The line runs
Without a flaw
The silver glint
On his royal pelt
The air sliced
As he raises his head.
Then suddenly a leap
As feet fluttering,
He shifts to another spot
He, bred on rivers
Skims the sea
But cannot swim
Why should he
Is it not enough
To be beautiful
And preside

2009

ROSEMARY CANAVAN

Placelore

Rams island
had rats as big as cats,
and a ruin where
one of the O'Neills
kept one of his wives,
they said.
The petrified forest turned up
sometimes in the rivers.
Killultagh: the blank
of trees on the old map,
or the hunt, a straggle of riders
in winter, one in a red coat.

Beyond our house
the lough went gold at night.
Birds craked in the hay,
and September was
the holiday for the potato harvest.
Our teacher wore a long skirt
and laced old-ladies' shoes;
when she beat a five-year-old
for blowing his nose, we all quaked.
In the master's room
big lads never learned past
the first five letters of the alphabet.
I feared his red-bellied stove
would set the place alight.
We'd come in for the radio:
'Find a space,' the English voice said.
'Now imagine you're a tree.'
I knew their warm, mossed
bark, the safety of their height.
To be one was absurd.

Home was a tramp along the hedge.
To the south, a school
with H-shaped football posts
was alien territory.
And down the fields the river
was an underwater world
where sticklebacks built fortresses,
and I had stones
to tell the height of every flood.
Francie took dollaghan from it
with a gaff he hid in our barn.
He taught me to play 'Davy Crockett',
told me that over the Lough
they were blowing up telephone boxes.
When he sawed Orange Aggie's bike
he had to go. She taught me
to sing 'The Sash'.
My uncle's stories of the Thirties:
how they'd dive for cover
when the bus crossed the Falls.
The radio with its green eye.
Athlone, Hilversum, the BBC
Home Service, Children's Hour…

The uncanny silence of night.
My mother, a Londoner,
alone with two infants
when my father had to go back;
the ghostly sweep of light
from the distant airport,
the lane black except
when the moon silvered it.

The strong-walled house
still stood when I came back.
If each makes holy
the place they came from
this place, more than any other,
is mine; not to be desecrated
by any that come afterwards
with gunshot or bomb,
whistle or growling drum —
so long as its stones stand
on their quiet earth.

ANDREA COHEN

Amsterdam, Hotel Silton

Three missed trains
before we got there.
Missing each other
at the bus stop,
at the station.
Hash under glass.
A chicken—if not
in every pot—in
ours, in the dining
room, by the requisite
fire, the red wine
redder and redder.
When at last
we went upstairs,
all the doors
on all the floors
were open—as
if nothing could
be forbidden.
It was. I
forgive you.

DAVID GARDINER

Frog's Love to the Scorpion

We swam the creek together.
I took your assurances &
trusted my heart.

I said I thought I had wings;
didn't know what they were for.
You laughed with me.

I took you onto my back
where you slept. I felt the weight
of your troubles.

I thought we'd nearly made it.
Then I woke you to your self.
Then it went wrong.

I made two mistakes with you.
My second one was my first.

After you stung me, we drowned.
I loved you the whole way down.

I remember what you said:

This all does not concern you.
None of it is your issue.
It is just in my nature.
I will love you forever.

I hear this as salt waters
hold me again quietly;
close around me &

you drift away in shadow

CELESTE AUGÉ

Start Over

So this is what it's like to start over:
to pick apart the mistakes hard woven
into each day—they drove me mad
but I knew them, chased my fairy tale
from decade to decade, groomed to fail.
I spent years becoming my mum and dad.
Lost years in the consumer choir trance,
ran around like all the other ants
to prove my group worth, had
my palms torn up on black briars.
I was a grown-up, always tired,
did what they told me on TV ads.
    I had given up on doubt.

Now I dream of getting spaced out,
finding a city inside the city,
holding hands with myself in the cold
re-reading old novels, covers rolled
back, balanced against my knee
on the air mattress, as hunger cross-fades
into hunger—taste and touch—afraid
of what it's really like to be,
of empty rooms, empty days,
empty faces. All new. All my mistakes
    out there, waiting for me.

GEORGINA EDDISON

My mother as Eve

The only time I heard
my mother speak Latin
was to confide
she and Dad practiced
'Coitus Interruptus'
(until they became
quite good at it.)
It replaced
'Vatican Roulette'
after too many
shots in the dark.

The day she confessed to the priest
he raged,
Adam's apple jigging up and down
against his roman collar.
'Your *husband's* immortal soul
will burn for all eternity'.
His hot words spilled
on stony ground.

So, she went home
and saying nothing,
took herself, her husband and his immortal soul
to bed for a threesome,
knowing that afterwards
there would be
one hell of a smoke.

from *Standing in the Pizzicato Rain*

GERARD HANBERRY

Encounter

I met my father today
on the road out from town
pushing his bicycle through the grey sea-mists.

Dead for years,
younger than me now,
he did not immediately recognise his only son.

Said I looked a bit shook
and why wouldn't I
given the circumstances.

He enquired about work and such,
we didn't go into much detail,
I lied a little, asked how he was getting along.

He wondered if there was
an All Ireland in Galway this year?
No chance, I said.

We never mentioned his accident,
how it all came to such a sudden end.
He looked at me once or twice.

Strange how time flies, he remarked.
Then the mists thickened
and he was gone.

NESSA O'MAHONY

Absence

Our regular route: cross the bridge,
up the hill, past trees,
along neat green squares
that front each house
in this suburban terrace.
Station wagons, sentinel
at each gate, disapprove
of each dog sniff, of lingering
for a twitch of curtains.
But nothing looks out
at this empty sky, bereft
of clouds, of movement.
Was it last year
that swifts carved their curve
here? Or the year before?
The nest on the burglar alarm
has crumbled, a winter's storm
washed away any other trace,
like the names of things
we knew only yesterday.

LEX RUNCIMAN

"Braced by Setbacks"

Teresa Deevy, Waterford Playwright, 1894-1963

I was a young woman deaf   yet heard the voices I made
I made them to listen and speak   hear and say *no*
to any want less ambitious than their hope   and wit
though urge of time and change come to naught

Say to me eviction   homeless a roofless room
in your own free state   say that I'll slap your face
What fault to thrive   what fault for a bit of lace   a bit
The Ireland I made knew wealth of guilt   accused Church

and fate   the law ever friendless injudicious cold
Hunger in the bones   what and where lives the right
and not the anger   the comfort and not the guilt

My sister's voice sounds

In memory's ear she berates me the saucer of milk
I'd set out for the milk-eyed cat that only ever made
no request   but sat on the back stoop under that little roof

and gazed at clean-pinned rain-leaden sheets
Though it wished   when I opened the door I'd not let it in
By setbacks braced   I was a young woman deaf
yet heard the voices I made   Since none could to me

speak than in their voices heard   I stared shameless
and read their lips   Glinty cars passed quiet as sheep
Sun on my skin said warm   Bluebells
reminded me of birds

JOHN CORLESS

Posts and Wire

                        divide the land,
keep sheep from grazing
and solicitors busy
where the wire doesn't work.

Brothers with borders.

Yet we all came with nothing
and will leave the same way,
coffins unable to accommodate
the vast tracts of land
acquired at auctions.
Their turn will come round —
underbidders will say farewell
beside the final acquisition.
The grass will grow
on both sides of the fence
                        regardless.

from *Are you ready?*

rob mclennan

Sunset, margins

1.

Such density

of colour. Braided palms. Facts carve
into sections, disproportionate

to their weight.

2.

Such simple prompts: air traffic
calculated, bear

direction, distance, volume.
Scan the gusto

of an image, undisturbed.

3.

Hard light, angles. Architecture,
background-soft and looming.

It demonstrates

a texture; illusions, climbed
and purified. And, at times,

imaginary.

4.

At no point,

speculates: how many ways
can you stare out this window,

carrying a glass?

A.E. STRINGER

The Contentment Museum

Antiques throughout, the clocks all stopped,
the elder gentleman our guide begs pardon
for the names that slip his tongue.
Antebellum jar of preserves split at the seal
in a dry decade, music boxes quelled
mid-song, a pristine white dress. The first
wife of the Colonel called the house *contentment*,
though ordeals ensued to undermine it.
A fainting couch swoons in a prominent
nook, where the weary patron may pass
a moment watching the human race
through columns on a sunny veranda beyond
the rippled window. Out on the highway,
few slow down to the pace of wonder.

A pin-cushion doll in her puffy dress is
impervious above the waist, porcelain.
Singular tabletop church opens to reveal
the maker and his bride at vows. Our guide
remarks a floor-cradle that may have held
twin sleepers. As he plays "When We
Were Young" on a saloon piano, a silk
quilt barely holds its patchwork together.
Now and then a mourning veil shivers,
careworn as the rice-paper fans
whose hand-painted gardens years
of sunlight have bleached into traces.

DOROTHY MOLLOY

My fireworks, the stars

My fireworks, the stars
exploding, over my head
tonight, whizzing around clouds, regrouping in
dense clusters, scattering
again, fading, falling,
shooting, hiding behind the
chimneys, nesting in trees,
and resting, finally, in the glass
wells of my binoculars.

The stars explode over my
head. Dogs bark as they
crackle, sizzle, fizz and pop
across the sky. The three cats
leap into my lap, eyes big as
saucers, ears pointing backwards.
Claws hook, tails twitch.

My stars flare like matches
unsteady as sulphur flame
in the quiet nothingness of the
sky. I reach up and pick them
one by one like silver daisies
out of the black field over my head.
They glow and tinkle like bells.
They are quite prickly.
They burn as I string them round my neck.

from *Long-distance Swimmer*

STEPHEN ROGER POWERS

Pretending We Live at Highclere Castle, Where *Downton Abbey* Is Filmed

My eyes can't stay open anymore, let's say.
In this game it'll just be pretend. Climb up these stairs with me
and call down goodnight to the other tourists in the foyer,
never mind what they might think of us.
Hampshire is full of poseurs who write their own chronicles,
and for now this house is ours.

Evening has ended, imagine, and a few from our modest dinner
soiree might linger for a while after we've gone up
to retire. Attendants will have spread our bedclothes out
for us. Water basins stand arranged. Ixion couldn't have sought
this more completely, you know. Leave me
in the corner with my Latakia for a quarter
hour while you get ready, and when you come out
I will have bluebells crowning
the trunk at the foot of the bed.
Lausanne will be waiting for our arrival
in the morning, like all the other cities
we dream of. Youngberries in a china bowl
next to a bottle of champagne, for midnight, beg
to be eaten one by one, sweeter
by hand, in the dark. One-horse carriages pass by
on a dirt road, their lanterns reflecting in the mirror
above the fireplace. Unbolt the door and let in
the hall breeze when the candlelight gets too airless.

Masquerades such as these end at the top
of the stairs, where we pretenders must turn back because
the sleeping suites are closed to visitors today.
And so now here we are. Rhododendrons
grow more colorful when you pronounce
them rhodendenrods. Right down this gravel pathway

we can find a park with enough for the taking.
Yellowhammers have beaten us there. Marzipan shared
from a rucksack-tattered box is plenty for both of us.
Extravagance like this worries me that your gentle
breathing will tickle my shoulder just one night,
and that's all there is.

GABRIEL ROSENSTOCK

Rud ab ea é nach bhfaca mé cheana

Rud ab ea é nach bhfaca mé cheana
Lon dubh
Ag piocadh as éan dá chineál féin
Ó thráth go chéile féachann sé i leataobh
San áit ina bhfuilimse
Ciontach mar dhea
Loinnir fhuar ina shúil
Ciontacht dá laghad ní bhraitheann sé ar ndóigh
Is cuma gur éan dá chineál féin a thit go talamh
Níl geis ar bith ann
A choiscfeadh lon dubh ar éan dá chineál féin a chéasadh

Is mar sin, leis, le briathra a ghoineann
Conas a éiríonn siad
Conas a ligtear dóibh éalú
As cuas éigin sa chroí nár caitheadh solas fós air?

It was something I hadn't seen before

It was something I hadn't seen before
A blackbird
Pecking at one of its own
Now and again it looks to one side
To where I am
As if in guilt
A cold glint in its eye
But of course it knows no guilt at all
It doesn't matter that one of its kind had fallen to the ground
No taboo exists
Forbidding a blackbird to torture one of its own

And so it is with hurtful words
How do they arise
How do we allow them escape
From some cavern in the heart not yet explored?

2010

VALERIE DUFF

Reflection

for M

Habitat branches
Near asphalt,

Trailing vines

We track mapless.
Hear the bird-calls.

They reply to pressure,
Boot phosphor,

Still ponds. My son,

You and I are
Spruce fall.

We fit beneath
The dripping canopy

Notch the needle

Bed beneath our feet.
Rain-stripped stumps

Reflect the planets

We can't see.
Take on faith

Existence, rings

Aligned to deep, wrenching,

Muddy mitochondria,

Powerhouse of fern

And net, open
On all sides, lowing frogs

And in the pond, the sky.

JOHN MORGAN

The Sinner at Six

Into the candled dark where haloed strangers
mingled in jigsaw-puzzle windows, Lily,
my Irish nursemaid and first love, snuck me
whenever my Jewish parents nodded.
Back when the Mass was still in Latin,
one Sunday in my boredom
I begged to hold the string of holy beads
she counted on for luck and in
my fidgets twisted it until it broke
apart and spilled its tiny white
and purple jewels into my lap.

Shame wet my cheeks and terror
seized me by the throat. I knew
that I was damned and, worse, Lily
might also go to hell for what I'd done,
and hell was like the front yard leaves we heaped
each fall and lit, each leaf a separate soul
that shriveled curling inward as it flamed,
then turned to smoke and ash. In hell, they said,
you burned like that forever. But seeing
my stricken face, she asked me why,
and when I unpeeled my young fists full
of tiny lights, she brushed my tears away,
and whispered that her beads could be restrung.

BERTHA ROGERS

Blue Beak Speaking

The apothecary door mirrors need,
images your *self* conspired from nothing.

You are a dog, a wolf, a coyote
Your under-face waits.

That physician in the reflection
a walking smile. *It's world-death,*

his wide teeth intone, *these open*
sores disease's beginning.

Plead. No answers are given.
The smile laughs, white coat swaying.

You mark seasons in your head.

In the forest, a crow's wings rent
from torso, scattered over dry needles.

Someone, something, anyone's game.
Nearby, Crow's skull shows on duff,

eye holes watch, jaw hinges, a maw,
and blue-black, that beak *speaks.*

Your talons, a twig, raise beak up.
You, like Crow, position it with

precision. This is the truth of it
physician's killer yap, *yapping.*

You are change, you are the canid you,
only this lonely morning, reflected.

C.J. SAGE

Go Greyhounds

It could be a particle of dander that ruins
my whole day and sends me reading hardship's
texts hour by hour. The stiffened hips
of racetrack breeding dogs make my eyes water,
get me posting Buyer Beware signs and begging
for change. Yum is not what I think when I think of meat—
fish or otherwise. I think of how a spine breaks under-thumb.
The hotel where I was raised had a mole problem;
less attractive was the double dose of poison
brought in by fair-skinned owners in leather boots.
Check the manes of trained horses for the gum of jockeys.
If there is pay involved, a majority will play.
You follow the ponies while I mimic the whimpered hounds.

JULIAN GOUGH

Seven Fake Zen Poems

I

Here we go, again.
Another drawing of a pen.

II

Here we go, again
Fake zen
is still zen

III

Here we go
Again
Go we here

IV

Look
A mountain
How amusing

V

Look
A volcano
How amusing

VI

Look
My death
How amusing

VII

Look
Amusement
How amusing

from *Free Sex Chocolate* (2010)

NOËL HANLON

So This Is It

So this is it she said

once she moved into the hospice bed
placed in the room she'd only ever used as storage

out of the cushy chair in her living room
where she would ask me to cut off the oxygen
when she smoked with her nimble legs tucked under her

while I sat beside her Monday afternoons
learning how to embroider and heard
who she had loved in her life
her face mirroring mine if I showed surprise

she showed me the colors of clothes she adored
tea towels she'd adorned with flowers and cows
warned me of the strained times with her daughter

told me what worried her awake in the nights
how she feared she'd brought this all down on herself

she had said in the very beginning *we can't talk about dying.*

MARY MADEC

This is the Place we enter the River

where water flows
deep and calm on New Year's Eve.

Later, as Spring comes, we will watch
for salmon leap, leaves on trees.

Warm in the ice-house
we dream human dreams.

Through the silence of night
the trees drop heavy blobs
of rain onto the Velux

like pearls or beads of hematite
they roll slowly down the roof
until the first timid light

of the New Year. You make tea
and we sit up and sip
the dark liquid as if it were a healing potion,

our half-formed thoughts
disappear with wisps of steam.
We are in the riverbed

where the pearl of great price
glistens like a salmon's eye
waiting for us to find

that love is deeper still
like a bedrock
we might never reach

in this lifetime.

CYNTHIA HARDY

Cosmos

(For Joe Enzweiler)

They aim
toward the arc of sky,
small suns
a child might crayon:
thick pink rays,
center yellow stipples—

cupping the light,
pink and purple blooms,
frill of leaves, small curls
of green. I wait

to tell you how
they bloom and spread
all summer, to hear
your astonishment:
a flower that name,

the place we all live.
The sky,
translucent porcelain
like the bottom of a cup
gleaming faint light
where the potter thinned
the clay. The lean stalks

of Cosmos, so tough,
the blooms vibrating
in the breeze. You will
want to know this.

AIDEEN HENRY

Elephant

My mother loved an emergency,
any emergency.
With six children she rarely lacked opportunity.
From rescuing a woman with a pram
from a shower of golf-ball hailstones,
to rushing a bleeding child to casualty,
encasing a scalded hand in ice
or driving hell for leather to the vet,
a poisoned dog convulsing in her lap,
to an overdose or two
and some slashed wrists.

Garden emergencies fell within her domain,
screwing interconnecting rods
to clear a blocked drain,
chasing a rat with a shovel,
few things pleased her more.
'As mo radharc' she'd bid us,
banished, real work to be done.
'You're not an elephant'
said my small brother
as he watched me try to move a rock.
'Get mommy!'

Lifted away from the humdrum
of meals to be cooked,
tidying and sorting,
cajoling and curbing,
admonishing and yelling.
The going in close to be there for the worst
and the pulling away,
finally, to force each of us
to consolidate
then tunnel beyond her,
to our own lives.

NOEL KING

Casting for Sea Trout

My father
made sure his footing was secure,
bent under the wind
and cast as far as he could.

I never remember him catching anything,
definitely nothing we could cook,
but he enjoyed the trying.

I see him all at once —
as a young man, just a man, and an old man.

He fished here the day Armstrong landed on the moon.
He fished here the day mother
went into labour with me —
they had to send someone to catch *him* that day.

He fished here today
where we found him;
the tide gone out,
his left palm
stuck on the rod handle,
his right fingers reeling,
entangled in the fishing wire.

MARY MULLEN

Recipe for Starting Celestial Spring Things

Build a woodstove out of a 55 gallon drum,
　　　　fit with 6 inch stovepipe, airtight door.
Build a greenhouse around the stove, cover with heavy plastic, staple tight.
　　　　Plug draughts with duct tape.
Sow for-get-me-knots, snapdragons, Livingston daisies, cabbage, arugula,
　　　　peonies, cauliflower, broccoli, calendula,
　　　　cosmos.

Add two three foot lengths of spruce logs into the stove each night at nine.
　　　　Damp down.

Compel your sister to wake each morning at three o'clock to heft
　　logs into the fire.

Water the plants, cup by cup, twice weekly in mid-day sun.

Insert Hale-Bopp comet, frost with apricot gleam from the stars until
　　the 59th parallel glows.

　　Be mindful that somewhere between the sixth and sixteenth day
　　　　of rising at three
　　your sister will be dusted by the Big Dipper.

　　　　　　　　　She will become drunk on beauty.
　　　　　　　　　She may create her own galaxy.
　　　　　　Or, at the very least, make a bed on the brittle snow.

Let the mid-day sun warm. At night, the reflection of stars on snow
　　　　will thicken the urge for love.

JOHN WALSH

An Explanation of Sorts

These are the days after
after the dust
after the questions
with no clear-cut answers.

These are the steps
seemingly important
ones we did not hesitate
ones that cost us sleepless nights.

This is where we are
bar-coding the experience
braving faces, anxious
it might still fall through.

This is not to say
given the chance again
we'd do the same
knowing what we now know.

This is not to say
we are certain
how far we would go
before we take a different turn.

RICHARD W. HALPERIN

The Man in the Red Shirt

When two of Rückert's children died,
He wrote four hundred poems in a year.
Comfort. Privilege. Gift.
And if instead
He had turned his face to the wall,
He had the right.

Luxembourg Gardens, summer, 2015.
I have paid for my table; a cup of coffee did it.
The sun a platinum pan, reflecting blaze from another
Source. The young, the old, are rimmed in crimson,
After-images of colour, time and place
One luminous blob. There is no difference here
Between peace and utter defencelessness.

Marie de Médicis once walked these paths.
It was her garden. A man in a red shirt
Walks one now. In 1942, people came here
Of an afternoon. At closing, some went home
To hide again in an attic. This, I cannot write about.
Like Rückert, I must keep to my own experience,
To my own dear roses, dried or, one senses, fresh.

The man in the red shirt.
In a dream, he would be an aspect of myself,
Or a meaning larger than myself.
Here, a man in a red shirt is a man in a red shirt.
One comes to a park
For a holiday from meaning.

LARRY JAFFE

I Am Refugee

I am refugee
Nothing is my own

I have no home
No city
No country

I am refugee
I have no food
No clothing
No shelter

I am refugee
I have tears
I have despair
I have misery

I am refugee
My government bombs me
The rebels shoot at me
The United Nations ignores me

I am refugee

Nothing is my own but

I have my honor
I have my morality
I have my love

I am refugee
I am refugee

ELAINE FEENEY

The Harvest

There is nothing in the old Tuam beet factory
only a greasy fluthering of Natterer's bats
and some gnawing weasels.

Once the full silos were emptied out, gathering began again,
bring in the next harvest, pregnant on a town promise
who plucked her beets from well-drained ground.

Bring your harvest to the side-door, ring the bell, check them in.

Throw away the bruised, pay the grower for the clean ones, pay the grower
for the fresh ones, pay the grower for the ripe ones, pretty ones, weigh them.

Tip them to piles, make little beet hillocks, line them straight, singular,
inspect with an old blackthorn stick, poke them, extract precious stone, then
gravel unable to be consumed, extract the bitter, slash the beets to cosettes.

Extract the unneeded, the inedible.

Cast them away over the ditch or take them to the pit in the dark of night,
move across the concrete slab, opening it, side-step the weasels.
Mind your ankle flesh. They'll eat the rabbits and the sugar,
they'll sit on the slab spreadeagled and salivate.

It's rumoured they'll hunt you down out the Weir Road after matins,
or midnight mass, naked of your cassocks, and rip the cornea from your
eyes, then feast on it.

They'll even come after your soul. And chew it. Refuse to release it.
Don't interrupt their funerals, they'll pull the skin from your hide and salt
all belonging to you, knee-cappings and featherings, cast a weasel spell.

Close over the concrete slab, quickly, blank your thoughts, bless yourself.

Don't look at the small skulls
Don't check if the hair is still growing
Don't take a deep breath. Do not breathe.

GLENN SHEA

Ashmita

Older girls mostly and some young women,
but a few little gigglers too, among the solemn
faces of the poor. Barrettes and bracelets, their best
smocks and jeans, lined up by the city hall,

a bird-bright sari here and there. Nakushi,
the first girl is named, I find out, and
Nakushi, the second and third, and Nakushi
the seventeenth and sixtieth and ninety-third to

the two hundred and twenty-second Nakushi
around the corner by the paper shop.
Unwanted, the name means in Marathi, which
means in plain English they were just girls,

not boys, dragging up the tail end
of too many births, dowries required now
to get rid of them, mouths for the food
you didn't have, so many more useless wombs.

But at Satara today they could change their names
if not their genders. At the official district ceremony
they could come away with the gleam of a new
certificate naming them a goddess or a star.

Nakushi went in and came out Aishwarya,
like the actress; Nakushi two came out with
the enhaloing name of Savitri, like the
Hindi goddess, to be followed by once-Nakushi,

now Vaishali, who is beautiful and good.
My favorite is fifteen year old Nakushi,
who chooses to be Ashmita, which in Hindi
is "tough" or "rock hard." I wonder

what safety their names will be to them
but just for now and for who knows how long a moment
they are new-made, with a certificate to show it.
Wear your names well, I can wish them. Ashmita: rock hard.

CHRISTOPHER LOCKE

What The Dead Know

There are not enough pleasures
to simplify the spirit.

—Charlie Smith

The dead do not visit me at night; at 3 a.m., I do
not sense their vaporous bodies gliding over my
bed as they reveal some mortal prophecy: "Avoid
the morning train," or "A fire awaits you at the bakery."
Nothing. Just me split and pulled from the char

of a receding dream, alone in my sheets as night
counts the insomniac stars, the neighborhood
crushed by heaps of silence as no dog unravels
on its chain, no loitering Camaro sprays *Van Halen*
against our petrified rosebushes. How can the dead

know I would prefer their blank company, their insolent
calm to all this ordinary nothing clogging the avenues
of my sleep as I lie here and think of my stepfather
and how almost every night he sees whole lines
of the dead enter his room as if taking numbers, closing

in on him, telling him they await not in fire but in silence,
and he will be addition by subtraction, and that they
will lift him up to the others breathing behind the clouds
in their melancholy and their robes, lift him by the wrists
as if he were just cut down from some holy machine.

2011

DREW BLANCHARD

No Delicacy

—for James Liddy

As I flew from the bicycle into a field of stone, I knew there was no perfect way of remembering, no way of unbreaking things. Believe me, James, there's plenty of news to share, but my notes are hidden well. The photographs have been sold. Your beats, your verbal beatings agreed that two wheels are no way to travel on any road. As I flew through the wet-white air, I learned Newton's laws and then the impenetrable magic of stone. Travelling through the air, though, is never really flying: We know that gravity turns airtime into mathematic equations that equal falling. Try this: without thought or hesitation, jump from a distance that scares you. You will land before you feel fear or pain. Put your hand on a stone and you get to know the cold beauty of life. Put your hand in the dank, dark earth and you get to know death. Put your hand in water and you see Gerty MacDowell on Sandy Mount and get wet. James, I know this is not funny. Jack Spicer radios us: Transistor, transmissions, transistor: let go. The rooms need furnishing, James. The furniture is disappearing. Suppose I didn't land in a field of peat and stone, of blood and bone and we landed in Morocco for a week of brown drinks and yellow food and unclean hotel rooms. When we left County Clare there was the normalcy of climbing stairs. Before I drove away, I waited for you to ascend, for your light to click on. That night I knew the rooms were furnished, the radio signals sent. As I flew from the bicycle I saw small swarms of gnats in the evening sun, agitating themselves and the world. When I landed in the field of peat and stone I knew that I would never see two shores as clearly again.

PRIMROSE DZENGA

Masking my pain

I hold my pain by the hand I take it to the river
I drag it by the ear, all the way down,
Down the path to the bottomless pool
To drown it, hide it, wash it, bleach it, change it
To leave it there for a while

I hide my shame behind my smile
I carry it with me to the table beneath my garments
I seat on it, stomp on it, dance on it
To mask its face for a while
To avert its gaze from my eyes

I take a thimble and needle to my shame
I spin it into a yarn and hand it over to the loom
I weave it all night, lovely shades and patterns
To take my needle and thimble to it in the morning
To make myself a gown in which to hide

I take my pain to the woods at night
I bury it into the ground with wild flowers
I water it with my tears, and keep a vigil, wait for it to sprout
To watch it turn into blooming rosebuds wild and free
To smell its scent purified by the earth

I take my shame to the rainmaker
I dance with her and beseech the skies
I feel the tears of heaven drench me to the borne
To make my flesh reek, stink, and sticky
To putrefy the air with my secret cloak

I befriend my pain, it stands with the hair on my skin
I befriend my shame, it's the centre of my heart speaking
To look them in the eye, as equals
They shake their heads in whispered disappointment

We will walk to the river
Run to the forest, like wild gazelle
Sit at the table, like old friends
Whisper to the loom, dance with the rainmaker
And make a shroud that fits all of us
How long can we run, hide and mask each other.

After we came to this, I left you, the pain and the shame
would destroy me at last.

JOHN FITZGERALD

Books

Compared to my desktop, the shelf is a coffin.
Keeping a book once it's read is antisocial.
Sure, I might refer again from time to time, but never do.
Not once, any of them.
Meanwhile, space becomes a commodity.
Old ideas seem less important,
can be moved to the garage
to die of mold in dusty boxes.

A book begs for giving again and again,
to live on until attributes tatter,
to speak such a story as must be retold.
The dreams! Imagine how insightful they can be.
They have notes in their pockets, somewhere.
No space in the trash to add another paper ball,
those already fallen wads, ignore for now.
Let the mind be happy with itself.

The more thoughts share, the more they prosper.
They start to notice patterns, measure probability,
assume shapes carved of light,
a flower, maybe a rose, and doesn't that gray look like a dolphin?
No, more a happy shark so laugh along.
I'm addicted to all these words.
They go to naught, and I keep compiling more.
I've accumulated myself in a drowning waste.

Don't be greedy, spread it around.
Say so in your own mean image.
Represent thoughts, inert emotion.
Each belief in existence remembers death a little every day
or loses consciousness.
There lurks this ever-present need for intake, outgo, trade,
a waking and writing it down in the moment—
an unending flux of information.

ALLAN PETERSON

Writing and Trying

On the water I smell diesel before it gets here,
hear the tug pilot playing Poison for the crew.

Signals are coming fast and I am writing and trying
to keep up signaling so often to so many receivers
they are almost certainly missing and misunderstanding.

But they don't stop, they are sharing imperatives
and my part is filling white pages with fingerprints,
blood types, notebooks with clues.

Perhaps I am making too much of the worm thrash
when I turn the compost, the last rain flashing mirrors
from the cups of the spiderwort, applying translations

to the semaphores of wings, but the whole world
passes through this room, and the persistent oak branch
cannot be urgently clawing at my window for nothing.

ADAM WYETH

Anatidaephobia

Anatidaephobia is the fear that somewhere
in the world there is a duck watching you.
No matter where you are a ringed teal
stares down its long bill searing your skin.
You may be on the lavatory 12,000 feet
above sea level and yet you turn cold
as the leer of a mallard stares up through
the bowl. The trauma often goes back
to a time in childhood when the victim
was scared or injured by a duck. Perhaps
they were flapped at in a park then tripped
and scuffed their knees. But anatidaephobia
can sneak up on you out of nowhere,
it can appear like the seasonal migration
of whooper swans to the lakes.
Anatidaephobia is irrational, it is a creature
with wings that cuts through everything,
it is the all-seeing eye of a jealous duck.
There is no duck in the sky and yet people
will kill to tell you there is a duck.
While the condition is rare it is possible
that somebody somewhere will develop it
now. There are various evolving suppositions
across a wide spectrum of science and medicine
on anatidaephobia, many of them ironically
appear to be pedalled by quacks. Nevertheless,
propounding theories on quantum mechanics
make it even more probable that there is
a duck looking at you. There is a duck.
There is always a duck. It is a creature
with wings that sees through everything.
It is what soaks you when you wake
in the middle of the night. Some people
let it fall off them like water. Others drown.

DRUCILLA WALL

My Mother Questions What Is Normal

I can hear her toss the walker
across the room
and move by clinging
from thing to thing
to the kitchen counter.
Her phone is on speaker.

Can you hear this racket?
Three geese are parading
from the bathroom to the front door
and will not listen. How did they get in?
And these big gold fish are shimmering
in the carpet by the closet. Of course,
they cannot understand speech
like the geese can, but who put a fish pool
in here? What a real Einstein, that one.
And there was a little boy. He won't
do his homework. He better learn
his times tables or they might keep him back.

You remember how we used to say them
together like a jump rope rhyme. That's how
you learned them. Those fish are not real.
I know that, but there they are.
You are going to tell me this is not normal,
but what is? What is normal after all?
And where does normal get you?
Where does normal get you? Tell me that.
Tell me that. Tell me that. Tell me that.

Oh, Mom, hold on to that counter.
Whatever you do, don't move.
I'll get there as fast as I can.
I will be in the form of your daughter.

PAUL KINGSNORTH

Drystone

With my white hands I planted an orchard
of pippins, russets, codlings. I don't know
if it will last. I water them.
I did it for me, not for you.

I made promises I couldn't keep
but I meant them. Probably
that means nothing to you now
but the light is still the same
when it catches the drystone in the morning.

There are things that change so slowly
no animal eye can match them.
Every day time leaks from this universe
into another, and I cannot follow it over.
I would have taken you there
but I am stuck on this hill
in my four dimensions, scrabbling after wisdom
and apple pips, my grafting knife
on my belt, my head in the clag
that has come down from the fell again
this day and hidden everything.

JOSEPH LENNON

D'Origine

Winter returns here as *granita*.
Spring, a wicker trap for salmon,
opened in a flood. Fall fell apart
like a dropped sack of chestnuts bursts.
August feels as immovable
as the bench where I sit by
an alfalfa field in violet bloom.

Last spring, rain swelled its planks,
now summer bakes them open as
a barn's bricks fall in, books fall apart,
words fail over what we say.
Today I read about fasting
in pages written by the long dead
about the longer (if-ever-living) dead.

St. Patrick broke the chains, sharpened
the axes of wood cutters. He spit on rocks
and broke them into trinities, freed
by fasting on the slave master.
Deep shade grows by the ruined barn,
where a black dog leans in—now
his limping owner passes, leash in hand.

Now a woman from a southern
continent, a man with old trainers on,
holds a watch to sell to break his fast.
Migrants walk up Italy from wars
fought at a summer's pitch.
Hunger has been their name,
whispered in Syria, Libya, Niger.

They continue swimming
as they sit at the edge of markets,
still slip over fences, into tunnels,
as they chat in broken phrases.
Hunger begins to warm the belly
as cicadas sing under a sky
that cools like an oven.

JOHN McKEOWN

The Mask

There's a mask behind this one,
which weathers life far better;
and a body that goes with it,
light, and graceful as water.

There's a mask behind this one,
that perhaps keeps the ageing one in place;
which bears the brunt of the damage,
until this one falls away.

This is a mask which must be worn off,
along with its body, graceless as clay;
leaving the one behind to go its own way;
a shadow, freed, or the wind ruffling water.

STEPHEN MURRAY

The Dead

1.

Here are the

        Dead.

    The flesh and mortal bone

Dead.

    A bronze bust encased in stone

             Dead.

The horseman, the clerk and the Red; the stoic heroic, the soldier, the
poet, the sculptor, the weaver, the cobbler, the baker, the altar boy
turned coffin maker, the journalist and the timber merchant's lad.

    Lined up against the wall and riddled with lead.

    Here are the
    Dead.

    Invincible. Immortal. Unbreakable.

             Dead.

2.

Strung up by the neck in the shed.

Dead.

Frozen to death in your shop doorway
Dead.

The almost living and the not quite yet
Dead.

Clothes folded upon our shores. Vast armies neck deep, submerging nameless. The faceless and the vanished, the disenfranchised and the banished, the Late Late, Bosco, An Garda Siochana and the HSE.

The Father, the Son and the Holy Ghost.

Here are the
Dead.

Invisible. Mortal. Unspeakable.

Dead.

WILLIAM WALL

The shit fox

this luminous night's ice moon
electro-plating the garden in pewter
& a salty rust-dog
travelling in the garden's underwear

rummaging the cotoneaster
autumn's evidence
wilderness in small places
hunger makes few friends

no songs come to starving creatures
& they spare no alms
but tomorrow when the sun rises
I know I will walk the lawn

& find the fox's stinking shit
a black twist in the garden's green
a full-stop between the door
& the blank sheet petrified to the line

JULIAN STANNARD

Eternal Lunch

Curious how the middle classes never tire
of salmon. I've been sitting at the table
for fifty years — and the potatoes are lovely.
They're from the garden and the beans?
They're from the garden too. And the beetroot!
Yes mother, I have the distinct impression
the beetroot has risen up like a garrison
of legionnaires, from the garden, the lovely garden.

Everything's from the garden.
Fecundity! Fecundity! What?
Even Jenny, I believe, is from the garden.
I'd like to cover her with crème fraîche.
Is the salmon, I ask, also from the garden?
Of course not silly boy, the salmon is
                              from Scotland.

I can't breathe very well
and I'm clearing my throat
and now I'm saying it:
I'm saying, I've been sitting at the table
for fifty years and I'm wondering
if I might get down.

What on earth would you do once you were down?
my mother asks and my sister's saying
He'd run around the garden
and climb a tree and smoke a ciggy.
Yes, my mother says, and in any case
you can't get down until you've eaten
                              everything.

I've eaten rivers of salmon and fields of potato
and I've eaten so much beetroot
that I'm beginning to hallucinate.
I think dear mother I have eaten quite enough.

What about Jenny?
What about Jenny?
It's true of course
that nothing of Jenny
has passed my lips.

Oh Jenny of Woking give me your arm,
give me some homemade chutney
and a glass of ginger beer and I'll wash you down.

Dearest Jenny.

PADRAIG O'MORAIN

The infant Jesus to his mother

I watched you pick up a feather
out the back, beyond the shed.
You smiled at it then hid it
in your pocket with the others.
You touch their smoothness under cover.
You think I do not notice.
My father says your stillness scares him
when you seem to turn to stone
and sit staring at the air.
He wants to ask what's wrong with you
but you are lost to your imagining,
not hearing him but listening
for Heaven's whisper at your ear,
a thunder of wings in the room.

MAJELLA CULLINANE

Finale To The Season

We're not there yet, but there are hints; in the pink-red clasp of sorrel
the cicada easing a pitch lower, shedding its voice. The wind
changing direction like the act of entering a room and forgetting
what it is it came in for. The sky tinged in blue-lavender,
spools of cloud whipping over the hills like wounds.

You are primed towards spring in the North, the light
drifting in a little more each day, like the black letters on this page
as they move across the white space, which remind me
of crows stalking frozen trees, or your breath hard and quick
as you sleep in the room we once shared, each in our own narrow bed.

Here, the hours are darkening, and in the undergrowth,
leaves are getting ahead of themselves, turning burgundy, copper.
In an old wives' tale a grey warbler is a sign of rain,
or in the clearing now, a moment where
the season's murmurings are breached, and enter our dreams.

PATRICK KEHOE

Places to Sleep

i.m. Ivan Kelly

Places to sleep, like the corner of a floor
On Calle Aribau; in the post-Christmas frost,
A place to lay the head, a mattress
On the tiles, whatever my late friend

Provided by way of bedding, and the casual talk
Around the lamp of an indeterminate hour:
Before we went out or after we went out?
That is forgotten and gone as accursed time.

PAUL GRATTAN

Last Remains, or, Maurice Neary's Epiphany

for Joseph, on our China Anniversary

Remember the Lion King
And the sloe eyed Echo
Clubbing in the Jakes
Remember the Dealer, singular
Sweater, and the weary Provo
Leaping from his mantle
At the peal of a mortis
Bollixing the lock, remember
Tenebrism, one pint of breaking
Light, and the Saxon stiletto
Bone bright, unbuckled
As a bit of a Party starts to kick
Off, remember Sir Edmund
His auld dear, Elizabeth
Dressed as cadavers
For the funerary slab, necrotic
Hub of St Peter's Close, still
Lives turned hard, mostly fruits
And vegetables, a horsey arse
A cup, it might be Santa Maria
Del Popolo, or Drogheda
Lachrymose shift of a Bishop's ring
To where one pulls dolmen bellied
Lumbers from The Earth, painted
Yon rancid shade of Williamite
Umber, a gift to sing, O sing
Of the Blessed Head, like a Jock
In a box, how shadow persecutes
The mouth, the brain, the nasal
Fleece, wherein the dead recover girls
Rent boys, so Nowth, so Dowth
All parted gorse, all terracotta Kings

O' chassis, emboweled, divested, churls
Or others like them, rehearsing
To be caught, your man, mid-hurl
At the window, on Juno's wings, you know
He was quite famous, in the RA
Back in the day, or is it a shite hawk, skirls
Like a pict in Roman Gaul, above the Quay
In the yet to be disinterred 1980s, O
Pine, *Them's dirty bitches, Mr Neary* —
A horse, the geese you herd, & Paul.

JUDITH MOK

A Cold Poem

for my father: Maurits Mok

For me to reach my father's poem
And see the mountain road
Where he hugged me after a month of summer camp
And pre-teenage intrigues.

I showed my father the river where I caught my trout
And let it go in its silver and slime
I showed him the tree where the eagle perched
The tents and tables
The wild artichoke growing underneath my hard crib
Raw and edible
A place in the sky where lightning struck
Every evening
And the grass circle where we whispered and danced
As I danced towards him
When I was his child full of his poetry
But when I saw him on that mountain road
With his red 2cv behind him
Shining in the stark Provencal sun
He was my father who lifted me up in his arms

It was not high enough:
For the fish to be a trophy of liberty
The artichoke a triumph of discovery
For me to be dancing Judith again
Like in that line of my father's poetry

from *Gods of Babel*

KEVIN SIMMONDS

Drain

A framed photo of Padre Pio is on the pizzeria wall
I took his name at Confirmation

On holy days his hands opened
There's film of this

I first saw stigmata in a movie about a nun so pure
she'd been chosen to bloodlet

Serving God like that was too severe
the calling too specific

If the wounds closed, what then?
How'd you know your standing?

I was twelve and who's to say
if this was the earliest of my trauma?

I seek suffering like the shade of an arcade of oaks
Still after all these years

Yet the shade is what burns and shuts out
a forgiving and endless sky

NUALA NÍ CHONCHÚIR

The Birds of Madrid

From the café window
we watch chaffinches
muddle around a feeder.
The sight makes our talk flit
from hummingbird to dove
to steadfast kingfisher.
I style you a cautious Icarus
— no avian daredevil, you —
you will not travel skywards,
to let wax melt,
to have feathers wilt.
And I am not the sun.
But still, I hope,
you won't censor your flight.
Soon, surely, you will lift
both wings and soar.

2012

CYNTHIA SCHWARTZBERG EDLOW

Bathsheba, A Downpour, and the First Twig

There is no functional utility to a Rembrandt.
Bathsheba, with her brief goblet breasts and blessedly
commodious belly, those muffinesque hips
and the freak-sized man-hands.
The croissant-shaped golden drapery
conspiring behind her, and the downward
maidservant, her excruciatingly
complicated carnelian silk cap.
Any painter worth his salt knows any
woman does not bathe in her jewelry.
Any painter first measures a ring finger
not to extend half the length of a thigh.
Yet such pungent detail in the servant. Someone
you could see on the street
and recognize.
The other painters fret in the sunny square.
"Poor Remy. You tell him; I can't!
I go to his home tomorrow for supper."

Then comes a day of dark and slanted rain.
The everywhere hurrying to be out of it.
Trees mute with birds. Rain
thick at the stone curb, frothing wavy and white.
He removes Bathsheba from the wall,
raises her above his head.
Down the street he goes
dry and glad.
He may fancy he hears woodwinds or chimes.
Some technology is intuitive.

Everywhere daily a bird pulls its shelter together.
Almost any high structure will do.
A common maple branch, a horizontal metal pole.
The unlikelier the location, the wilder the marvel.

Using what would be to a man
only a thumb and forefinger, the first twig
would seem always to fall or fail during the trip
to get the second. Stay wisp, stay
wisp of a twig, so I might return with a second,
a third, and soon, a floor of safety, soon
finer filaments of twigs, and grasses,
plant down and human hair,
all contrived circles, bowled tighter and
softer up in radiant warmth and protection.

As a painter swirls the brush upon the palette:
the gathering of mud
by the feathery, beating breast
and the full body then swiped across the furrowed bark,
the moisture of bird spew mixing
with mud, this glue fixes the first twig's
anchor down.
To get back to where the need to be is.
Where there is the expected.
Two lavender grey eggs.
Some technology is the earth
right under your feet.

REBECCA MORGAN FRANK

The Moon's Magnetic Field Once Came From an Asteroid

When you walked in
it was like recognizing

the moon when he returns.
His lover bites his cheek; she

has no choice. All we see
is the dissolution, then await

the reconstruction.
Each time, the sky

yanks her into his orbit.
I want to say *I'm sorry*.

I want to say
You win. Our bodies are like

the confessional booth these
poems are stuck in. Even

the priest can see that sin.
You'll be all spit and honey—

or maybe I'm the poisoned
flower gnawing on its own

lip because it has no hands
to reach for you. Only words

that are as useless as the pollen
for saying anything. I continue

to serve them even with your hands
around my throat from across

the room. Your voice is home,
I answer it like a bat guided

across the atmosphere. This
is a narrative that cannot end

well but wants to, but must.
I'll continue to go down kicking

and you'll be sweet as anything
until you bite back. No it can't

end here—we won't let it.
It's been billions

of years since the asteroid hit
the moon: clearly some

magnetic fields can be sustained.

SCOT SIEGEL

Stars From A Well

When she awakens from
the dissipating dream

she leaves in folds of wool
impressions,

not of sun dancing on
cold leaves,

but love in the creases
of the blanket

where her body was,
where the folds still hold

the warmth of the dream
she rose to leave

to pull the blinds back,
to let the light in.

ANDREA POTOS

In The Musée de L'Orangerie

immersed
in the oval room,
no compass but water
and light,
willows
draping dusk
and mirrors of cloud,
lashes of reeds
and rushes,
lilies
and roses widening to air—
all this transcribed
by the eyes of the painter nearly blind—

you can do nothing
but sit in the center
of silence. Tears break
through the surface of your life.

DONNA L. POTTS

Seducing Spock

"To Nimoy's great surprise, Spock became a sex symbol."

I.

A high school girl stumbling into sex dreams she seduces him,
that half-human, half-Vulcan from the old Star Trek.
"My dear, this is highly illogical," he says wearily,
eyebrows incredulous, dark eyes, slits,
thin-lipped mouth an embrasure.

He nonetheless permits her to remove
his snug steel gray shirt and black clinging pants.
As she unpeels his special Vulcan underwear
he gasps, *not logical, not logical*
but soon his gasps melt to whispers.

Spock was Leonard Nimoy, a Jew from Catholic Boston
who knew how it felt to be alien.
Irish and Italian kids called him a Christ killer.
He learned Yiddish to talk to his Russian grandma
Who spoke nothing else.

He stole his Vulcan salute from
a sacred hand position of orthodox priests,
whom he bravely glimpsed while others
covered their eyes with prayer shawls
for fear of being blinded by divine light.

NBC worried he looked too Satanic,
and asked that his character be dropped;
 "the 'guy with the ears' will scare the shit
out of every kid in America," they said,
so they airbrushed away his sharpness.
He later wrote a book, *I am not Spock*,
still later, *I am Spock*.

II.

In pictures of you as a uniformed,
white blond child in Berlin,
You hold your *Schultüte*, the cone of treats
nearly as big as you, which your parents
gave you when you started school.

Later, you would watch
Star Trek reruns dubbed in German,
dress as Spock for a costume party.
With your mother, you made the ears
from modeling clay, heated them,
and glued them to your own ears,
which hurt like hell, and
they never stayed in place.

Then she ran off with someone else,
leaving you with a father who'd
been drafted at eight by the Nazis.
Years later you'll watch *Downfall*
with him in Berlin, remember German
children were victims too.

I'm more like Spock than anyone you'll ever meet,
you assure me, and I recall the Vulcan brain
striving to subdue a human heart,
your heart pounding as you run
from the hospital where your child's
life hangs in the balance, then run from your wife,
then from your lover. *Not logical.*

It so happened that everyone wanted Spock,
but nobody, not even Nimoy, knew how to be him.

SARAH CLANCY

Desire runs rings around me (and I don't mind)

Women with your many slanted humours
and me with mine: you saunter in on fearless
and resourceful feet with your adaptable hands
your appropriate limbs and those flexible minds.
You hold me as you would a child's hand
a sharp blade, an injured bird, a half wrung neck
an amulet. You play me like an old accordion
easing out its leather skin until like a kite skylarking
on its thin strings, despite myself, I sing. Women
you go everywhere to waste like an unlamented wind
keening itself through a rusting iron gate, or a harbour full
of empty sails — you just lie at ease and wait. Women
you can ride your fleetfoot ponies roughshod over
anything you want and they'll never balk, never falter
never doubt you — your time has always come.
And you need me about as much as old news,
as a fortune teller's lie, or yesterday's horoscope today
but come in and run your rings around me, I won't mind
— I love how women know things, I find them wise
and this is what the empty fool in me desires.

PAUL CASEY

Last Wildflower

for Rosie

I scaled the cliffs of Moher
to write about the tourists
trekked south till there were no more
barriers, signs of stick men falling
to where I could breathe
alone

right up at the edge where I have always been afraid
                    of imagining
that I have always been
                    and forever will be   falling
    imagine
              being afraid of *imagining*
                                        falling
and let go
          spilled
                    back
                         eyes to sky
clutching burren blossoms   picked for you

I went in gannet-deep
shot straight into the air
to reclaim my still form
then danced
in the tower of Moher
above the clear blue day

Trace memories of this scene recur
mitochondrial microfilm coaxed open by the sun
these cliffs those islands, the fall
and lay of it, the width & breadth of it
the countless known unknowns
like Mog of the Hundred Battles

or why Clare isn't in Connacht.
But writing as I walk now
should this ledge crumble
please know you were
the last wildflower
on my mind

LEAH FRITZ

After Orleans

Sometimes a poem is empty at its heart,
a work of art whose words are stacked like stones
in a cathedral — strong enough to hold
the arches high, to point the steeples, to
impress; and like a tall, eternal space
hard and cold where no one living sleeps,
the dead encrypted underneath (but, oh
how beautiful it is!), inhuman, yes,
not meant for comfort but to awe, where we
who think ourselves inferior to those
whose vaults we contemplate — above and yet
below, forever below — emerge into
the sunlight or the rain refreshed as if
in leaving awe behind we've left our death.

COLM KEEGAN

Bering Strait

i.m. Rachel Peavoy

We've been crossing this frozen ocean
snowblind in a perpetual storm.
Our tribe has endured this trial so long
we almost forget where we're from.

Beyond the horizon, our destination
hope, an approaching thaw
and here the question that burns in our gut
what to do about all that we've lost.

Sacrifices we were forced to make
those we left so the rest could keep going.
We are bound to all that we have given up
it lingers in our wake like a ghost.

How many bodies have we left behind
their voices calling out in the snow?
Are we going to go back and save who we can
or keep marching for fear of the cold?

AFRIC McGLINCHEY

Immortality

When you run in naked, dive underwater,
I become erratic, an addict
hearing the want, roar of the bay.

Such intensity, like looking
at my feet, deep animal gestures
on a yoga Monday.

I know it's morning
and the stars have fallen,
but coming from your eyes

is this light, where lightning starts,
and after seeing it,
I want not to die.

I've never had immortal things —
well yes, for a time
there was god, a guardian angel,

but now, there's you,
and I must apologise
for asking

for this shimmering
wonder palace, and you, naked,
underwater, forever.

JOHN MURPHY

Iris and Hermes

And our special powers? Winged feet
to patrol the shifting borders,
the contested zones of occupation,
flimsy aces lashed to our ankles,
ligaments of luck and kilter fluttering
below the sheets in a valley running
south of the neutral zone — here, a lifetime's
worth of weights and measures sweats.

Back to back, all things being equal,
a sort of river commerce flourishes
between us — nothing so glib or slick
as double entry, contracts for difference
or gilt returns, just a night trade of rounding
errors, hedged bets, and devaluations,
the arbitrage of psychopomps,
the reinvention of fire.

PEADAR O'DONOGHUE

Tuesday

(After Spring Fugue by Harold Brodkey)

Awake. Alive. Another day.
Half asleep. Stretch out leg, other half empty.
No morning glory. No birdsong.
Still alive, dry mouth, backache, right wrist hurts,
new bicycle, handlebars wrong.
Eyes sore, late night, every night late lately.
Cornflowers, Chalk Hill Blues, poetry, Spring Fugue.
And with one giant limp, Peadar is free of the bed!
Chance the mirror, Homer Simpson replaced by Homer Simpson's Dad.
Grandpa Simpson, I'm Grandpa Simpson.
Kettle boiling, fly enters room, bluebottle, buzzes off,
lots of blue today, am I feeling blue?
I ache all over, I'm breathing through my dry mouth,
water, need water, take medications, silence,
the computer hums the keyboard clicks under my sore wrist,
one finger dabs 'Tuesday'.

THOMAS LYNCH

Genesis 3

In Defendante Ferrari's panel of
Eve Tempted by the Serpent only a
filigree leaf frond from a sapling tree
tastefully obscures her mons veneris.
For the moment she is still ignorant,
not yet embarrassed by her nakedness —
how God, mannish in his heaven, fashioned her.
Later she'll get blamed for everything,
her comeliness and breasts which in this painting are
those of a fourteen or fifteen year old,
will become sources of sweetness and of guilt.
The serpent's head is an old bearded man
leering at her, all lechery. "Yes, yes,"
it must be hissing as she bends the branch
and reaching upwards with her perfect hand
takes hold of the fruit of the Tree of Knowledge.
This is the last hour of Paradise,
the girl and her consort oblivious to
good and evil and their ramifications.
Their bites of the tree's fruit not yet taken.
The fig leaves are only fig leaves;
their genitalia not yet shameful,
the creator still happy with creation.
The pendant canvas in which Adam appears
ready to give into all temptations
has been lost, alas, to the centuries.
Nor can we know how he held her at the end,
grateful for her succor and constancy.

ILSA THIELAN

Homage to Darkie

the wild dog of Ballyreen

Like a landmark you sat
on the cliffs of Ballyreen
wild dog
once dumped at the roadside
as a young pup
now a big black sheepdog
with white markings
only the photographs
of a kind man
leaving food for you
when you were still a pup
revealed your age

I saw you there
your belly hanging low
your ribs showing
through your long fur
waiting for the anglers
at the Fisherman's hole
to throw some food your way
wild dog
always lingering
in a distance

I promised you
to bring food every day
and I followed you
deep into the canyons of Ballyreen
but never could touch you
I found the den
you lived in
and retrieved your litters
to find homes for them

one by one
often crouched down
on the earth
and limestone pavement
for a long time
and you
with bare teeth over me
warning me

you taught me
when the time was right
for your young ones to go
you taught me
the ways of nature
the ways of wilderness
beautiful dog
with the brave soul
of a Shewolf

you never killed
you dug up roots to eat
and taught your young ones
to do the same
I observed and learned
saw you living close to wild goats
and hares
often ravens on your back
waiting to pick the leftovers
of the food I had brought
kind people
left bones for you
near the cliffs of Ballyreen
where they had seen you
a landmark
a legend

few were hostile
for no reason
and threatened to kill you
I tried to catch you
dear dear Darkie
many hours
desperate to save you

there was silence
no wind
no waves
such silence
even the ravens were gone
such silence

when a pale sun
touched the islands
and the sea turned silver
I had my arms around you
a collar over your head
to bring you home
dear dear Darkie
bring you home
where there was
warmth and love
bring you home alive

a rock
somebody had thrown
at your head
affected your eye sight
and an Xray
of your lungs
showed a bullet
stuck at a rib
close to your heart
shot
many years ago

you survived it all
brave animal
I was blessed
having met you
could feed you
and bring you home
to live with you
for many years
beautiful dog
gentle spirit
of the Shewolf

DAVID McLOGHLIN

Easter Vigil

—For my wife, Adrienne

And then there was the absolute dark the church went into
before the fire vault was lit—baptismal font, fontanelle—
shadow licking the faces of the good priests, parents,
the trim male-couples, a baby in a stroller,
a corpulent man with cropped hair, hawk eyes,
two rows across, near children—shadow flash
   it's him.   Shake it from my eyes. *I am a faulty*
damaged prism.
               No. Breathe   for community,
and the God space: empty room. You smile, squeeze my hand.
Love, it's been a hard belay, to being here again—
like climbers tracking across a face, searching
for hand holds, to a path up—but you anchored the rope.

ANNE FITZGERALD

The Price of 1965, Near Archbishop Palace

Under November's wet darkness you enter
Drumcondra's tree lined respectability, push
in a low sliver gate towards St. Joseph's
fanlight guiding you up its diamond aisle
like a nave to this red bricked three story
Georgian door nurse Gallagher opens. Lets
night in and the one you carry day 'n night
for nine months to this anaglyptic hallway,
narrow as a birth canal, dimly lit shadows
climb walls, little by little, beyond return
to a top box room. Do you lift the sash
window, let the outside in, or not come
out till I leave your womb, hurting as if
the man who left half the idea of me.

Roses ramble your wallpaper incarceration,
traces branches that do not match
like how this came to pass, and the unlikely
bonds that will betray. And as your waters
break your pelvic floor widens what
will be given up, what'll not be talked
of becomes clear, as I appear crown first
under the eye of the sacred heart's red light
into the hands of nurse Gallagher, who
cuts our cord, (according to a well buried
birth certificate up in Werburgh Street); who
hands me over for a fist full of Lady Laverys
rolled up in a black velvet band like a Roman
candle, to a nun in a Hillman making for the ferry.

JOHN MacKENNA

The Turning of the Year

(For Angela)

And so the year begins to turn,

its back towards the waning of the light,

its face to all that lies ahead.

And we stand here,

our backs against the wind and rain,

our faces towards the lifting sun

and everything begins again:

this joy; this life; these days;

this love.

HUGH McFADDEN

Homage to Patrick Kavanagh

Once more I went down by the River Fane
again, on a sunny summer's day,
below the old stone bridge at Inniskeen,
following the Patrick Kavanagh way

and I sat by the flowing brown river,
watching it flow, eleven years after
my first visit one day in September
in the year two-thousand and four, for your
anniversary, Patrick Kavanagh.

On the day of my first visit I saw
a white butterfly flit by brown water,
but on this day it was an Emperor
butterfly I saw settle softly
on the dew-wet grass by the river.

It was a sign, another reminder,
marvels are seen in the ordinary.

AIMÉE SANDS

Gangle and Boot

What a plain man you are, plain like a hand-cranked
sifter, its worn red knob and the futility
of trying, oh plain like applesauce, strained

and sweet, the tang of the stubborn
pulp after pressing, you know, the pattern
you make with tin cookie cutters, the flaps

of dough left hanging, I'm like that too,
the marrying of the scorned and lonely self,
the lid of the bread bin drawer that squeaks

when you slide it back, no one
uses that now, but I can smell the crumbs
from those old, stale years, rescue inconceivable,

the raisin maid dark in her red box
where your shame lies, and mine;
This is a kind of rescue, isn't it:

the dog-brown honesty in your eyes,
your common threads, that plaid flannel shirt,
the stray hairs above your first button.

2013

PATRICIA BRODY

Floating Away, Not

Yesterday in Kundalini we floated our arms
thanked our liver, our kidneys.
My sister has one kidney

only, with "mets" on her liver
and lung. Two weeks after they found these

tiny henchmen, they called with new news: "Hi,
this is the oncologist calling about your brain."

Today she starts chemo after five days of radiation. I'm listing
to the right, to the left –
not to shock, or make you go *Awww*.

Listing shocks   to remind us how we lean
west, east: don't know
how we'll make it home. ≈ ≈ ≈   So I started this poem about floating.

How lovely to stroll, meet your darling, on Dover beach
                          to hover
over ripples like a tern. No, terns

fly well over the surface. To say how much
how much I want to float away —

                                        from grief, not over
my sister,   who says I've grieved her
since her birth
                    float above — a long, withdrawn "you" who shines
no light

for Jill or me. I don't mean god, but a drowner, with a few good lines —
                        "Ahh, *let us be true!*" – who urged me

to float right off his pillow, over grief, over Death –
                                        over the rosy earth

but would not show me how to
                              float
                              back
                              down

                                              or linger —

or let me stay
in his sliver-of-glow,   so I could save her.

HÉLÈNE CARDONA

Twisting the Moon

Now is the time to know
that all you do is sacred.

—Hafiz

We shared the coast of Maine in June,
      hundreds of whales, lobster
         sandwiches, buttermilk pancakes
            and a room in Bar Harbor with antique tub.
They're now a cloister of shadows loved,
      goldsmith of the music of time.
         She left when circumstances met.
I dream of offering her strawberries on sacred moons,
      healed by the beauty of memories,
         ready to start over as if knowing nothing.

Étreinte de la Lune

C'est maintenant le moment de savoir
que tout ce que tu fais est sacré.

—Hafiz

Nous avions partagé la côte du Maine en juin,
      des sandwichs au homard, des spécialités de crêpes,
         une chambre et sa baignoire d'antan à Bar Harbor
            et des centaines de baleines.
Ces ombres forment à présent un cloître adoré,
      gardien de la musique du temps.
         Elle est partie par la force des circonstances.
Je rêve de lui offrir des fraises lors des lunes sacrées ;
      guérie, je le suis, par la beauté des souvenirs,
         prête à repartir comme si de rien.

LARRY O. DEAN

I Had a Good Time With You at the Jewel Last Night

for Deirdre

I had a good time with you at the Jewel last night.
I appreciate you letting me park by the cart corral,
even if it is farther from the door than other available spaces.
Even though we were held up a bit by the morbidly obese man
mumbling to himself at the Redbox just outside the door
whose stance overlapped about thirty percent into our path,
and once inside, there was an avalanche of on-sale oranges
as a throng of shoppers on their way home from work and in a hurry
caught wind of the discount and dove at them like a flamboyance of flamingos,
and as we deftly sidestepped this commotion, only to be hemmed in
by a near-collision with three other carts, everyone stopping
to squint at illegible expiration dates stamped on pre-washed salad bags
just as the artificial thunderstorm effects began and the misters
refreshed the piles of recently replenished produce.
I had a good time sighting the young couple dressed
like Hutterite hipsters clutching Drano and Dog Chow, who disappeared
like UFOs between aisles just as they have done a handful of times in the past.
I had a good time despite the whippet-thin woman who loudly and enthusiastically
regaled her companion about all her upcoming "appointments," lying down
on the floor near the bunches of flowers developed with built-in obsolescence
designed to wilt and jettison petals the day after you brought them home.
When the firetruck and ambulance pulled up, nobody hurried
since they all seemed to recognize her, and one of the EMTs paid for a Diet Pepsi
on his slow saunter out, hoping for an emergency-free rotation to enjoy it as his leisure.
I had a good time hearing the two Somali cab drivers laughing
near the Lotto ticket self-service machine, between fares and between worlds.
Even though you caught me admiring the UGG-booted, teutonic blond whispering
    into her iPhone,
whose hand basket held Oreos, Marie Callender's Comfort Bakes Chicken
    & Broccoli Alfredo,
and a bottle of chardonnay, you let it slide
on the way to the check-out—not the lane with the shortest line,

but with the mildly autistic or OCD bagger who gets riled if our cart isn't
    in *just* the right spot,
because he has his job down to an anal-retentive art most of the time,
    being fast and fastidious
and dependable, unlike the others who throw caution to the wind,
    or more specifically,
cans and bottles and potato chips indiscriminately, not caring the way *he* cares,
philosophizing just under his breath, stationed at the terminus of the conveyor belt
bearing our perishables into his outstretched hands. Even after
unloading the cheap plastic bags of purchased products—some full, some holding
only an item or two, perhaps thematic, such as cotton balls and grapes (round),
or tortilla chips and Hershey's KISSES (airtight)—I smoothly eased the cart
into the skeleton of another, ready to be centipeded back inside the store later
by one of its lot-roaming, turn-taking employees, and we were gone.
I had a good time and hope you had a good time, too.

LORI DESROSIERS

Ice Fishing in the ICU

Therapeutic hypothermia…refers to deliberate reduction of the core body temperature in patients who don't regain consciousness after return of spontaneous circulation following a cardiac arrest.

— www.americannursetoday.com

The nurse shivers as she works
despite her down coat.
Bare hands check
my husband's breathing tube
the respirator's click and hum.
She replaces an ice pack under his arm,
hangs a new bag of Propofol.
She seems to be talking as she
smiles at me through the glass
then opens the door to let me in.
I want to hold his hand
but am not allowed to touch.
It will be thirty hours
before they can wake him.
*I was telling him a story about
ice fishing*, she says.
Something to dream about.

AMY DRYANSKY

Trompe L'Oeil

Every time the sky gets out of whack, too much
this or that, I get out my conscience. A set of tools.

I went to art school. I'm trained in perspective,
proportion. I'd never push a foreground

smack up against a background, even if
the middle ground was all over lilies, or *putti*

or wise men bearing gifts. I'm not taken
with beauty, though some days I could crawl

right into Rembrandt's *chiaroscuro*, Durer's
clarity. He and I share initials. I didn't say

genius. I don't imply, the way Brueghel does,
making his *Icarus* a study in humdrum:

humans and animals alike distracted, bored,
oblivious to the spectacle of Daedalus' son

drowning. Can you blame them? It's almost
time for dinner. The boy barely makes a splash.

PETER JOSEPH GLOVICZKI

Love on a Cold Evening

My mother buys a standup light and sets it up in the
living room. Everything looks brighter: it's
Thanksgiving Day—I had turkey with my girlfriend
at her family's house. They live in a college town;
it's where I went to school. For you, I'd name each
star; the night sky would light this room.

IVY PAGE

Recovery

Fighting to live. All negotiations
are on your terms,
but you constantly change the rules.

Never knowing if you will lock *me* inside
or reach out to the edge
of what you can bare
and break, for me.

I want to kill you.

A slow death is the only way to go.
Ripping apart my broken will,
sinking your teeth further in,
stealing my moments.
Leaving only fragments.

Your face, a killer,
drawing deeper
lines on an already withered face.
From beneath the rubble,
the broken bits, I scream.

Your spiraling body winds
itself around the darkest parts of me.

JAMES RAGAN

A Room on the Irish Coast

Outside the shadows graze on sea holly.
I have known this room in light.
At any moment the May sun will leap across
the field to steal a glint from beds of aster.
There is little time to fill the ceiling panes
with night or peel the darkness off the shades.
The thinking here is gold in hue.
Rays that flutter through the blinds,
sheer as scrims, are kaleidoscopic,
latticed down between the light outdoors
and the slats of books within. There is no black
or white into which the mind need go.
I would think the sun might want the curtain
nearer, and of a sort that shimmers,
to show how vast and infinite are the whims of color:
emerald, sienna, indigo. All day their palette
reflects the bold insurgence of the writer's soul.
I could leap into the flow of it, barreling like a thought
along the Cliffs of Moher or down to Aran shoals,
a phrase shifting here or there, a syllable revised
like dunes or waves in poetry or prose.
All day the night imagines
how in passing through the shade
of only half the world, the light has lost
what essence of a soul the room still knows,
how the mind inspired, with all its splendor failing
like these words, might endure beyond their telling.

STEVEN REESE

The Going (Notes on the Text)

Allons!, no stoppage, for there is no staying.

> "Allons! [Let's go!] we must not stop here," cries
> Whitman in "Song of the Open Road." Compare
> "stoppage" in "Song of Myself": "There is no
> stoppage, and never can be stoppage...."
> "For there is no staying" translates Rilke's
> *Denn Bleiben ist nirgends*, in the first
> of the *Duino Elegies*. More literally, *staying*
> *is nowhere.*

the waiting now just long enough, the call
to depart irresistible: *lève l'ancre!*

> The first line here translates *Certera ya la espera*,
> in Jorge Guillén's "The Departure" (*La salida*).
> Whitman's "Song of the Open Road" speaks
> of "an irresistible call to depart."
> *Lève l'ancre* ("raise the anchor"), "Sea Breeze,"
> (*Brise marine*), Stéphane Mallarmé.

and here are the places left behind
with a furtive tear, *labitur ex oculis*
nunc quoque.

> *Voici les lieux que nous laissons* ("Here are
> the places that we leave") says Saint-John Perse
> in the prose-poem "Chronicle" (*Chronique*).
> "A furtive tear" alludes to the *romanza* sung
> by Nemorino in Donizetti's opera *The Elixir*
> *of Love (L'elisir d'amore)*; "A furtive tear
> appeared in her eyes," it begins (*Una furtiva*
> *lagrima/Negl' occhi suoi spuntò*), a tear
> which Nemorino reads as a sign of Adina's love
> and of the elixir's magic power. He is
> right about the love, wrong about the elixir,

which is only cheap burgundy.
Ovid's Latin, describing (in *Tristia* [*Sorrows*])
his last night in Rome before going
into exile, says "it [a tear] falls from my eye
now, too."

*Des terres nueves, par là-bas, et nos poèmes
encore s'en iront sur la route des hommes*
**(I swear I never will translate myself
at all)**

Saint-John Perse's French here combines portions
of the prose-poem *Winds (Vents)*: "New lands
out there, and our poems will set out again
on the road of men."
The English is Whitman's "Song of Myself,"
a commentary on his own poem, its method.

Neue Weite, **wider and wider expanding,
outward and outward and outward.**

"New expanse," says Rilke's German, *Sonnets
to Orpheus*, I.11, which ponders a constellation
and the human bent for figures, tropes.
Whitman, gazing up at the stellar systems in "Song
of Myself, says: "Wider and wider they spread,
expanding and always expanding, / Outward
and outward and forever outward."

**as when language goes on great streets
of silence.**

ESTHA WEINER

... to the sea again

In the waves
the voices of the lost
are found

In the gentle lap
or the undertow
the whitecaps whisper
the beloved they know

Or the whitecaps spit
their relentless snare

Either way they drown
us. It's why we're there

TERENCE WINCH

On the Boat

for eamonn wall

I went on a little visit in the rain today to the Diaspora,
and it was such great fun. We had tea, we had beer,
and later we assembled in the vestibule for the Christening.
The bartender sang a lamentation, as the ushers from the nine
o'clock mass mispronounced the baby's name. Satan was there,
of course, and we all renounced him, as is the custom. We also
renounced many others of whom we did not approve. For example,
Bob Hope. Jimmy Cagney danced on the table, his ass sticking
out as always. Der Bingle sang a song about Frank Sinatra, stressing
how much he didn't like him. A half century fell off the shelf
and my name broke apart into a million pieces. That's when
they put me on the boat, told me not to come back until my
passport was as thick as a book with no name by Michael Lally.

JOHN W. SEXTON

Minnow Mermaids as Blue …

The minnow mermaids can fit two-dozen
into the cupped palms of your hands.
Beneath the surface of the pond
they are a choir of splintery light.

Young boys have kept them in jam jars
listening to them sing plaintively
when the moon shines bright on the sideboard;
watched as they darkened over the weeks,
became nothing but sluggish fish.

A princess might keep one, just one,
in a waxed purse full of water.
A little darling to be shown to her friends,
fed with midges or nibs of parsley.

Princes have kept them in onyx basins
as a council of prophecy.
They swim to the left: bad luck.
Good luck if they swim to the right.

Mixed luck if, while swimming in the river,
one swims into your ear.
Once there she'll charm your mind.
Sad luck certainly if two take an ear each.

On summer days they will frolic wantonly,
showing no concern for the world.
And it's many you'll see then, squirming
in the beaks of kingfishers.

EDWARD DENNISTON

The Chair

for Samuel, one day old

Someone has bothered to beachcomb this turquoise
marine-blue, sea-green plastic chair, to bury its looped legs
into the sand and marram shelf, skewer them

with a length of sea-scoured groyne—to have them
held fast, facing south into Tramore Bay
just above tide-reach

at the nose of the spit where tides
moonwise, gorge the Rinneshark.
The chair's a radiant thing,

a sitting place to take in the offing
these Spring days of bright blue sky,
warming sun, a steely northerly—your birth's

happened-upon weather. My feeble pilgrimage
and rite: to walk the length of the beach,
sit on a turquoise plastic chair, give thanks

for the stem cell wonder that has you
made manifest, birthed and shored
for your Mum and Dad.

The surf's easy swell is on its way in;
an untidy chevron of Brent geese
head lagoon-ward, fly close and low

readying themselves; like them,
you have that mystery mechanism
that won't be denied, the need

for journey, sustenance, safe haven
and all that compass, desire-path stuff.
Little human, more than ever I'm spring-struck,

taking my time on this turquoise plastic chair
of thanks, fabulous as it is, as I see it,
washed up in honour of your hereness;

and whether or not the chair's in situ artfulness
survives human, wind or tide, it doesn't matter,
soon, with you in harness in all your outdoor gear

we'll stroll beach and burrows,
for journey's sake; extemoporise
about colours and weather and sand

and tide and bird noise
and where the turquoise chair is,
or might be, or was, the day you were born,

right at the spit end - free of explanation
or the knowhow of time passing
when you and I Samuel will be alive.

RITA KELLY

We know our Milton...

for Carmel Cummins,
Inistioge, Co. Kilkenny

I had no hint, no clue even,
Of the song that you were singing
All those years ago. No.

I had no idea of you;
Who you really were then
who you are now.

The Northwest, you said.
I saw an immense place
Of cold air, very cold air.
A far-reaching, wind-swept emptiness.
Some great trek, a mission perhaps
To reach other ways and passages
To new lives. New beginnings.
To leave the old confined and restricted you
Behind by a stream of turbid water washed
Down from swollen lands, higher grounds
Of scant grazings, marginalized places where
Old words survive, old ways of viewing the world,
In isolated realities. A word or two like *sceach* after
Sceach scattered on the landscape. Blackthorn.
Thorn indeed beneath the pure white flower.
The black-stemmed walking stick, glazed bark.
The bitterness
Of the small blue-black berry as if it held its luminous colour
Like face powder, a soft dusting — but oh the bitterness
Until there were almost tears; and the taste solidified
In the mouth, along the tongue. So often we test the world
with our tongue
Not just when we are young and primordial
Before we can tell the story, before the story can tell itself.

Faces and families, families and faces, always asking,
Always already knowing.

When the bluebells fill the woods with joyfulness
They will know, the familiar faces, who see that joy
That you have already gone, left for the new life;
A paradise beyond our fear of fading bluebells,
Of May giving way to high summer, to the scamper
Of little feet along the headlands of the fields
You know so well from all the differing angles,
The lengthening of the light until there is no light
But the lonely sound of a prowling fox —
The single contraction of the heart, yours, the ewe's
Fearful for its baby, for its *leanbh*, the beloved
Whose force and presence enriches the land.

Beneath the dampness of the forest's floor
The bluebells will retreat and wait
And wait until the year's heart has thawed again
To bring bells bluer than her eyes
Out of the dead ground.

North west Orient rings some bell,
It is a contradiction too—
Going in both directions,
Diametrically opposite
To you and to my idea of you.
Within the convention of the familiar orchards,
Wooded places, little tucked-away churches,
Limestone bridges, hazel in the hedgerows
And fields full of cereals to sweeten the air of the city.
Rape-seed yellow blinds with its unbroken generosity,
As we pass it by. We think too of you,
Of her, in that other place, that northwest windblown place.
That you would lose her there.
Lose her forever.
I had no idea of all that pain,
Of all that love,
I had no idea of your world.

RAINA J. LEÓN

Birthplace: N 39° 55' 37.43"

The vessel splits. Water soaks pedestal legs,
thick to their trembling fat, waddling columns
beneath still heavy core. She pushes,

expels like other women. Her sister
labored only minutes, but that child trusted
hands to catch, to unmuffle the scream

with a swipe. This child bicycle-churns feet,
trusts no one to bring her to earth safe. Blood
that sticks. Breach. She will not return to turn.

Scalpels cut the fabric skin,
stretch mark asylum. A body
sets out; infection sets in. A babe

alone, still hungry from vestigial morphing.
She despised her mother's *fat, I'm getting so fat*,
and spite-swallowed her own twin,

like *This is life-fat* and *Mine*. Now,
girl-girl unfurls her cries with the swaddled throng,
while her mother weeps a week, childless,

her breasts dry, solitary confinement
of staph, hearing other women's babies
cry for milk.

NICKI GRIFFIN

The Old House

Rain fills each hoof-made pock mark
down to where the ditch hits tarmac
and the boundaries are anybody's guess.

All the known places are submerged,
rusted droops of barbed wire,
sentinel trees splitting field from field.

Maybe I should have stayed on the road,
stayed with the predictable,
but I wanted to come to the house from behind,

catch it unawares, trick it into being
what it used to be. I wanted to peep through
the kitchen window and see you there.

Over in the distance the town lights come on
but I turn my back, keep on into the dusk,
mud glooping round my wellies, sucking.

When I get there the garden is under water.
Someone else's mother walks across the room.

DANIEL THOMAS MORAN

Here, in the Afterlife

We each keep those things to ourselves,
The long midnights which followed
days behind a locked door.

We contain the pain of our engagements.
The hollow aches, the tightened scars.
The memory left behind in a severed limb.

We had always been nomads without tribe,
Walking the dunes in our chest,
believing the promise of our mirages.

Silently we marked the dates in our head,
Walking cautious around the ditches
so as to not to slip or be swallowed.

We, each lived though many days,
knowing the many and not the other,
Believing one day we would meet us.

We imagined a kingdom of tall trees,
staying green through winters,
Set over hills where snow came to sleep.

We imagined the syllables of water,
chanting its *berceuse* in the darkness,
Lighting upon a peculiar forever.

MARK A. MURPHY

The Wedding Crow

On the red brick chimney
up there,
quite out of reach of man's affairs —

feeds the black crow,
now and then preening
her dumb show in the sizzling heat.

We do not wait for her to be pleased,
translate the way
that man might perceive

the crow's *kaww-kawwing*,
but turn instead to where the eye is deceased,
expurgated from the flesh-eaten socket of a vole.

Poor vole! We cry,
but never, *Poor crow!*
Oh no, not the lowly crow to make us swoon

over the newborn in the nest —
her crowy savagery had already begun
with jagged claw and beak

long before the bespoke cruelty of man.
So comes the crow, long before
the dreaded wedding bells

and the clip-clop of wedding shoes
on sun baked paving stones,
incongruent in the long upswing

as our own unflattering repose —
where love's lost once more,
long lost in petals of the white rose.

2014

CAMERON CONAWAY

Painted Over

—*for Thầy (Thích Nhất Hạnh)*

For the first time your voice
unfurls as lotus into the sunlight
of my ears. No filter, no need
to plug in to listen—just you,
two cushions away, guiding me
to the seed of my 12-year-old self,
and me, sitting here in Ayutthaya,
drifting back to Altoona, to wounds
I've painted over in thick brushstrokes,
to pants pulled down, the backhand
that bloodied my mouth, the helpless
watching as my sister took worse.
You tell me to see my father
as a 5-year-old boy picking up pebbles
in a stream. His hands are so small.
Minnows swirl around his bare feet.
He is so gentle. You tell me to see
myself as a 5-year-old boy, picking
up pebbles beside him in the stream.
Minnows swirl around my bare feet.
We are both so small; our hair so soft.
We make up a game where we see
if we can toss pebbles and get them
to land on the surface of a large stone.
He tosses first and misses. Then I toss
and miss. He tosses again and misses
again. I do too. We decide to leave.
My foot slips on green algae, he reaches
his hand out to me. You place your hand
on my shoulder. It is so warm. My eyes
are crusted shut from dried tears. They
open and you are there and I am here.
An hour has passed. You whisper:
When you stand please walk as though
your feet are kissing the earth.

EDWARD MADDEN

Park

Dublin, winter 2011, after my father's death

Rain in the park, near dark, the trees
leaning over the wet walks,

bark washed slick and black, the leaves
a pale gold, glowing, cold,

and the faint smell here of something
sour, the pond funky with ducks

and gulls, mounded leaves moldering,
and my heart, here, far

from home, thick with memories of my father,
those last moments. It's not

that things had to be said—the dead
keep speaking after all—just

how quietly they speak,
how quietly.

ROBERT McDOWELL

From Here On, Dragons!

That's what the mapmakers wrote on their maps a long time ago
To name the mysterious, big blue spaces nobody had ever been to.
Amend that. Nobody white, with lots of gold to blow, had been to them.
The mapmakers didn't think about that, or where the gold came from.
Who cared whose wrist it was torn from or whose severed head it fell off of
As a drunken mercenary fumbled the basket catch? It was hard enough
Making a map an explorer would trust to guide his fleet
Before his blundering ambition made his dream obsolete.

JEAN KAVANAGH

Glass

A sea bird dives
into the mirror
of the fjord,
seeks its prize,
as if there is no border
between water
and the air.

And on the island
we look for our
own treasures,
unearth forgotten jewels —
the right words
caressed into the quiet,
cloud-shadows
caught up in sunset,
and that minute, after,
where the sea
is brighter than the sky.

I was woken,
like to the sound of rain
falling on the camp;
found inside a moment,
an end unto itself, intense,
but not without reward.

There are scattered
keepsakes
on the shore —
complete again,
in smaller pieces;
opaque, worn smooth,
no longer fragile,
yet still transparent
at their heart.

JACQUELINE KOLOSOV

There are those who hide ghosts in manila folders

Silence is so accurate
—Mark Rothko

Here again, your birthday
And I find Rothko lingering

Between frayed bands of color
How he tried to buttress the mind

By containing the light
You lined the windowsills with bottled glass

Blue as night, blue as the forlorn soul
Clouds sift morning closer now

*

The morning she found you
I stood among the Rothkos

Your soul had escaped by then
Having slipped inside

The trace of line that bleeds
Into the horizon

A lone pair of footprints
Ink-blue in each book's margins

And those light-filled bottles
All that remained

From now on I will grow older than you

*

When will the white-winged terns arrive
Black bodies sleek as night's turn

To light, these carriers of distance
Bell beat of wings, silence's metronome

Now only waves of white, memory's
Waves, and the mind's heights

Unfathomable
Your footprints remain and the blue—

*

Once you dreamt of a great ship
Anchored on a rock cliff

How clean the mind is, you told me
Afterwards, and how quiet the sky

From now on I will grow older than you

KELLY MOFFETT

Chickens do not Fly

What else has she learned? The yard circles a kind
of green like the egg sac in the science chart.
In the pen, nine hens, two rabbits. A baby
with a brush in its lap. On the wall, a red stag.
At night frogs are Buddhist monks chanting.
She keeps too much. He gives too much.
He does not explain magic to her. That in the tissue box
there is another tissue box and in there a calendar
that tells where all of us have been. Nine dogs
in nine cages. Three cats in three beds. She doesn't
share well. He does not share well. She does not
believe that he believes in sweetness, but the gods—
they show her. And so she carries (as ants carry)
the dead and Hitchcock gives her her moment:
a hall, a door, a hall, a door, a hall, a door.

MARY PINARD

Poet

for Estelle Travers Smith

I was living then
in the West, nine years old
and already also

old with loss, my mother, your
niece, gone swiftly, finally
elsewhere, as had others

from the distant family—
grandmother, grandfather,
uncle—also gone, and gone long

when you took me in,
showed me how to make
a stroke, its precise angle, brush

or pen tip to paper, a pressure
that once given, stayed,
uninterrupted, a keeping

deep in
the in,
so that later,

when you left, one more
rupture, your own stroke
piercing every plane,

I could remember you,
your veined hand, jade-ringed
guide, you

taught me autumn, color, that
turning air, and how I could
draw it best by breathing,

beat by beat, deliberately,
like this, I heard you say, *I am*,
I am, *iamb*, *iamb*.

JO PITKIN

Ferry

From blue shoals and bleak shores
a squat ferry pulls its white flag
of gulls in its slow, heavy wake.

Its cargo of tourists headed home
laughs, coughs, drinks, and swears
in a tongue I cannot bear to hear.

Over the swaying railing I lean
to touch the churning dirty tide,
to catch the first flinty rock

broken from the thumb of jetty
jutting out from the gray land
that bars the *you* from *me*.

Into the harbor's narrow neck
the bow inches like a black fin
tearing through the sea's silk.

Disgorged from a steely corridor,
I do not plant a flag or stoop to kiss
the gritty beach beyond rough surf.

Instead, I fly through metal gates—
the portals of your distant life—
and rush past clods of reunions

to greet the interruption of your city,
your curve of ocean, your salty air,
your brick and soot, your tinny rain,

the sudden lifting of boundaries.

LAURA-GRAY STREET

Shift Work I (Loray Mill, 1929)

They had a bell would ring any time
they was leaving or coming or anything
and let you know you had so much time
to eat or sleep or smoke, day or night,

on or off your shift. The mill run regular then.
They'd blow a whistle when it was time
for lunch, for break, to change out lines.
If the whistle blew otherwise, there'd been

an accident. It was only a matter of time
before you stopped worrying who'd died.
Back then we knew all about such things,
prayed the bell would ring for quitting time.

They had clocks on every line.
When your machine wasn't running,
you made nothing for your time.
Day and night, whistles blew, bells chimed.

And that's the way it went a long, long time.

JOSEPH P. WOOD

After Baika

Dumbfounded as I'd never been:
Newborn slimed in meconium.

The Space before her first cry
I charged like a quadruped. Still
The cherry trees bloomed too soon . . .

Snow fell: dandruff, confetti.
A nurse placed a mask on my wife's sweaty face.

The river had ice chunks.
The river had guppies.

A defibrillator was hauled from the corner.

And nothing broke the monks' chant.
And smoke spiralled the rock garden.
Fields shot everywhere. None were aflame.

from *Fold of the Map*

LISA MARIE BRODSKY

The Purpose Explained

When asked about your children, point to
the divorce of their parents: hair-tearing,
tear-sopping, and how step-loving
is rocky and hard on your bare,
naïve feet.
Moods tangle and tatter, change with the weather,
all noised up
like I love you —
I like you not.

When asked about home, smell
the wood smoke wafting through your childhood.
Turkey, crocheted sweaters, marshmallow chocolates,
Christmas a new magic
every time it snowed.

When asked about comfort, sit
on your mother's bed
stored in the attic for safe keeping.
Do not sneeze or cry; do not light
the snuffed-out memories.
Listen for echoes, but there'll be no advice
for the weary parent, just scratches on wood
from passing mice.

When asked about suffering, know
it stood for something. Do not call the ashes black
or the tears dry and wasted.
Your lullabies have purpose; these children aren't cursed
because you sometimes warble and shout.

Call them *drenched roses having thorns.*
Call them *overlooked candles needing wicks*;
call them *little grace-givers.* Call it all
something to write home about.

And it will click at some point:
The fighting and loving and breathing the same air
day after day. How questions don't always need answers
and living goes by faith in the unexplained.

EDWARD O'DWYER

And Each Other

It was settled then, that's what we were going to do.
And mutually agreed, thank goodness.

It'd be just like when we were kids, we said,
lovely nostalgic notions filling up our heads
of those days, the rainless ones.

We'd have ourselves a big jumble sale, but an adult one,
because it's a long time since we've been kids —
even when we've acted like them, we were not kids.

Next fine day, we agreed, yes, we'll do that.

I'll shout jumble sale at everyone and anyone I can see.
I'm good at shouting, I have years of practice
when it comes to making myself heard.

We'll get a roll of those tiny stickers,
like in those old shops you don't see much of anymore,
where the prices of items are all handwritten,
the sale recorded, (handwritten), in a dishevelled ledger.

The kids in the neighbourhood will be disappointed
we've not got much of interest to them
but, luckily, kids are not any concern of ours.

The microwave, Waterford Crystal or Grandfather clock
wouldn't appear in too many Santa letters, you say.

Yes, best keep them well away, I say, what with
all those bits and pieces in the drawer — yes, that drawer.
We'll put up a sign so there's no confusion. *ADULTS ONLY*.

My golf clubs and tools will fetch a bob or two,
and your jewellery, and maybe in its new homes, as well,
the nicest things will be said, fine compliments
be made at last to their loveliness.

Great, you say. Yes, I say, equally looking forward to it.

We'll split everything 50/50, fair is fair.
Wonderful to be able to agree so easily now.
Such a fine idea, a jumble sale — selling it all off.

Good we can be so reasonable, under the circumstances.
The next fine day. Gone. All of it...

SANDRA ANN WINTERS

The Clock Tower

Stone upon stone the bell tower rises outside my window,
a protestant ruin of the village church. You belonged
to Drishane Castle. You belonged to the people.
The ringer gently bowed to the lintel, climbed
narrow stone steps spiraling, to call worshipers to holy communion.
Years later, Tidy Towns filled your belfry with a white-faced clock.
I raise the linen shade, wake to your dial. Black Roman numerals
go round and round. You move through my tea and egg.
I notice the time as I am off to the shop for the *Guardian*
and lamb. You are my companion as I play with poems
and read *Passing Through*. I stroll in the deep grass,
rubbing old tombstones, no longer legible.
You move through my days until you wane in the light
of the evening and fade at the unfairness of fate.

2015

NEIL SHEPARD

Lines Written at Tyrone Guthrie

(Tyrone Guthrie Artists' Centre, Ireland)

1

The wind is up: it wipes that placid look right off the face
Of the lake and turns to frowns and wrinkles all content.
Times like this, I'm bent on fame, embarrassed as I am
To say it, and all my equanimity goes slack or turns
To grimaces as the wind comes up: the last flowering
Trees are blown to hell. A bell in the wind signals the start
Of the hell-hound race. My mind makes them lap the track
And howl when only one can win: the rest conspire to eat him.

One angry down draft: ripples start on the far shore and fan out
In vectors violent as a temper tantrum or a Chinese fan
On whose face one reads a hundred years' war: cherry blossoms
Scattered onto blood trails; a flock of storks disordered in the air,
Buffeted upside and down, tumbling under boot-heels
Of the marching army. Oh, how my mind makes a mess
Of something simple as a springtime gale! You'd think
That reputations were for sale, and not earned the hard way:

Word by word. There is no grace. The wind hurries the clouds
Along at a pace too fast for thunder or the lightning strike.
They're just wild, like leaderless, spooked stallions or grey-
Hounds who've lost the track, the comfortable oval upon
Which their brilliant speed begins to look like art, like smart
Intention, and not some useless burst of energy that blows
The whole pack in a frightful, confused tumble off a cliff,
The wind whirling in their anxious, dying ears: *if, if, if, if.*

This morning's world is wild with wind: if we're not rooted deep
And stiff with a resistance, like trees surviving by the shore,
we're blown to hell and back before we know it. To bend
is also useful, and to bow, and to let the wind blow itself

out through the shaded spaces between our ribs where a clinging
nest might be. Let the wind blow away, let it bundle its violence,
without a mind at the reins, let it blow over hills and down to the sea.

2

One more sunny day in which there are no answers.
Well, the trees haven't needed them for a million years.
And the common justification — that they've got a hundred
Spring-times in their veins before they rot — is not much better
Than what I've got. They'll fall and fuel a Resolute and end
As ash. I'll skip the step in which I warm men's bones,
But I too will end in a furnace. The lawn-man comes to trim
The grass, as if it mattered. The Irish bluebells, thick
Along the path, teach green a blue thing or two for a quick
Week before they pass. Are they happy, sad? Do they care?
Am I asking the right proprietors? Let's take the largest lens
We've got, place it on the sky and look back to the Big
Bang's near-beginning, a mere million years from the Original
Nothing, when out of the blackest asshole farted gases
That with a scratch and match burst into suns and solar flares —
And tell me if, in that god-damn first springtime, there's matter
that matters. No, I'm not just nattering on, though yes, I am, I'm doing
what we do in the midst of twiddling thumbs in a void, I'm voiding myself
of expectations, of heavenly vacations, of hell's glam-hot coastline, and
I'm going to take my god-damn time with a chaise longue, dragging it out
on the new-clipped lawn to lie in nothing but uncertainty, not a day more,
just today's alluring sunny skies under which I'll wish and wish for rain.

3

Two hours rambling over gorse-studded pasture. I'm hoarse
from shouting yellow yellower than the sun and more vanilla
than aether! Even the swans honk their approval of my out-
and-about and general brightening of the disposition. In this
country where every second shadow's attached to a sinner,
they drink to excess but follow the hedgerows and stumble home
for dinner. Agnostic as I am, I haven't talked to god
along a nature trail, nor met a god I ever liked that wasn't
in a lotus posture: not Buddha — for I'm fond of women

and prefer Guanyin meditating amidst the marsh marigolds
or Mary, cross-legged, sniffing roses in a topiary manger,
or someone out of time like Gaia-Tellus who I believe
as I believe the Earth is round and spinning on a phallus.
I'm lost. We're lost. God cast us out when Modernists
Miscast him or wished him dead. And he's been dead
Ever since, or turned his back on us, a black monolith
In space the greatest telescope can't penetrate. We've lost
The light from that old signal that goes back before the Big
Bang. That's why our postmodernists obsessively observe
The sky for signs of icy H2O in distant universes and track back
Now almost to the blast of the first Big Whimper, perhaps
Just a temper-tantrum God'd thrown from another unbelieving
Swarm of stars and planets, our parallel, our oldest lesson before
Our sun was warm. Hell, what can I know beyond the mute
swan's honk who, if his name were true, would be original
as silence, or sin, or sun, though I'm told there's a hiss and hum
from the gases. We're perfect asses here on earth. What's it worth
to know that gods are gone, ghosts are phony, the fore-known
and the after-known are ignorant of us and us of them? It's worth
my life, I guess, my sixty years vexed by the cradle that rocked me
from my first foundations, to my earnest vernal search, to my selva
oscura in the dark woods of middle life, to this very moment
growing always closer to the age of god who is ageless, unless
I clap my hands and scare off the swans and sing for all I'm worth,
Though it be nothing, a yellow stain and sting along the hedgerow home.

JUDITH BARRINGTON

The Book of the Ocean

They've all written their books: the wind
with its scattering of seeds, its steady erosion
of terraced hills, histories carved in the gray faces
of cliffs whose grief it transcribes into song.

Rain with its poetry: quick rivulets or pocks
that rattle on the roofs of our minds. And sunshine
with its golden tales: honey in the mouths
of heroes; warriors who blaze and die young.

The book of the ocean is the greatest
and most neglected. It floats in shadows
under rock shelves; it laps at the edges
of dreams—a reminder of the deep dark

into which we dive nightly, a reminder
of the moon that hauls us and hurls us
on the brink of wrinkled lands where once
we staggered ashore, trying to become human.

> It is written on wavy scrolls at the tide line;
> It is written as a crab on a dry desert rock;
> It is written in green and indigo, sometimes a wash;
> It is written to be studied from space or through
> the mask on a diver's face;
> Its comedy splashes our feet.
> Its tragedies writhe in the tides of the night.

Like it or not, we are turning the watermarked pages
their words hissing in our ears with blood and with salt
while the moon grows fat, then wanes to the sweetest sickle.

TODD HEARON

See-Saw

For Lionel and Kempie, on their eighth birthday

And in the tumbling heights
     where April's earliest green
tangles with sunfall

     somewhere the unseen
bird-of-two-tones
     balancing the moment, both

here-and-there, then-and-now,
     high/low, heigh-ho and so
it goes, the old see-saw

     singing out in memory
with a springling chickadee
     now your half-flown see-saw years

have flown.

YUN WANG

Seascape at South Padre Island

Dolphins part sargasso curtains
to observe
ice mountains in the sky
shape-shift into a brush-painted
pine forest

Salt-sprayed men extend themselves
into the sea
through fishing poles
Buckets fill with striped fish
gasping to death

Scarlet sunset

A procession along the jetty:
men and women in black suits
each holding a long stemmed red rose
followed by a young blonde
a white-gowned infant in her arms

Our blood speaks the tongue
of the gleaming sea
Dolphins the leaping angels
of the continuum
etch it in scrolls of moonlit water

GEORGE MOORE

The Crow in Some Mythologies

was a woman who could change form
was *Badbh Catha*, the "battle crow"
riding a horse, a sign of disaster for the armies
who encountered her

was a woman and goddess, a female
war-deity, whose black and scavenger ways
were the gist of her indifference
were her defining mark

were the intrusion of death
at crossroads and on rings and currency
on the coin with its power to transform
carried her, who was paramount on the horse

was ubiquitous and omnipotent
before forests were cut and cities burned
was forever at the scenes of bloodshed
searching out the ones who would not believe

was carved in stone and forged in bronze
was etched in wood
and with wings lifted, soared across plains
and pages where the winds bay

was purplish black in age but never gray
for gray was the dawn and the battle crow
was forbidden that one hour to haunt the fallen
who shortly would be hers forever

NICHOLAS McLACHLAN

The Stag Party

for Noel Berkeley

It's unbalanced, this men-only gathering
on the bank of the river Barrow,
but we're here, at the end of a narrow stem
of country lane upriver from town,
standing beside a head-high trailer,
preparing to embrace
the opposite ends of a two-man canoe.
They're fibreglass dug-outs,
heavy and round-bottomed,
buoyant but skittish.

It's balance, the instructor says, as he demos
his rule of thumb position for the paddle,
counts nine syllables per stroke,
and kneels to show the kind of quarrelling
two blades must do to guide a boat.
I'm looking on from the bank.
I can see the river gliding by,
wide, silken, slow-moving.
Perfect for play acting upon,
for corkscrewing and games of Chicken
though I know there's danger further on,
a weir and white-water rapids to negotiate.

It doesn't matter that we haven't time
to master our canoes because the weir
will make men of us. I feel its power
through the floor of the canoe.
It hooks us with its fish-strike bite and drags.
We slow race back to face it right
but it swallows us in a single gulp
and coughs us up in shallows
among tree roots and hanging branches.

Yet again sensing comes before seeing:
the rapids are close at hand.
I hear cascading water, louder now,
thirty miles of river backing up behind us,
tonnes and tonnes of the stuff.
Next thing, we are suddenly dropping twenty feet
by way of a submerged cliff
into a hole which nature has plugged
with granite boulders the size and symmetry of small cars.
It is through this we are expected to slalom.

Of course, being men wasn't enough.
The river won and turfed us out half-way.
When I came up for air — without my glasses
but with my feet on the bed of the river —
my reaction was shock, laughter, relief.
As for my dear friend, he was already away,
purposeful in his march through the water.
In a moment he will reach the riverbank
onto which the man he has become will step.

OWEN GALLAGHER

Straight Up

When she grasped what I considered big,
stuttered *Is that it?*
I fumbled with the zip.

For a decade I thought myself unfit,
destined to drift
with lads unable to get onto the pitch.

Until I was referred to a page-turner
for the inadequate,
What men can do with or without it.

If things for us go amiss, let us persist
with this artificial aid —
which I believe is strapped on like this.

RUTH O'CALLAGHAN

Death

places a lace handkerchief
over her nose, lifts her gown
clear of urine and other matter,
slowly rises through the stairwell.
She knows the ache for escape

lies on the tagged walls - the young
yet to realise the release she offers.
Her ringed fingers caress a scab
of steel: the handrail flakes.
On the fourteenth floor she slips

casually past the slick young man
whose smile reflects his work is done.
Death bends gently, notes
her silver bangles will not wake
the old woman. Death appreciates

the young man's art: commitment
to detail leaves the carpet unmarked.
Her dimpled wrist brushes a speck
of saliva as she adjusts the teeth
loose in the mouth. She closes her eyes.

Death does not dawdle.
She will follow him or his twin sister
across the arc of this city to visit
the righteous or the fashionista:
the twins do not differentiate.
Their time is precious.

STEPHEN BETT

Back Principles (52) : agoraphobic

Big spaces are
made of this

Phoenix to Yuma
—terrifying

The christ to
the buddha ...
terrifying too

Hold my back (pls)
the landscape
would break
it in halves

Agoraphobic,
big space

Holding emptiness
in my hands

PHILLIP CRYMBLE

House Burning Down

Walking side by side along the pavement, cold
and weak from sleep, we each take turns to push

the fold-out stroller, keep our little boy in motion
through the clamour of the market-going crowds

and would-be witnesses to mishap, bald calamity.
The corner house at Regent Street and Charlotte

won't stop smouldering. Beleaguered, smudged
with smoke, and soaked in flame-retardant foam,

it sputters like an all but spent volcano. Passers-by
stare sheepishly — take pictures with their phones.

A barricaded spectacle's like open water chummed
with crates of mackerel. Frank voyeurism levels us —

absorbs as it enthralls. An excavator nudges down
the lath and plaster walls. We stop a while, cinch

up our coats, agree to carry on — make haste towards
the market stalls — in search of something warm.

TREVOR CONWAY

Play

I could never escape goalposts:
Between the pillars of brick walls,
The shadows of bridges built for trains,
The wooden frames of a house-in-progress.

Like a dog distracted,
I became Marco van Basten,
Eyeing a long ball, assessing my angle.
I was Cantona once, my school collar turned up.

Freed by the confines of tar and lines,
I'd sweat at the sight of a metal frame
Designed to keep caravans from car parks.
One time, I was tackled by a puddle.

It's dangerous for me to drive through towns
Where pitches flaunt their green allure.
Gaelic posts strike above dull walls,
Thin as stalagmites.

There's pain in my knees, my hips.
All this for just a bit of play.
With a pen, I find new fantasies,
Days devoted to rainbowed worlds.

A ragged web shivers by my window,
As though a ball had burst the net.
At the desk, I play, someone else for a while.
The book closes — I'm me again.

BERNADETTE CREMIN

Cherry Pink

Seagulls graze on sky above the nursery,
clouds yawn and stretch apricot and violet
into powder blue and china white. Night

is late. In the playground a swing sits still,
overlooked by a squad of toys that squat
on the sill poking fun at the empty yard.

Cherry pink chalk matchstick men march
across tarmac, the wooden horse needs
a child on its back, a lick of paint. Night

is late. It's the anniversary of Mr Perry's
death. They found him a year ago today
swinging like lead from his garage roof

in a zero of rope. The news was translated
for the kids by parents reduced to innocence
and a rash of gossip spread across the tabloids

before anyone said a word. I remembered
the date on the bus, got off at the wrong stop
to come and feed the birds.

2016

MILLICENT BORGES ACCARDI

The Mass

The priest who devours
himself as sacrifice
invokes the Latin words
for
Take this
my body
Take this in memory of me.

Burn this house
He says, burn it
with the secret
fire of philosophy,
a fiery form of water.

Burn it with supplication,
honor among the willful,
his own brand of
vertical theology,.

Make life into sudden
Food,
Wine for a bloody immaculate
escape.

Burn this
He says taking
what
he can separate from each palm:

the right-hand pages, the references
to eternity, the Song
of Solomon, the great voices
of Jack in the Pulpit.

Reverence.
Burn this he says,
Letting his soul
savor pain
uncrowded by regret
or remorse. Burn this,
smaller and smaller
thing
like a piece of paper
like a soul
burning in
circles from the sun
Like nothing
I have ever seen before.

Entirely, he steps outside
his world,
Not knowing
what he has been given
is
a prayer.

If not this birth—
This earth
A burning,
this wonderment
without smiles--
then nothing at all.
Yes, nothing, he says.
He says. Nothing.

JENNIFER HORNE

The Spartan Wife

Historians will say of us that we were a warlike people.
No. Our men are warriors, our women fierce and used to sacrifice.
But on those rare evenings when a cool breeze rises from the plain
and the men are released from camp for the night,
what joy! We kill and roast the best meat we have,
send the children to gather more sticks for the fire,
for tonight we blaze, though our flames be seen for miles.
The children asleep, my man at my side, we wrestle like two opponents
meeting suddenly in battle. Muscle for muscle, will for will, we struggle,
roll over, meet in sweetest combat, both defeated, both victorious.
Historians will say of us that we were a warlike people.
They might note, somewhere, that the men camped no farther
Than the distance they could hear their children's laughter.

ADAM TAVEL

The Nineteen Nineties (Abridged)

There was the usual shortage of saints.
There was much discussion of slimming
              down. After growing in brand & variety

    peanut butter earned its own shelf.
Teens made a mockery of flannel
              living secure in the faith that they

    were the first to believe in nothing.
Except at Christmas, everyone gave up
              on letters. Beautiful strays were fed

    & put to death. No one wanted to cross
the bridge. No one trusted water
              from the tap. Sleet warmed its end

    on clay roofs of gophers.
Like small grains of rice
              satellites left Earth beaming back

    sitcoms. All our wars
were small & in their smallness seemed
              for a time complete.

IAN WATSON

Hedge

for Pearse Hutchinson

With the engine of the world asleep,
the old men stare out to where the sea is,
sniffing where the wind used to be.

Grief lies like curled leaves on the land,
lies with the lightness of the dead wren in the hedge
on the shoulders of the drinkers.

The hedge is where the schools were,
hunched against the wind
where they could smell the sea.

With the hedge there was no wind; now
without the wind there is no need for hedges.
The dead wren lies with the lightness

of her hatched eggs
in the skeleton of the hedge.
Should the wind return,

she will blow like tumbleweed
down towards Doolin across the field.
The view is a half-moon through branches;

the silence lies like lightness
in the frost, the ash of wren-skull
still as pebbles under ice.

Old sheep sniff unsheared;
the hatched eggs of the dead corn
scratch like voles' feet on cobbles.

MARIE CADDEN

Gynaecologist in the Jacuzzi

Is it himself? Well well.
Hard to tell without the trappings.
For a moment I thought it was the butcher

but there now, he knows me,
gives a thin fig-leaf smile
remembering my nether parts, perhaps,
then in to his chin underwater.

Above the whirlpool of legs
we float and chat, mouth platitudes,
keep his years of vulvic rummaging
under water

until he stands,
extends a naked hand
without shirt cuffs or camouflage.

In that trade, a man
should stay fully dressed.
How can you shake hands
with your ransacker
when his rubbery limbs
are dribbling to the toes,
empty trunks still bubbling
from massage jets?

I hand him his towel.
My vagina and I look him in the eye.

THOMAS LYDEN

Rhythm and Shadows

The darkness hangs about her
There are shards draining her cheeks
She came a great distance, from an ancient road
And visions creep from her aura
If you see her dance on a headland
She'll be burning like a mad dog
I have not been able to touch her
For a long time –
She bends to a rhythm of her own
And talks about celestial doom
She burns her anger in the dance,
Throwing arcs and shadows
To a wind that understands.

KERRIE O' BRIEN

Rothko

They found him
Hunched over a
White sink
All his beauty let out.
I think of him in his studio
East Hampton 1964
Wooden beams
Stained,
Concrete floor
Sitting back in a dark green chair
Head tilted, cigarette in hand
Peering at his creation
Layers and pain
Towering before him
Lost to it,
One mere man
What he gave

I see him with wings

Immersed in his
Low lit hush
Portals — expanding
Crimson lilac
Burnt orange, greys
Weighted hum
Solemn yet violent
Fire, heart
Bloodsweat
Spilling out
So close and strange
Holy
People weep before them
Sacred —
What we do to each other
And give
Without knowing.

KARL PARKINSON

I Saw Walt Whitman Today

In a DVD rental shop, just as Ginsberg did once in a supermarket.
He was wearing a hat, blue jeans, brown boots of the worker,
a tin whistle in his breast pocket and of course the fabulous long
    white beard.

He browsed through the music section,
maybe he was looking to see if they had his songs there?
I wanted to go over and say "Hey Walt, how the hell are ya?
What do you think of the 21st century?"

Ask what he thought about the Internet, Facebook and Youtube?
If everything written about him on Wikipedia was true? Was he gay,
    bi or straight?
Would he place the laurel on my head, could I touch his beard?

What did he think of the States? Democracy? Was Obama doing alright?
But then I thought, nah, he probably doesn't want to be bothered,
I'll wait till I meet him again some night in a bar and have a chat
    over a pint.
So I blessed him with a smile, left the shop with a song of my own
    playing in my head.

ALVY CARRAGHER

Canal bank moon walk

I want the sky to be monumental, but it won't cooperate,
better to think about the moon, to stalk the walk of moon talk,
once, you pointed to its round orb, said *it's a mystery for lovers*,
I laughed, but you never meant to be funny

I don't dance like Michael Jackson or know like Kavanagh,
Who would have understood the way you spoke,
always filling each syllable with meaning,
you saw the magnitude in each blade of grass,
those clumps of green hulking with metaphors

I sit on the bench, where you said goodbye,
the place where you first told me your sadness,
we watched a furled swan unravel as if to crack our skulls,
you said something about beauty or transience,
I saw only its hard beak, capable of bone break,
back then, I must have been scared of everything,
fear of swans, mostly, and dying without saying anything

as for the canal, in all its borrowed romance,
you pointed at our trapped reflection,
said *we're stuck in a moment of time*,
and I cursed your brain magic,
I felt nothing, no shimmer, just a watery fish-grave
full of coke cans and slouched condoms

after you left, I started to see others —
doctors, bankers, anyone without a thought for the canal,
I keep their kisses, they don't make me feel insignificant,
they don't know about moonwalking canal banks,
or how you gave me night-time flutters,
they see the dead water that I see,
their scarves are thick and braced for winter,
they all have warm skin, not like,
your cold hand pointing at the moon

PHIL LYNCH

Tossa Revisited

Two lovers
one scooter
the martyr Vincent
observes their kisses
from his carved out window
high above the old town square

the church clock chimes the hour
pews empty and quiet now
in the night as in the day
I walked the empty aisle
to count the steps
from door to altar

lizards dart in and out
from behind a light
half way up a wall
they pause to take stock
of the comings and goings
a drunk with a can
and a one-legged man
make their different ways home

silhouetted two floors up
my thoughts run rampant
a balcony of memories
the only sound
the pouring of another glass

all is well
in the old town
tonight.

DEVON McNAMARA

Vale of the White Horse

Up through wheat fields
from the standing stones
along King Alfred's cattle road,
border of hawthorn, loosestrife,
sedge, we walk the flints, the wheel
ruts of civilization. Out here
long groundswells, russet, amber,
reach for the edges of the known world,
beeches rise and woodland oak,
dark strokes of coppery blue
beneath the sky, and we reach too
for news of Amali's huge Rhodesian
Ridgeback at the vet in Sri Lanka,
for directions down through thistles
to the chalky Hackpen Horse,
for water, for the right word
filo, for shade, for history,
for each other.

Two horses, white,
one tall, and one a pony,
appear on a dappled path,
their riders, Dane red, Saxon gold,
explain our way, their accents
courteous and musical.
Good afternoon.

We miss the castle of earth
and grass, go down beside
its ramparts into the combe,
speaking of time
here
in Elysium.
The Roman road cuts
west of us.

In the pub
the loud men say
you didn't walk that far.
Salty, we know the truth,
outside, savor its
swart touch, before
we find the bus stop
in the silent town
grown silent ourselves
as if we'd been singing.

Biographical Notes

MILLICENT BORGES ACCARDI is the author of four poetry books: *Injuring Eternity*, *Woman on a Shaky Bridge*, *Practical Love Poems* and *Only More So* (Salmon, 2016). The recipient of fellowships from the National Endowment for the Arts (NEA), Fulbright, CantoMundo, Creative Capacity, the California Arts Council, Fundação Luso-Americana, and the Barbara Deming Foundation (Money for Women), Accardi has been in residence at Yaddo, Milkwood in Cesky Krumlov, Fundación Valparaíso in Spain; Jentel, and Vermont Studio Center. She holds degrees in English literature and writing from California State University, Long Beach (CSULB) and the University of Southern California (USC).

NADYA AISENBERG was former Adjunct Associate Professor of Women's Studies at Brandeis University. Over the years, she was also a teacher of English at Tufts University, Wellesley College, and the University of Massachusetts at Boston. In the 1980s, she co-founded Rowan Tree Press, which published 30 titles. She was also a co-founder of the Cambridge Alliance of Independent Scholars and on the Board of Directors of the Writers' Room of Boston. Born in New York City, she graduated from Bennington College and earned a doctorate in English literature at the University of Wisconsin. She was a frequent contributor to literary journals such as *Ploughshares, Angi, Poetry* and *The Southern Review*. She is the author of the monograph, *I Fall Upwards: Images of Women and Aging in Contemporary Women's Poetry*, published by the National Policy and Resource Center on Women and Aging, Heller Graduate School, Brandeis University, Autumn 1997. Nadya passed away in April 1999. Her collection, *Measures*, was published by Salmon in 2001.

M.G. ALLEN is the author of *The Bitter Word* (Poolbeg 1998) and occasional poems and short stories. He lives in Dublin and works in an advocacy role in one of Ireland's leading social justice organisations. He is one of the co-founders of Salmon Publishing and a joint editor until 1988.

PAUL ALLEN taught courses in poetry, form and meter, and writing song lyrics at The College of Charleston, in Charleston, SC, USA, where he was Professor of English. His poems have appeared in a number of journals, including *Northwest Review, Southern Poetry Review, Cimarron Review, Southwest Review, Ontario Review, New England Review, Iowa Review, Puerto Del Sol*, and *The Southern Review*, as well as in several anthologies. He has received the South Carolina Arts Commission's Individual Artist Fellowship in Poetry twice, the Mary Roberts Rinehart Award (George Mason University), the Vassar Miller Poetry Prize from the University of North Texas Press, the South Carolina Academy of Authors Fellowship, the John Williams Andrews Narrative Poetry Prize from Poet Lore, the Distinguished Research Award from The College of Charleston (2007), and a Pushcart (XXXII, 2008). His books include *American Crawl* (UNT Press, 1997), *His Longing* (FootHills Press, 2005) and *Ground Forces* (Salmon, 2008).

TIMOTHY ALLEN was born in New York. He lived in London from the age of three before moving to Galway with his mother and stepfather in 1981. He received his BA from UCG (now NUIG) and his Teaching Diploma from the University of Limerick. He currently teaches French at secondary level and lives in County Clare with his wife and daughter. His poem that appears in this anthology was written when he was 13.

NUALA ARCHER's first book of poetry, *Whale on the Line*, (Gallery Press, 1981) won the Patrick Kavanagh Award. *Two Women, Two Shores*, poems by Nuala Archer and Medbh McGuckian was jointly published by New Poets Series, Baltimore & Salmon Press, Galway, Ireland, in 1989. *Pan/ama*, a chapbook, was published by Red Dust, New York, in 1992. *The Hour of Pan/ama* was published by Salmon in 1992. She has taught at Yale University. She was also director of the Cleveland Poetry Centre and associate professor at Cleveland State University. She currently lives and writes poetry in Cleveland, Ohio.

CELESTE AUGÉ is an Irish-Canadian writer who has lived in Ireland since she was twelve years old, when her family moved from the backwoods of Northern Ontario, Canada. She is the author of Skip Diving (Salmon Poetry), *The Essential Guide to Flight* (Salmon Poetry) and *Fireproof and Other Stories*

(Doire Press). The World Literature Review has said that "Celeste Augé's poems are commendable for their care, deep thought, and intellectual ambition", while the Anna Livia Review said, "Fireproof is a remarkably strong debut into the world of short stories and will begin to build what is undoubtedly going to be a strong readership for the author". Celeste has a Masters degree in writing from NUI Galway. Her poetry has been shortlisted for a Hennessy Award and she received a Literature Bursary from the Arts Council of Ireland to write her poetry collection Skip Diving. Her short story 'The Good Boat' won the 2011 Cúirt New Writing Prize for fiction. She lives in Connemara with her husband and son, a stone's throw from where her mother was born and reared.

LELAND BARDWELL was born in 1922 and grew up in Leixlip, outside Dublin. She has published five novels, including *Mother to a Stranger*, a bestseller in German translation, while her memoir *A Restless Life* was published in 2006. A short story collection *Different Kinds of Love* was reissued in 2012. Her poetry collections include *Dostoevsky's Grave* (1991), *The White Beach: New and Selected Poems 1960-1998* (Salmon), *The Noise of Masonry Settling* (2006), and *Them's Your Mammy's Pills* (2015). She lives in Sligo and is a member of Aosdána.

JUDITH BARRINGTON has published four poetry collections: *Horses and the Human Soul*; *History and Geography*; *Trying to Be an Honest Woman*; and, most recently, *The Conversation* (Salmon, 2015) and two chapbooks: *Postcard from the Bottom of the Sea* and *Lost Lands*. Among her awards is the Gregory O'Donoghue International Poetry Prize for 2013. She is also the author of *Lifesaving: A Memoir* (winner of the Lambda Book Award and runner up for the PEN/Martha Albrand Award for the memoir) and the best-selling *Writing the Memoir: From Truth to Art*. Judith has been a visiting writer at many universities. She teaches in the USA, Britain, and Spain and has been a faculty member of the MFA Program at the University of Alaska, Anchorage.

MARCK L. BEGGS lives by a lake in Arkansas with his wife, Carly, and a lot of animals. He is the author of four collections of poetry: *Blind Verse* (2015), *Catastrophic Chords* (2008), *Libido Café* (2004) and *Godworm* (1995). He also edited the *80th Anniversary Poets of the Roundtable of Arkansas Anthology* (2013). His poems have been published in numerous journals and magazines, including *Oxford American*, *Denver Quarterly*, *Poet Lore*, *Missouri Review*, *Exquisite Corpse*, *Toad Suck Review*, *Arkansas Review*, *Excelsior Review*, and *Common Ground*. In his spare time, he sings and plays guitar in the folk-rock band, dog gods. In 2009, he was selected by PETA as one of the top-10 sexiest vegetarians over the age of 50.

MICHAEL S. BEGNAL has published the collections *Future Blues* (Salmon Poetry, 2012) and *Ancestor Worship* (Salmon Poetry, 2007), as well as the recent chapbook *The Muddy Banks* (Ghost City Press, 2016). He has an MFA from North Carolina State University and has been nominated for a Pushcart Prize.

In 2011, Copper Canyon published MARVIN BELL's *Vertigo: The Living Dead Man Poems*. His newest book is a back-and-forth of 90 paragraphs with writer Christopher Merrill titled *After the Fact: Scripts & Postscripts*, to be issued in 2016 by White Pine Press. Long retired from the Iowa Writers' Workshop, he serves on the faculty of the brief-residency MFA program based in Oregon at Pacific University. Salmon published his collection *Wednesday*, a selected poems, in 1998.

SARA BERKELEY grew up in Ireland and now lives in a rural valley near San Francisco with her husband, daughter, dog, cat, and varying numbers of fish. She has had six collections of poetry published: *Penn* (Raven Arts Press/Thistledown Press, 1986), *Home-movie Nights* (Raven/Thistledown, 1989), *Facts About Water* (Bloodaxe Books/New Island Books, 1994), *Strawberry Thief* (Gallery, 2005), *The View from Here* (Gallery, 2010) and *What Just Happened* (Gallery, 2015); also a collection of short stories *The Swimmer in the Deep Blue Dream* (Raven/Thistledown, 1992) and a novel *Shadowing Hannah* (New Island Books, 1999). Her poetry has been widely anthologized, and nominated for a Pushcart Prize and the Irish Times Poetry Now award. When she's not making vast sums of money as a poet, she works as a hospice nurse.

STEPHEN BETT is a widely and internationally published Canadian poet. His earlier work is known for its sassy, edgy, hip... caustic wit—indeed, for the askance look of the serious satirist... skewering what he calls the 'vapid monoculture' of our times. His more recent books have been called an incredible accomplishment for their authentic minimalist subtlety. Many are tightly sequenced book-length 'serial' poems, which allow for a rich echoing of cadence and image, building a wonderfully subtle, nuanced music. Bett follows in the avant tradition of Don Allen's New American Poets. Hence the mandate for Simon Fraser University's "Contemporary Literature Collection" to purchase and archive his "personal papers" for scholarly use. He is recently retired after a 31-year teaching career largely at Langara College in Vancouver, and now lives with his wife Katie in Victoria, BC. Salmon published *The Gross & Fine Geography: New & Selected Poems by Stephen Bett* in 2015.

DREW BLANCHARD holds a BA in Journalism from the University of Iowa and an MFA in poetry from The Ohio State University. In January of 2009 he received a university research grant to work with the novelist Iván Thays in Lima, Perú and in the summer of 2010 he was a graduate student scholar at the National University of Ireland, Maynooth, a scholarship provided by the International Association for the Study of Irish Literatures. His writing has appeared in *Best New Poets, Notre Dame Review, Guernica / a magazine of art & politics, Blackbird, Meridian* and elsewhere. Winter Dogs, his debut collection, appeared from Salmon in 2011.

EAVAN BOLAND was born in Dublin in 1944. Her collections of poetry include *23 Poems* (Dublin, Gallagher, 1962); *The War Horse* (London, Gollancz,1975); *In Her Own Image* (Dublin, Arlen House, 1980); *Night Feed* (Arlen House, 1982); *The Journey* (Manchester, Carcanet, 1987); *Selected Poems* (Carcanet, 1989/Pennsylvania, U.S.A., WW Norton & Co Inc, 1991); *Outside History* (Carcanet, 1990/WW Norton & Co Inc, 1991); *An Origin Like Water – Collected Poems* (New York, W.W. Norton, 1996); *The Lost Land* (Carcanet/ W W Norton 1998); *Code* (Carcanet, 2001); *Against Love Poetry* (W.W.Norton, 2003); *Domestic Violence* (Carcanet/ W. W. Norton, 2007); *New Selected Poems* (Carcanet, 2013); *A Poet's Dublin*, with photographs by the author (Carcanet, 2014); and *A Woman Without a Country* (Carcanet, 2014). Her other work includes a collection of prose writings, *Object Lessons* (Carcanet, 1995); and with Mark Strand she has edited *The Making of a Poem, A Norton Anthology of Poetic Forms* (WW Norton, New York/London, 2000). Her awards include a Lannan Foundation Award in Poetry, and an American Ireland Fund Literary Award. A member of the Irish Academy of Letters, she is Professor in Humanities at Stanford University in the USA.

ROSITA BOLAND was born in County Clare. She has published two collections of poems, *Muscle Creek* (Raven Arts, 1991), and *Dissecting the Heart* (Gallery, 2003), as well as two travel books *Sea Legs: Hitch-hiking the Coast of Ireland Alone* (New Island, 1992) and *A Secret Map of Ireland* (New Island Books, 2005). She won the Hennessy Award for First Fiction in 1997. A journalist with *The Irish Times*, she has travelled extensively.

Born in Dublin in 1959, DERMOT BOLGER is one of Ireland's best known writers. His thirteen novels include *The Journey Home, Father's Music, The Valparaiso Voyage, The Family on Paradise Pier, New Town Soul, The Fall of Ireland, Tanglewood* and *The Lonely Sea and Sky*, published in 2016. His first play, T*he Lament for Arthur Cleary*, received the Samuel Beckett Award. His numerous other plays include *The Ballymun Trilogy* and a stage adaptation of Joyce's *Ulysses*, which recently toured China and is the subject of a forthcoming documentary on BBC 4. A poet, his ninth collection of poems, *The Venice Suite: A Voyage Through Loss*, was published in 2012 and his New and Selected Poems, *That Which is Suddenly Precious*, appeared in 2015, containing a revised copy of the poem first published by Salmon. A former Writer Fellow at Trinity College, Dublin and Playwright in Association with the Abbey Theatre, Bolger writes for most of Ireland's leading newspapers and in 2012 was named Commentator of the Year at the Irish Newspaper awards.

PAT BORAN (b. Portlaoise, 1963) is a poet, publisher and broadcaster and lives in Dublin. He has published 15 books of poetry and prose including *Waveforms: Bull Island Haiku* (2015) and the prose memoir *The Invisible Prison* (2009). His work has been translated into half a dozen languages and he is a member of Aosdána.

EVA BOURKE has published six collections of poetry, including *Gonella* and *Litany for the Pig* with Salmon and most recently *piano* with Dedalus Press. Her work has appeared in several anthologies of Irish poetry in translation, an anthology *Landing Places. Immigrant poets in Ireland* as well as *Watching my Hands at Work. A Festschrift for Adrian Frazier* (Salmon). At the moment she and Vincent Woods are putting the finishing touches on *Speaking of Music*, a collection of writings in prose and poetry by contemporary Irish writers on music, to be published in 2016 She has taught poetry for many years at U-Mass Boston and NUIGalway and is a member of Aosdána.

RORY BRENNAN has published four collections of poetry, *The Sea on Fire, The Walking Wounded, The Old in Rapallo* and *Skylights*, a collaboration with the Greek artist Euphrosyne Doxiadis. His work has appeared in many journals and has won the Patrick Kavanagh Award among other literary prizes. A Dubliner, he is an ex-director of Poetry Ireland, was a lecturer in Communications in Dublin City University and has worked in broadcasting with RTE. He has travelled widely in the Far East and lived for long periods in Morocco and Greece.

HEATHER BRETT was born in Newfoundland and raised in Ireland. She has been editor of Windows Publications since 1992. She has also been Writer-in-Residence for counties Cavan, Louth, Offaly and Westmeath. She has published four collections to date — the first, *Abigail Brown,* was winner of the Brendan Behan Memorial Prize and the most recent is *Witness* (2015).

LISA MARIE BRODSKY is the author of *Motherlung* (Salmon Poetry, 2014) recognized by the Wisconsin Library Association as a 2014 Outstanding Achievement in Poetry, and the chapbook, *We Nod Our Dark Heads* (Parallel Press, 2008). Her poetry, fiction, and creative nonfiction have appeared in various literary journals, most recently *riverSedge, VerseWisconsin*, and *The Mom Egg Review*. Lisa is on faculty of All Writers' Workplace & Workshop and teaches workshops and online classes about creative writing as a balm for emotional wounds. Lisa is a wife, stepmother, and advocate for chronic lyme disease, all of which can be gleaned from her most recent writings. She lives in Evansville, Wisconsin, with her husband and three stepchildren and is at work on a third poetry collection. www.lisamariebrodsky.com

PATRICIA BRODY's first chapbook, *American Desire*, was selected by Finishing Line Books for a 2009 New Women's Voices Award. Her second collection, *Dangerous to Know*, was published by Salmon Poetry in 2013. Many of the poems are in the voices of "forgotten women writers." Brody's work has appeared in many journals including *Barrow Street, International Journal of Feminist Politics, Western Humanities, The Paris Review* and most recently on *BigCityLit, Verse Daily, Levure Litteraire.* She is currently teaching Seeking Your Voice: a Poetry & Verse Memoir Workshop at Barnard College Center for Research on Women and taught English comprehension and American Literature for many years at Boricua College in Harlem.

PATRICIA BURKE BROGAN is a writer and visual artist based in Galway. She is the author of Eclipsed, one of the first plays to tell the story of the Magdalene Laundries and was inspired by Patricia's experiences as a young novitiate. After seeing the horrendous goings on, Patricia decided that becoming a nun was not for her. Instead she decided to highlight the plight of these women in her writing. The play has since won many awards, including a Fringe First at Edinburgh Theatre Festival in 1992,[1] and the USA Moss Hart Award in 1994. To date, there have been well over 60 productions of Eclipsed on three continents. Since then, Burke Brogan has continued to write two more plays, Requiem of Love and Stained Glass at Samhain (Salmon, 2002), and has also released a number of poetry collections. Her latest work, *Décollage New and Selected Poems*, was launched in October 2008 at the Galway City Museum. She was awarded an Honorary Master of Arts, honoris causa, by NUI Galway.

SIMMONS B. BUNTIN is the American author of two books of poems, Riverfall and Bloom, both published by Salmon Poetry. His award-winning poetry and prose have appeared in numerous North American and European journals and anthologies. He is the founding editor of the acclaimed international journal *Terrain.org: A Journal of the Built & Natural Environments*, for which he also writes a regular editorial. He is the recipient of the Colorado Artists Fellowship for Poetry, an Academy of American Poets prize, and grants by the Arizona Commission on the Arts and Tucson Pima Arts Council. He is an avid photographer, website designer, and all-around rabble-rouser who lives with his wife and two daughters in the Sonoran desert of southern Arizona. Catch up with him at www.SimmonsBuntin.com.

SAM BURNSIDE was born in County Antrim and now lives and works in the city of Derry where he was founder and first Director of the Verbal Arts Centre, an educational charity he established in 1992 to promote literature in all its forms. He is the author of *The Cathedral* (1989) a long poem that won the Sunday Tribune/Hennessy Literary Award for Poetry in that year. His work has attracted a number of literary prizes, including an Allingham Poetry Prize ; the University of Ulster's McCrea Literary Award for Literature and a Bass Ireland Award. His poetry has been published and broadcast widely. He has also published *Walking the Marches* (Salmon, 1990) and *Horses* (1993), a handmade book published in a limited edition by Ballagh Studios and with woodcuts by the Canadian artist Tim Stampton. He published *Fahan Mura* in 1995 (with an introduction by the Donegal poet Frank Harvey). He is represented in *The Great Book of Ireland* and in *The Crazy Knot* (1996), collaboration between Ulster writers and artists. He is the author of *Writer to Writer* (1990), a discussion of community-based writing initiatives; he has edited *Ourselves and Others* (1998) a gathering of children's poems and *The Glow Upon the Fringe* (1994) a collection of essays that celebrate the literary heritage of the north-west of Ireland. In 2001 he devised an exhibition in celebration of the city of Derry's contribution to literature and produced an accompanying publication *The Magic Circle* that includes an extensive bibliography of contemporary writers with Derry connections. He was guest editor of Issue 99 of *The Honest Ulsterman*. Sam Burnside holds the degrees of BA, MPhil and PhD. He was awarded an MBE (in 2012) for services to the arts.

CATHERINE BYRON was born in 1947, the child of a Galway mother and a father from Southern England. She grew up in Belfast, but moved at seventeen to England to read Classics and Medieval English at Somerville College, Oxford. In subsequent decades she has lived and worked in Scotland, England, Derry, and most recently in Dawros in Donegal. The flora and history of that coast, and the lifelong friendships she has enjoyed there, are central to her sense of self, and her poetry. She write for the page, the voice, and the web, always hungry to embody the matter of this world in these different textual media, and to collaborate with visual and sound artists. Her most significant long-term inter-arts collaboration has been with Dublin-based artist and calligrapher Denis Brown. His cover design for her sixth poetry collection, *The Getting of Vellum* (Salmon, 2011), incorporates details from his large work *Couple*, illuminating words from Byron's poem "Crypt." She is also the author of *Out of Step: Pursuing Seamus Heaney to Purgatory* (1992).

MARIE CADDEN was the winner of the Cúirt International Festival of Literature 2011 New Writing Prize for Poetry. In 2012, she placed 2nd for the Westport Arts Festival Poetry Prize and 3rd for the Francis Ledwidge Poetry Award. She was shortlisted for the Bradshaw Books/Cork Literary Review Poetry Manuscript Competition in 2013 and 2011, for the Over the Edge New Writer of the Year Award in 2013 and 2010, and for the Desmond O'Grady Poetry Competition in 2012. She was longlisted for the Fish Poetry Prize in 2013. Her work has appeared in *The Recorder* (USA), *THE SHOp, The Stony Thursday Book, ROPES, Revival, Boyne Berries, Skylight 47* (of which she is co-editor). Her debut collection, *Gynaecologist in the Jacuzzi*, is published by Salmon in 2016.

LOUISE C. CALLAGHAN was born in 1948 and brought up in County Dublin, Ireland. She now lives in Dublin, close to her four children and many grandchildren. Her poetry collections are *In the Ninth House* (Salmon, 2010), *The Puzzle-Heart* (Salmon, 1999) and *Remember The Birds* (Salmon, 2005). She compiled and edited *Forgotten Light: An Anthology of Memory Poems* (A & A Farmar, 2003). Her poetry, which is widely anthologised in Ireland and England, is included in the *Field Day Anthology: Vols IV & V.* She completed an M.Litt in Creative Writing at St. Andrews University in Scotland (2007) receiving a First Class Honours in her poetry dissertation.

ROSEMARY CANAVAN was born in Scotland in 1949. She was brought up in the North of Ireland, and after forty years in Cork now lives in France. Her first collection of poems, *The Island*, was shortlisted for the Vincent Buckley Poetry Prize (University of Melbourne, Australia) and her second collection, *Trucker's Moll*, appeared in 2009 from Salmon. Other publications include children's books, translations of French short stories and anthologies. She is currently completing a third collection of poetry, and a biography.

MOYA CANNON was born in County Donegal. Her first collection of poetry *Oar* was published by Salmon Poetry in 1990. *Keats Lives* (Carcanet Press, Manchester) is her fifth collection of poetry. She is a winner of the Brendan Behan Award and the Laurence O Shaughnessy Award. She has been Editor of *Poetry Ireland Review* and was 2011 Heimbold Professor of Irish Studies at Villanova University P.A.

HÉLÈNE CARDONA is a poet, literary translator and actor, the recipient of numerous awards and honors including a Hemingway Grant and the USA Best Book Award. Her books include three bilingual poetry collections, most recently *Life in Suspension* (Salmon Poetry, 2016), and *Dreaming My Animal Selves* (Salmon Poetry, 2013); and two translations: *Beyond Elsewhere* (White Pine Press, 2016), and *Ce que nous portons* (Éditions du Cygne, 2014). She also translated Walt Whitman's *Civil War Writings* for the Iowa International Writing Program's Whitman Web. She co-edits *Fulcrum: An Anthology of Poetry and Aesthetics*, is Co-International Editor of *Plume*, Essay contributor to *The London Magazine*, and co-producer of the documentary *Pablo Neruda: The Poet's Calling*. She holds a Master's in American Literature from the Sorbonne, taught at Hamilton College & Loyola Marymount University, and received fellowships from the Goethe-Institut & Universidad Internacional de Andalucía. Publications include *Washington Square, World Literature Today, Poetry International, The Irish Literary Times, Dublin Review of Books, The Warwick Review* & elsewhere.

ALVY CARRAGHER received a First Class Honours in her MA in Writing from The National University of Ireland Galway, where she focused on poetry. A Pushcart nominee, she has been listed for many prizes including: Over the Edge New Writer of the Year, The Gregory O'Donoghue Award and The Cúirt New Writing Prize. She is a two-time All-Ireland Slam Poetry Finalist, a Slam Sunday Winner, Connaught Slam Champion and a Cúirt Grand Slam Poetry Champion. She has performed at many festivals throughout the country, and abroad, including: Cúirt International Literary Festival, Edinburgh Fringe Festival, Electric Picnic, Body and Soul, Lingo Spoken Word Festival, and Imagine Waterford Arts Festival. Her poems have featured on RTE's Arena on several occasions. Her work has appeared in various publications. She is also an award-winning blogger, and her blog *With All the Finesse of a Badger* has been archived by the National Library of Ireland. *Canal Bank Moon Walk* (Salmon Poetry, 2016) is her first collection.

PAUL CASEY's début collection *home more or less* was published by Salmon in 2012. It was followed in 2016 by *Virtual Tides* (Salmon). A chapbook of longer poems, *It's Not all Bad*, appeared from The Heaventree Press in 2009. He has published poems in journals and anthologies in Ireland, the US, China, Romania, South Africa and online. Aside from writing poetry he is a multimedia artist, teacher, events director, editor, occasional filmmaker and poet in residence each May for Carechoice, a group of elderly homes in county Cork. He also edits the annual *Unfinished Book of Poetry*, verse written by secondary school students in Cork city and runs multimedia and creative writing courses for adults at the Cork College of Commerce. He is the founder/director of the non-for-profit poetry organisation, Ó Bhéal.

Poet and publisher SEAMUS CASHMAN founded the Irish literary publishing house Wolfhound Press in 1974 where he remained publisher until 2001. He has four published poetry collections: *The Sistine Gaze: I too begin with scaffolding* (Salmon, 2015), *Carnival* (Monarchline 1988), *Clowns & Acrobats* (Wolfhound Press, 2000), and *That Morning Will Come: New and Selected Poems* (SalmonPoetry, 2007). He co-edited the now classic anthology, *Irish Poems for Young People* (1975, 2000); and in 2004 compiled the award-winning *Something Beginning with P: new poems from Irish poets* (The O'Brien Press). He was one of three English language judges (with Yusef Komunyakaa and Debjani Chatterjee) for the first International Mamilla Poetry Festival in Ramallah, Palestine in 2013, and edited its English language anthology. A poetry workshop facilitator, he has given poetry readings in Ireland, England, Wales, the UK, Belgium, Saudi Arabia and in Iowa and Wisconsin, USA. He is an emeritus International Fellow at the Black Earth Institute (USA), where he edited the 'Peaks & Valleys' issue of their About Place online arts journal. He has four adult children. From Conna in County Cork, he now lives in Malahide near Dublin.

DAVID CAVANAGH's four books include *Straddle*, *Falling Body*, and *The Middleman*, all published by Salmon Poetry, and *Cycling in Plato's Cave* from Fomite Press. His poems have also appeared in many journals in Canada, Ireland, the U.S., and the U.K., and in anthologies such as *The Book of Irish American Poetry*, from U. of Notre Dame Press, and *So Little Time: Words and Images for a World in Climate Crisis*, from Green Writers Press. David's work has been nominated for a Pushcart Prize and supported by grants from the Canada Council for the Arts and the Vermont Arts Council. Born and raised in Montreal, he lives in Burlington, Vermont, and is chair of Interdisciplinary Studies at Johnson State College.

For seventeen years, JERAH CHADWICK was a resident of the Aleutian Island of Unalaska, where he first went to raise goats and write, living in an abandoned WWII military compound eight miles walking from town. From 1988 he taught for and directed the University of Alaska extension program for the Aleutian/Pribilof island region. He holds degrees from Lake Forest College (Illinois) and the University of Alaska Fairbanks and is a recipient of an Alaska State Council on the Arts Writing Fellowship. Chadwick's poems have been published in numerous journals and anthologies in the U.S., Canada, and Ireland; and he is the author of three chapbooks, including *The Dream Horse* (Seal Press, Seattle) and *From the Cradle of Storms* (State Street, New York) as well as the collection *Story Hunger* (Salmon).

PATRICK CHAPMAN was born in 1968. *Slow Clocks of Decay* follows *Jazztown* (1991), *The New Pornography* (1996), *The Wow Signal* (2007), *Breaking Hearts and Traffic Lights* (2007), *A Shopping Mall on Mars* (2008), *The Darwin Vampires* (2010), *A Promiscuity of Spines: New & Selected Poems* (2012) and *The Negative Cutter* (2014). He has also written an award-winning short film starring Gina McKee and Aidan Gillen; and many episodes for children's animated television series broadcast around the world. His audio credits include writing adventures for *Doctor Who* and *Dan Dare*, and producing B7's 2014 dramatisation of Ray Bradbury's *The Martian Chronicles* for BBC Radio 4. This starred Derek Jacobi and Hayley Atwell, and won Silver at the 2015 New York Festivals World's Best Radio Programs. Chapman's writing has won first prize in the Cinescape Genre Literary Competition, been shortlisted twice in the Hennessy Awards, and received a nomination for a Pushcart Prize. With Dimitra Xidous he edits the poetry magazine *The Pickled Body*.

GLENDA CIMINO was born in Atlanta, and moved to Ireland in the early seventies. She worked in social research and evaluation for ten years, then co-founded, with seven friends, the legendary Beaver Row Press, publishing poets such as Paula Meehan, Brendan Kennelly and Eithne Strong from a handpress. Her collection of poems, *Cicada*, was published by Beaver Row in 1988. She lives in Dublin.

SARAH CLANCY is a page and performance poet from Galway. Her current collection is *The Truth and Other Stories* and was published by Salmon Poetry. She has two previous collections to her name, *Stacey and the Mechanical Bull* (Lapwing Press, Belfast, 2011) and *Thanks for Nothing, Hippies* (Salmon Poetry, 2012). Along with fellow Galway poet Elaine Feeney she released a poetry CD, *Cinderella Backwards,* in 2013. She has been placed or shortlisted in several of Ireland's most prestigious written poetry competitions including The Ballymaloe International Poetry Prize and The Patrick Kavanagh Award. For performance poetry Sarah has won the Cúirt International Festival of Literature Grand Slam Championships and has twice been runner-up in the North Beach Nights Grand Slam Series. She has represented Connaught in the All-Ireland Grand Slam Championship twice, and in 2013 she was runner up in the finals. This year she won the Bogman's Cannon People's Poet Award for 2015. Her work has been published in translation in Slovenia, Poland and Mexico. She is on Twitter @sarah-maintains and can be contacted by e-mail at sarahclancygalway@gmail.com

ANDREA COHEN's poems have appeared in The New Yorker, The Atlantic Monthly, Poetry, The Threepenny Review and elsewhere. Her books include Furs Not Mine (Four Way Books), Kentucky Derby (Salmon Poetry), Long Division (Salmon Poetry), and The Cartographer's Vacation. Four Way will publish her fifth collection, Unfathoming, in 2017. Cohen directs the Blacksmith House Poetry Series in Cambridge, MA and the Writers House at Merrimack College.

MARY COLL is a Limerick poet, playwright and broadcaster. Publications include *All Things Considered* (Salmon, 2002). She has made numerous contributions to RTE Radio One and RTE Lyric FM. She has had stage productions of *Excess Baggage* (2007) and *Anything But Love* (2010) at The Belltable Arts Centre, and radio plays commissioned by RTE *Drama On One*, as well as writing lyrics for the Choral Work 'Spirestone' and two art song cycles in association with the composer Fiona Linnane. A new play, *Diamond Rocks: Sunset*, was commissioned by The Lime Tree Theatre, Limerick in 2014 and a second collection of poems entitled *Silver* is due for publication in 2016.

CAMERON CONAWAY is the author of *Until You Make the Shore* (Salmon Poetry, 2014) and *Malaria, Poems* (Michigan State University Press, 2014). His work has been supported by the Pulitzer Center on Crisis Reporting and the International Reporting Project, and has appeared in Newsweek, NPR and the Stanford Social Innovation Review, among other outlets. Follow him on Twitter @CameronConaway.

TREVOR CONWAY, a Sligoman living in Galway since 2005, writes mainly poetry, fiction and songs. His work has appeared in magazines and anthologies across Ireland, Austria, India, the UK, the US and Mexico, where some of his poems were translated into Spanish. Subjects he's drawn to include nature, creativity, football and people/society, especially the odd ways in which we look at the world. In 2011, he was awarded a Galway City Council bursary. He is a contributing editor for *The Galway Review*. His debut collection of poems, *Evidence of Freewheeling*, was published by Salmon Poetry in 2015. See trevorconway.weebly.com.

JOHN CORLESS lives and writes in County Mayo, Ireland. His poetry is a mix of political, satirical and rural and has been described as "Paul Durcan meets The Sawdoctors." He has an MA in Creative Writing from Lancaster University (2008). He writes poetry, fiction and drama. His work has been published in magazines and collections worldwide. His first collection of poetry, *Are you ready?*, was published by Salmon in 2009.

PATRICK COTTER has published a verse novella and two full-length collections. He has received the Keats-Shelley Prize for Poetry.

ROZ COWMAN was born in Cork in 1942. She is a teacher, poet, and literary critic. Her collection, *The Goose Herd*, was published by Salmon in 1989. Her non-fiction includes *Our Daily Bread: A History of Barron's Bakery*, with photographs by Arna Run Runarsdottir (Cork, Onstream Publications, 2011). She received the Arlen House/Maxwell House award in 1982, and the Patrick Kavanagh Award for Poetry in 1985. She lectures in Women's Studies at NUI Cork, and lives in Cork.

BERNADETTE CREMIN has published four collections of poetry, most recently Papercuts: New & Selected Poems (Salmon, 2015). Her work has won various awards. Her one-woman show 'Altered Egos,' six poetic monologues depicting six untidy lives, was awarded Arts Council of England funding after being made runner-up Best Literary/Performance Piece at the Brighton Fringe Festival. Cremin has collaborated with musicians, film-makers, scientists and photographers. Her first spoken-word CD, "Sensual Assassins", was released by State Art in 1998 and was followed in 2015 by a second spoken-word CD, "Guilty Fist". Her film work includes the film *Inside Skin*; and her photography work includes *Birth* and *Science* (Promise or Threat). She reads her work extensively in the UK and Ireland.

PHILLIP CRYMBLE was born in Belfast, and emigrated to Canada with his family as a child. He holds two Bachelor's degrees, and in 2002 earned his MFA from the University of Michigan, Ann Arbor, where he went on to teach for a number of years. The recipient of several Canada Council for the Arts Professional Writer's grants, his work has appeared in *The North, The Stinging Fly, BRAND, Iota, Oxford Poetry, Causeway, Cúirt Annual, Abridged, Crannóg, The Moth, Revival, Burning Bush 2, Poetry Ireland Review, The Salt Anthology of New Writing*, and numerous other publications worldwide. In 2007 he published a short collection with Lapwing and was selected to read in Poetry Ireland's annual *Introductions* series. His first full collection of poetry, *Not Even Laughter*, appeared from Salmon in 2015. Phillip now lives with his wife and son in Fredericton, New Brunswick, where he divides his time between serving as a poetry editor for The Fiddlehead, and pursuing a PhD in American Literature at UNB.

VICKI CROWLEY was born in Malta and much of her early childhood was spent in Eritrea and Libya. She was educated in England and Malta where she trained in Architectural Drawing. She has lived in Gibraltar, Sierra Leone and Cameroon with her Irish husband before settling in Galway in 1970. She is a visual artist and has worked and exhibited extensively in Ireland and abroad. Her travels and treks throughout her life in all the continents including Antarctica have greatly influenced her visual and written work. Her illustrated collection of poetry, *Oasis in a Sea of Dust*, was published by Salmon in 1992 and her memoir, *Beyond the Ghibli*, was published by Breadfruit Books in 2015.

MAJELLA CULLINANE was born and raised in Ireland. She became a New Zealand resident in 2008, where she still lives. She has previously received a Sean Dunne Young Writer's Award for Poetry, the Hennessy XO/Sunday Tribune Literary Award for Emerging Poetry and also an Irish Arts Council Award to study for an MLitt. in Creative Writing at St. Andrew's University Scotland. She has been a Writer in

Residence in Ireland and Scotland. Her debut collection, *Guarding the Flame*, was published by Salmon in 2011. She is currently working on her next collection which will also appear from Salmon.

J. P. DANCING BEAR is editor for the American Poetry Journal and Dream Horse Press. Bear hosted the weekly hour-long poetry show, Out of Our Minds, on public station, KKUP for nearly 15 years and select shows remain available as podcasts. He is the author of several collections of poetry, three of which are Salmon productions: Conflicted Light (2008), Inner Cities of Gulls (2010) and Fish Singing Foxes (2016). His work has appeared in American Literary Review, Crazyhorse, the DIAGRAM and elsewhere.

GERALD DAWE, born Belfast 1952, lived in Galway (1974-1992) where he taught at NUIG. He is Professor of English and Fellow of Trinity College Dublin where he was founder director of the Oscar Wilde Centre for Irish Writing (1998-2015). He has published nine volumes of poetry since *Sheltering Places* (1978) including *Selected Poems* (2012) and *Mickey Finn's Air* (2014). His other publications include *Of War and War's Alarms: Reflections on Modern Irish Writing* (2015) and *Earth Voices Whispering: Irish war poetry 1914-1945* (2008). In 2008, Salmon published *Catching the Light: Views & Interviews*. He lives in County Dublin.

LARRY O. DEAN was born and raised in Flint, Michigan. He attended the University of Michigan, where he won three Hopwood Awards in Creative Writing, and Murray State University's low-residency MFA program. His most recent books include *Brief Nudity* (Salmon Poetry, 2013), *Basic Cable Couplets* (Silkworms Ink, 2012), *abbrev* (Beard of Bees, 2011), and *About the Author* (Mindmade Books, 2011). Selected magazine publications include *Berkeley Poetry Review, Passages North, Big Bridge, Keyhole, OCHO, Heavy Feather Review*, and *Artichoke Haircut*. Also a critically-acclaimed songwriter, Dean has numerous releases to his credit, including *Fables in Slang* (2001) with Post Office, *Gentrification Is Theft* (2002) with The Me Decade, and *Fun with a Purpose* (2009) with The Injured Parties. His latest solo album, *Good Grief*, is due in September. He was a 2004 recipient of the Gwendolyn Brooks Award. Seek him out at larryodean.com.

JOHN F. DEANE was born on Achill Island in 1943. He founded Poetry Ireland, and was formerly the editor of Dedalus Press. A member of Aosdána, he was shortlisted for the 2003 T.S. Eliot Award and the Irish Times Poetry Now Award. In 2007 the French Government honoured him by making him Chevalier de l'Ordre des Arts et des Lettres. His latest books include the novel *Where No Storms Come* (Blackstaff Press), the poetry collections *Snow Falling on Chestnut Hill: New & Selected Poems* (Carcanet October 2012) and *Semibreve* (Carcanet, 2015), and a 'Faith Memoir', *Give Dust a Tongue* (Columba, 2015). He lives in Dublin.

GREG DELANTY's latest book of poems is *The Greek Anthology, Book XVI*, published in the US as *Book Seventeen*. Other recent books are *The Word Exchange, Anglo-Saxon Poems in Translation*, WW Norton; and his *Collected Poems 1986-2006*, Oxford Poets—Carcanet Press. He has received many awards, including a Guggenheim for poetry. He is Poet in Residence at Saint Michael's College, Vermont. The National Library of Ireland acquired his papers from 1986-2010 and University College Cork acquired his papers from 2010-2015—to celebrate the UCC acquisition, Christopher Ricks gave a talk: 'Interrogative: Three Irish poets: W.B Yeats, Greg Delanty and Patrick Kavanagh'. [NOTE: Greg Delanty's original poem in Issue 15 of *The Salmon* was "Couple Walking." Greg requested we substitute it for this anthology with his poem "The Alien" which is reproduced with the kind permission of Carcanet Press (UK), publishers of Greg's *Collected Poems 1986-2006*, in which "The Alien" also appears.]

Originally from Longford town, EDWARD DENNISTON has lived and worked in Waterford since 1980, the city in which his Presbyterian ancestor lived and preached dissent in the early 18th century. Edward is a teacher of English and Drama. His publications are: *The Point Of Singing* (Abbey Press, 1999); *Eskimo Advice*, an ebook (Rectory Press & Hayrake Press 2007); *Interacting — 60 Drama Scripts* (Russell House Publishing, 2007); and *The Scale of Things* (Salmon, 2013).

LOUIS DE PAOR is a well-known poet in the Irish language. Born in Cork in 1961 and educated at Coláiste an Spioraid Naoimh, de Paor edited the Irish language journal *Innti*, founded in 1970 by Michael Davitt, Nuala Ní Dhomhnaill, Liam Ó Muirthile and Gabriel Rosenstock. He was awarded a

PhD in Modern Irish from the National University of Ireland in 1986 for his thesis on Máirtín Ó Cadhain. He and his family emigrated to Australia in 1987 and lived in Melbourne, where he wrote, gave poetry readings and broadcast in Irish on the Special Broadcasting Service (a network set up for speakers of ethnic languages). He was given scholarships by the Australia Council in 1990, 1991 and 1995. He returned to Ireland in 1996, and is now the Director of the Centre for Irish Studies at the National University of Ireland, Galway. De Paor has worked alongside several other Irish language writers, such as Seán Ó Tuama, with whom he edited a twentieth century anthology of poetry in Irish. He has also published academic works.

THEODORE DEPPE is the author of *Children of the Air* and *The Wanderer King* (Alice James Books, 1990 and 1996); *Cape Clear: New and Selected Poems* (Salmon, 2002); *Orpheus on the Red Line* (Tupelo, 2009); and *Beautiful Wheel* (Arlen House in March 2014). A new collection of poems, *Liminal Blue*, is due out from Arlen House in 2016. Ted holds an MFA in Poetry from Vermont College. A recipient of two grants from the NEA and a Pushcart Prize, he has been writer in residence at the James Merrill House in Stonington, CT, and Phillips Academy in Andover, MA. Last fall, his poem "Shouting at the Windows of the Night" appeared in the *Forward Book of Poetry*. Ted has taught creative writing in graduate programs in the U.S., Ireland, and England. He is on the faculty of the Stonecoast MFA program, and directs Stonecoast in Ireland. He worked as an RN for twenty years while teaching poetry and fiction classes. He and his wife, poet Annie Deppe, live in Connemara.

LORI DESROSIERS is the author of *The Philosopher's Daughter*, published by Salmon Poetry in 2013, *Sometimes I Hear The Clock Speak* (Salmon, 2016) and a chapbook, *Inner Sky* from Glass Lyre Press. Her poems have appeared in *New Millennium Review, Contemporary American Voices, Best Indie Lit New England, String Poet, Blue Fifth Review, Pirene's Fountain, The New Verse News, The Mom Egg, The Bloomsbury Anthology of Contemporary Jewish-American Poetry* and many other journals and anthologies. Her work has been nominated for a Pushcart Prize. She edits *Naugatuck River Review*, a journal of narrative poetry and *WORDPEACE*, an online journal dedicated to peace and justice. She teaches Literature and Composition at Westfield State University and Holyoke Community College, and Poetry in the Interdisciplinary Studies program for the Lesley University M.F.A. graduate program.

MARY DORCEY is an award-winning Irish poet, short story writer and novelist. In 1990 she won the Rooney Prize for Literature for her short story collection: *A Noise from the Woodshed*. Her bestselling novel *Biography of Desire* (Poolbeg) was published in 1997 to critical acclaim and has been reprinted three times. She has published five volumes of poetry: *Kindling* (Only Women Press, 1982), *Moving into the Space Cleared by Our Mothers* (Salmon Poetry, 1991), *The River That Carries Me* (Salmon Poetry, 1995), *Like Joy In Season, Like Sorrow* (Salmon, 2001) and *Perhaps the Heart is Constant After All* (Salmon, 2012). In 1990 she published a novella, *Scarlet O'Hara* (1990) contained in the anthology *In and Out of Time* (Onlywomen Press). Five of her eights book have been awarded major Literature Bursaries by the Irish Arts Council, in 1990 and 1995 and 1999, 2005 and most recently, in 2008. She is a member of Aosdana.

THEO DORGAN is a poet, novelist, prose writer, editor, essayist and translator. He has written libretti and documentary film scripts, and is a broadcaster on radio and television. His first two collections, *The Ordinary House of Love* and *Rosa Mundi*, were published by Salmon. Among his recent publications are: *Barefoot Souls* (2015), translations from the French of the Syrian poet Maram al-Masri; *Jason and the Argonauts* (2014), a libretto; *Foundation Stone: Towards a Constitution for a 21st Century Republic* (2013, editor) and the novel *Making Way* (2013). His most recent collection of poems, *Nine Bright Shiners*, from Dedalus Press, was awarded the Irish Times/Poetry Now Prize for best collection published in 2014. He is a member of Aosdána.

AMY DRYANSKY's second book, Grass Whistle (Salmon) was published in 2013 and received the Massachusetts Book Award for poetry. Her first, How I Got Lost So Close to Home, was published by Alice James and individual poems appear in a variety of anthologies and journals, including Harvard Review, New England Review, Orion, Salamander, and The Women's Review of Books. She's been nominated for several Pushcart Prizes and received honors/awards from the Massachusetts Cultural Council, MacDowell Colony, Vermont Studio Center and the Bread Loaf Writers' Conference. She has two children, lives in a small town in western Massachusetts, and is currently the assistant director of the Culture, Brain & Development Program at Hampshire College. Amy's alter ego, Pokey Mama, blogs occasionally at amydryansky.wordpress.com.

VALERIE DUFF is the poetry editor for *Salamander Magazine*, and she has received St. Botolph and Massachusetts Cultural Council grants for her poetry. She earned her masters degree in creative writing from Boston University and Trinity College, Dublin. Her poems have appeared in *Ploughshares, Harvard Review, PN Review AGNI, Zoland Poetry: an Annual of Poems, Translations and Interviews*, and elsewhere; her book reviews have appeared in *Salamander, Bostonia*, and *PN Review*. Her debut poetry collection, To the New World, appeared from Salmon in 2010. It was shortlisted for the prestigious Seamus Heaney Centre Prize . Valerie is a freelance writer and editor. She lives in Boston with her husband and two children.

SUSAN MILLAR DUMARS' debut poetry collection, *Big Pink Umbrella*, was published by Salmon Poetry in 2008; *Dreams for Breakfast* appeared in 2010, The God Thing in 2013 and Bone Fire in 2016 (all with Salmon). Her work features in *Landing Places*, Dedalus' 2010 anthology of immigrant poetry written in Ireland; and also in *The Best Of Irish Poetry 2010*. A fiction writer as well, she published a collection of short stories, *Lights In The Distance*, with Doire Press in 2010. She has been the recipient of an Arts Council Literature Bursary for her stories. Susan has performed her poetry in Ireland, Northern Ireland and the UK; in Athens and in Brittany; in New York, Chicago, St. Louis, Denver, Washington DC and Huntington, West Virginia; and in Geelong and Canberra, Australia. Susan teaches creative writing to adults at various academic venues; and to individuals with special needs through the Away With Words project. She and her husband, the poet Kevin Higgins, have run the acclaimed Over the Edge readings series since 2003. Born in Philadelphia, Susan now makes her home in Galway, Ireland with Kevin and their cat, Ziggy.

Born in Wedza, Zimbabwe on 20 February 1982, PRIMROSE DZENGA is a creative non-fiction author and poet. Her first book *The Unsung Heroine — Auxillia Chimusoro*, was published in Zimbabwe by Zimbabwe Women Writers (June 2009). She has been published in poetry magazines, and online with the US Embassy in Harare. Primrose has performed and read her poetry at several international festivals. Her essay on publishing in Zimbabwe was included in *Poetry: Reading it, Writing it, Publishing it*, edited by Jessie Lendennie (Salmon Poetry, 2009). Her greatest passion is to work with and write about issues that advance, empower and inspire women all over the world. Her collection, Destiny In My Hands, was published by Salmon in 2011. She currently lives and works in the USA.

GEORGINA EDDISON is a counsellor and psychotherapist. She lives in Kildare, Co. Wicklow. She has an M.Phil in Creative Writing from Trinity College, Dublin. She was the winner of the 2008 Listowel Writers' Week Poetry Competition for the poems which appeared in the subsequent volume, Standing in the Pizzicato Rain (Salmon). She has also been shortlisted for a Hennessy Award and was awarded first prize in poetry at the Dunlavin Arts Festival 2003. Her poems have appeared in, among others, *The SHOp, The Sunday Tribune, Cyphers*, and *Broadsheet*.

CYNTHIA SCHWARTZBERG EDLOW's poetry collection is *The Day Judge Spencer Learned the Power of Metaphor* (Salmon Poetry, 2012). Her chapbook is *Old School Superhero Loves a Good Wristwatch* (Dancing Girl Press, 2014). She won the 2012 Red Hen Press Poetry Award (judge: Cynthia Hogue) — the poem, "Super Dan Comics Question Box Series #18," was published in *The Los Angeles Review*. She won the 2014 Tusculum Review Poetry Prize (judge: Jericho Brown) for the poem, "The Timekeeper," published in *Tusculum Review*. She is also the recipient of the Willow Review Prize for Poetry, the Beullah Rose Poetry Prize and two Pushcart Prize nominations. Her poetry has appeared widely, including *American Literary Review, American Poetry Review, Barrow Street, Cimarron Review, Cutthroat: A Journal of the Arts, Fjords Review, Folio, Fourteen Hills, Georgetown Review, Gulf Coast, The Main Street Rag, Smartish Pace* and *Tahoma Literary Review*. Poems have also been featured in the anthologies *Dogs Singing: A Tribute Anthology, Drawn to Marvel, The Emily Dickinson Awards Anthology* and *Not A Muse*. New poetry is forthcoming in: *Dublin Poetry Review, Fulcrum, Iodine Poetry Review* and *Plume*. Her next full-length verse collection, *Horn Section All Day Every Day*, is forthcoming from Salmon Poetry in 2017. Blog: http://cschwartzbergedlow.blogspot.com/

JOSEPH ENZWEILER received a degree in Physics from Xavier University. He received a masters in Physics from the University of Alaska, Fairbanks. He worked for many years as a carpenter, stone mason and photographer during the summer and fall months, and spent his winters writing. Enzweiler published four books of poetry: *Home Country* (Fireweed Press, 1986), *Stonework of the Sky* (Graywolf Press, 1995); *A Curb in Eden* (first version by Salmon in 1999; revised edition by Iris Press in 2003); and, *The Man Who Ordered Perch* (Iris Press, 2004).

JOSEPH ENZWEILER was a poet & memoirist. Born in Cincinnati, he grew up in Ohio. He received a MS in Physics from the University of Alaska Fairbanks, and in 1981 built a log cabin home in Goldstream Valley north of Fairbanks. Joe published six books of poetry: *Home Country* (Fireweed Press, 1986), *Stonework of the Sky* (Graywolf Press, 1995), *A Curb in Eden* (Salmon, 1999); *A Curb in Eden: New Version* (Iris Press, 2003), *The Man Who Ordered Perch* (Iris Press, 2004) and *A Winter on Earth* (Iris Press, 2006). With his wife Karen Grossweiner, he completed a memoir, We All Worship Something, shortly before his death. His poems have been featured on *The Writer's Almanac, Verse Daily* and in numerous journals. Joseph died on April 16, 2011, aged 60.

MÍCHEÁL FANNING practised as a medical doctor in County Kerry. As well as his books from Salmon, he published several chapbooks and translations, as well as collections of poetry in the Irish language which are published by Coiscéim under his Irish name — Mícheál Ó Fionnáin. He founded and directed Féile na Bealtaine, an arts and politics festival, held annually in West Kerry. Mícheál died on Christmas Eve 2010 at the age of 56.

MICHAEL EGAN was born in Baltimore in 1939. He did his undergraduate work at the University of Maryland, and then took an M.A. in the Writing Seminars of Johns Hopkins University, where he studied with Elliott Coleman. His books were *The Oldest Gesture* (Baltimore: New Poets Series, 1970) and *We Came Out Again to See the Stars* (Galway: Salmon Publishing, 1986). In the early 1970s, he taught at UMBC, and then, in the 80s and 90s, interspersed among numerous trips to Ireland, he taught at the Maryland Institute, College of Art. He was working on an epic poem, Leviathan, in his final years. He was able to complete the first half of this work, some 85 pages, of which, sections were published in various journals, before his death in 1992. Since his death, his work has appeared in *Salmon: A Journey in Poetry, 1981-2007* and in the *FSG Book of 20th Century Italian Poetry*.

TYLER FARRELL was born in Illinois, grew up in Milwaukee, WI, was educated by the Jesuits at Marquette High School and Creighton University, and by layfolk at the University of Wisconsin-Milwaukee. He has published poems, essays, and reviews in many periodicals and anthologies (*The Book of Irish American Poetry* — UND Press and St. Peter's; *B-List: Contemporary Poems Inspired by the Saints* — Ave Maria Press), and a biographical essay for James Liddy's *Selected Poems* (Arlen House, 2011). He teaches writing and literature at Marquette University as a Visiting Assistant Professor and currently lives in Madison, WI with his wife and two sons. Farrell has two collections of poems published by Salmon Poetry, *Tethered to the Earth* (2008) and *The Land of Give and Take* (2012).

ELAINE FEENEY teaches English at St. Jarlath's College, Tuam, County Galway. She is considered as part of a growing band of new young political Irish poets. She won the North Beach Nights Grand Slam and Cuirt Festival's Grand Slam. *The Radio was Gospel*, Elaine's third collection, was published by Salmon in 2013. It followed *Indiscipline* (2007) and *Where's Katie?* (Salmon, 2010). She has recorded an audio collection of her work with Sarah Clancy, *Cinderella Backwards* (2012). Her poetry has been broadcast on RTE radio and television. Elaine was the Over The Edge poetry Competition judge in 2011 and NUIG's Sin Poetry Competition judge in 2013. She has performed at various literature and music festivals including the Cúirt International Literature Festival, The Ex-Border Festival in Italy, The Edinburgh Fringe Festival, The Vilenica Festival and The Electric Picnic. Her work has been published in numerous magazines including *The SHOp* and *The Stinging Fly*. Her work has been translated into Italian, Slovene and Lithuanian. Elaine grew up in Athenry, Co. Galway, where she now lives with her husband Ray Glasheen and sons, Jack and Finn.

ANNE FITZGERALD is a graduate of Trinity College, Dublin and Queen's University, Belfast. Her collections are *Swimming Lessons* (2001), *The Map of Everything* (2006) and *Beyond The Sea* (Salmon, 2012). She is a recipient of the Ireland Fund of Monaco Literary Bursary at The Princess Grace Irish Library in Monaco (2007). She teaches Creative Writing in Ireland and in North America. She lives in Dún Laoghaire, Co. Dublin.

JOHN FITZGERALD is a poet, writer, editor, and federal appellate attorney in Los Angeles. A dual citizen of the U.S. and Ireland, he attended the University of West Los Angeles School of Law, where he was editor of the *Law Review*. He is author of *Favorite Bedtime Stories* (Salmon Poetry), *The Mind* (Salmon Poetry), *Telling Time by the Shadows* (Turning Point), and *Spring Water* (Turning Point Books Prize). Other works include *Primate*, a novel & screenplay, and the non-fiction *For All I Know*. He has contributed to the anthologies *Human and Inhuman Monstrous Poems* (Everyman), Poetry: *Reading it, Writing it, Publishing it* (Salmon Poetry), *Dogs Singing: A Tribute Anthology* (Salmon Poetry), *Rubicon: Words and Art inspired by Oscar Wilde's De Profundis* (Sybaritic Press), and *From the Four-Chambered Heart: In Tribute to Anaïs Nin* (Sybaritic Press), and to many journals, notably *The Warwick Review, World Literature Today, MadHatters Review, Barnwood Mag*, and *Lit Bridge*.

GABRIEL FITZMAURICE was born, in 1952, in the village of Moyvane, Co. Kerry where he still lives. For over thirty years he taught in the local primary school from which he retired as principal in 2007. He is author of more than forty books, including collections of poetry in English and Irish as well as several collections of verse for children. He has translated extensively from the Irish and has edited a number of anthologies of poetry in English and Irish. He has published two volumes of essays and collections of songs and ballads. A cassette of his poems, *The Space Between: New and Selected Poems 1984-1992* is also available. He frequently broadcasts on radio and television on education and the arts.

MÉLANIE FRANCÈS was born in Paris, France, in 1972. She grew up in France, but lived for four years in New Delhi, India, as a child. As a college student, she discovered her gift for writing and developed an interest in the arts and American literature. She later moved to Montreal, Canada to pursue her graduate studies at Concordia University and obtained an M.A. Degree in English and Creative Writing. In 2001, she published her first chapbook of poetry, *The World is in your Head*, with Ginninderra Press in Australia. Her collection, Anatomy of a Love Affair: My life in the movies, appeared from Salmon in 2007). She currently lives in the USA.

REBECCA MORGAN FRANK is the author of two collections of poems: *Little Murders Everywhere* (Salmon 2012), a finalist for the Kate Tufts Discovery Award, and *The Spokes of Venus*, forthcoming from Carnegie Mellon University Press. Her poems have appeared in such places as *Ploughshares, New England Review, Harvard Review, 32 Poems, Southern Indiana Review*, and elsewhere. She is a founding editor of the online magazine *Memorious* and an assistant professor at the University of Southern Mississippi.

PHILIP FRIED has published six books of poetry. *Publishers Weekly* called his fifth book, *Early / Late: New and Selected Poems* (Salmon, 2011), "skillful and memorable." And British poet Carol Rumens wrote in *The Guardian* that his sixth book, *Interrogating Water and Other Poems* (Salmon, 2014), was "outstanding" and praised it for "the valor and vision of its protest." "Late in the Game," which appears in this anthology, comes from a new manuscript entitled *Squaring the Circle*. Fried's Web site: www.philiphfried.com

Born in Norway ERLING FRIIS-BAASTAD has spent most of his adult life in Canada's Yukon Territory where he writes a science column for the Yukon Research Centre at Yukon College. His publications include the books *The Exile House* (Salmon Poetry, 2001) and *Wood Spoken: New and Selected Poems* (Northbound Press/Harbour Publishing, 2004). He recently completed a manuscript for the collection *Fossil Light*.

Born and educated in New York, LEAH FRITZ's essays and journalism on the peace, civil rights and feminist movements resulted in two non-fiction books. She spoke at universities and in churches across the USA, and in debates on radio and television. Although she has written poems since early childhood, it wasn't until she crossed the Atlantic in 1985 that she accepted poetry as her true vocation. In Britain her work has appeared in several anthologies and in *Acumen, Ambit, Poetry Review, PN Review* and numerous other magazines. Having received an award and commendations in competitions from Jo Shapcott, Les Murray and Carol Ann Duffy, Leah Fritz served as an adjudicator on the Torriano Poetry Competition and for three years on the Petra Kenney Memorial International Competition, becoming an honorary patron. Her archives are at Duke University in America. Salmon published *Whatever Sends The Music Into Time: New & Selected Poems* in 2012.

OWEN GALLAGHER was born in Gorbals, Glasgow. He has family in Donegal and Leitrim and lives in London, where he worked as a primary teacher in Southall. His poems have been widely published in Ireland, Britain and abroad. He has won poetry competitions and awards for poetry from the London Arts Board and The Society of Authors. His poems have been displayed on London buses and in public places in Ireland, and were placed on the Listening Wall, at the Southbank Centre, London, as part of the Poetry International Festival, 2014. His collection, *A Good Enough Love*, was published by Salmon in 2015.

DAVID GARDINER is a writer and editor who currently lives in Chicago. From 2006 to 2010, he was founding editor of the international arts journal, *An Sionnach*. He has served as professor at Creighton University and visiting scholar at Boston College, New York University, Trinity College Dublin and the University of Ulster. Since 1989, when he attended the International Writers' Workshop at University College-Galway, he has commuted between Ireland and the U.S. He has written five books, edited ten and authored over sixty journal publications. Most recently, he was guest poetry editor of *Burning Bush 2* (Dublin). His collections with Salmon are *The Chivalry of Crime* (2015) and *Downstate* (2009).

PAUL GENEGA was born and raised on Long Island and educated at Georgetown, Columbia and Johns Hopkins. He is the author of five chapbooks and five full-length collections of poetry, the most recent being Salmon's *All I Can Recall* (2013). Over a thirty-plus year career his award-winning work has appeared in scores of literary magazines and journals, including *The Nation, Narrative Northeast, New York Quarterly*, and *North American Review*. Paul founded and taught in the creative writing program at Bloomfield College, New Jersey, where he also served for many years as Chair of Humanities. Recently retired, his legacy continues at Bloomfield through the Genega Endowed Scholarships in Creative Writing. Paul lives with his husband Jim and Welsh Springer Spaniel Brick at the edge of the majestic Hudson in Stuyvesant, New York.

PETER JOSEPH GLOVICZKI is a teacher, a communication researcher and a poet. His poems have appeared in *Hayden's Ferry Review, New Orleans Review, The Christian Science Monitor, Verse Daily* and elsewhere. His collections are: *Kicking Gravity* and *American Paprika*, both from Salmon. He is also the author of *Kicking Gravity* (Salmon Poetry, 2013). He works as an assistant professor of communication at Coker College in Hartsville, South Carolina, where he also serves as coordinator of the communication program. His first scholarly book is *Journalism and Memorialization in the Age of Social Media* (Palgrave Macmillan, 2015). His scholarly journal articles have appeared or are forthcoming in *Health Communication, Humanity and Society, Journal of Loss and Trauma* and *The Qualitative Report*. He holds a PhD and an MA in Mass Communication from the University of Minnesota, and he is a magna cum laude graduate of St. Olaf College in Northfield, Minnesota.

FRANK GOLDEN is a poet, novelist and visual artist. His novel *The Night Game* was published by Salmon Fiction in 2015. His previous novel, *The Two Women of Aganatz,* was published by the Wolfhound Press, Dublin. His last book of poems was *In Daily Accord* (Salmon Poetry). He has received two bursaries in literature from the Arts Council of Ireland and a number of other awards. He lives in the Burren, County Clare, Ireland. www.frankgolden7.com

JULIAN GOUGH was born in London, to Tipperary parents. When he was seven, the family returned to Tipperary. He was educated by the Christian Brothers, back when throwing a boy across the room was considered healthful exercise for both parties. At university in Galway, he began writing and singing with the underground literary rock band Toasted Heretic. They released four albums, and had a top ten hit in Ireland in 1991 with 'Galway and Los Angeles', a song about not kissing Sinéad O'-Connor. His first novel, Juno & Juliet, was published in 2001. His second, Jude: Level 1, came six years later. Jude: Level 1 was described by the Sunday Tribune as possibly 'the finest comic novel since Flann O'Brien's The Third Policeman'. In the UK, it was shortlisted for the Everyman Wodehouse Prize for Comic Fiction. In 2007, his story 'The Orphan and the Mob' won the BBC National Short

Story Prize -then the world's largest annual prize for a single short story. He also wrote the first short story ever printed in the Financial Times, 'The Great Hargeisa Goat Bubble'. In 2009, 'The Great Hargeisa Goat Bubble' was broadcast as an acclaimed radio play on BBC Radio 4. In early 2010, the Sunday Tribune chose *Jude: Level 1* as their Irish Novel of the Decade. His third novel, Jude in London, was published by Old Street in September 2010. 2016 sees the publication of his first children's book, *Rabbit's Bad Habits*, which Neil Gaiman called "a laugh-out-loud story", and Eoin Colfer called "an instant modern classic". Later this year, Picador will publish *Connect*, a novel for adults.

MARK GRANIER has published four collections of poetry, *Haunt* (Salmon, 2015), *Airborne* (Salmon, 2001), *The Sky Road* (Salmon, 2007) and *Fade Street* (Salt, 2010). His awards include the New Writer Poetry Prize, the Vincent Buckley Poetry Prize and a Patrick and Katherine Kavanagh Fellowship.

PAUL GRATTAN was born in Glasgow, Scotland, in 1971. He moved to the North of Ireland in 1995, and gained an MA in Creative Writing at the Poets' House/Lancaster University; studying under the late James Simmons. In 2002 *The Edinburgh Review* published his first collection, *The End of Napoleon's Nose*. His work has appeared in several anthologies including: *The New Irish Poets*, ed. Selina Guinness (Bloodaxe 2004); *Magnetic North*, ed. John Brown (Lagan Press 2006); *The New North*, ed. Chris Agee (Wake Forest 2008); *Landing Places*, eds. Eva Bourke & Borbala Farago, (Dedalus 2009). His collection, Daytime Astronomy, was published by Salmon in 2011.

ROBERT GREACEN (1920-2008) was born of Scots and Irish stock in Derry/ Londonderry on 24th October 1920 and lived in both urban Belfast and rural Monaghan. Experiences in city and county furnished materials for later poems and reviews. At Methodist College, Belfast, he discovered his gift for writing and developed an interest in leftist politics. Later, at Trinity College Dublin, he pursued a diploma in Social Studies and found friends in artistic circles. He has had an outstanding career, with poems published in Ireland, England, Scotland, France, and the United States, and several volumes in Ireland. After his retirement from a career of teaching English as a Foreign Language in London, he was nominated for membership in Aosdána, an association of 220 living artists in Ireland. Now resident in Dublin, he was honoured by his peers on his seventieth birthday, 1990, with a commemorative volume of poems. In 1995, he was awarded the Irish Times Poetry Prize for his *Collected Poems*. Salmon published his *New & Selected Poems* in 2006. Robert died on Sunday 13th April 2008 at the age of 87.

Poet and painter ANGELA GREENE was born in England in 1936 and lived from early childhood in Dublin. She was educated at Dominican College, Eccles Street and trained as a nurse at the Mater Hospital, Dublin. In 1988 she won the Patrick Kavanagh Award and in 1989 was short-listed for The Sunday Tribune/ Hennessy Literary Award. In 1987 she was a prizewinner in the Bloodaxe Books National Poetry Competition. Her poetry was published in Britain and Ireland, read on RTE Radio and BBC Radio Ulster and was performed in *Sunny Side Plucked* at the Project Arts Centre, Dublin. Her collection, *Silence and the Blue Night*, appeared from Salmon in 1986. Her deeply lived experience as woman, daughter, wife, mother, poet and painter is reflected in quiet, well-crafted and moving poems. The lateness of her arrival to contemporary Irish poetry and the quiet way she received her well deserved recognition, makes her loss, in 1997, all the more poignant.

NICKI GRIFFIN grew up in Cheshire but has lived in East Clare since 1997. Her debut collection of poetry, *Unbelonging*, was published by Salmon Poetry in 2013 and was shortlisted for the Shine/Strong Award 2014 for best debut collection. *The Skipper and Her Mate* (non-fiction) was published by New Island in 2013. She was awarded an Arts Council Literature Bursary in 2012 and has an MA in Writing from National Univeristy of Ireland, Galway.

RICHARD W. HALPERIN is an Irish-U.S. dual-national. He is widely published in magazines and journals in Ireland and the U.K. His three Salmon collections are *Quiet in a Quiet House* (2016), *Shy White Tiger* (2013) and *Anniversary* (2010). The latter has been translated into Japanese and French. Lapwing Press, Belfast, has brought out four chapbooks. The most recent of these is *Blue Flower* (2015). Mr Halperin reads at festivals and many other venues in Ireland and has begun giving bilingual readings in Paris, where he lives.

GERARD HANBERRY is an award-winning poet living and working in Galway on the west coast of Ireland. His fourth book of poems, What Our Shoes Say About Us, was published by Salmon in 2014. It followed on his 2009 collection At Grattan Road, also from Salmon Poetry, a collection the Irish Times said was 'bursting at the seams with fine poems'. Gerard Hanberry has also published a biography of the Wilde family More Lives Than One — the Remarkable Wilde Family Through the Generations (The Collins Press). He is a teacher of English at St. Enda's College, Galway and delivers a creative writing module at the National University of Ireland, Galway. He lives, overlooking Galway Bay, with his wife Kerry.

NOEL HANLON was born in Portland, Oregon in 1956. She lives on a small farm in the Willamette Valley with her husband, where they raised their two children. Her first book of poems, Blue Abundance, was published by Salmon Poetry in 2010.

CYNTHIA HARDY has published poems and stories in Permafrost, The Northern Review, Ice-Floe: An International Journal of the Far North, and Cirque: A Literary Journal of the North Pacific Rim. Her chapbook, We Tempt Our Luck, was a finalist in the 2008 Astounding Beauty Ruffian Press Poetry Chapbook competition. Her poetry collection Beneath a Portrait of a Horse was published by Salmon in 2010. She is a past recipient of an Alaska State Council on the Arts Individual Artist grant. She lives in Fairbanks, Alaska, where she teaches at the University of Alaska Fairbanks, dances, gardens, and tends the horses that appear in her poems.

MAURICE HARMON, a well-known critic, scholar and academic, has written studies of writers from William Carleton to Mary Lavin and Seán O'Faolain, from Austin Clarke and Thomas Kinsella to John F. Deane, Peter Fallon, and Dennis O'Driscoll. His pioneering anthology Irish Poetry after Yeats appeared in 1978. His reputation as a poet has grown, particularly with the publication of his acclaimed When Love Is Not Enough: New and Selected Poems (Salmon, 2010), which shows the range and variety of his work. His Dialogue of the Ancients of Ireland, a translation of Acallam na Senórach, the medieval compendium of poems and stories, was published in 2009.

CLARINDA HARRISS (Baltimore, Maryland) is a professor emerita of English at Towson University. For more than 40 years, she has been publisher and editor-in-chief of BrickHouse Books, Inc., a non-profit corporation which is Maryland's oldest literary press. Her most recent books are poetry collections, Air Travel, Mortmain, and Dirty Blue Voice; a short story collection, The White Rail; and, with poet Moira Egan, editor of Hot Sonnets, An Anthology. She continues to work with prison writers. Of Celtic origin, she has traveled extensively in Ireland and given readings in Galway and Clifden. Thanks to the wanderlust of her children and grandchildren, she has spent time in New Zealand and Argentina as well as snorkeling in Mexico.

ANNE LE MARQUAND HARTIGAN is a prize-winning poet, playwright and painter. She trained as a painter at Reading University, England. She returned to Co. Louth, Ireland, in 1962 with her husband Tim Hartigan where they farmed and reared their six children. She now lives in Dublin. She has published seven collections of poetry: Unsweet Dreams (Salmon, 2011), To Keep The Light Burning: Reflections in times of loss (Salmon, 2008); Nourishment (Salmon, 2005); Immortal Sins (Salmon, 1993); the award winning long poem with Anne's drawings, Now is a Moveable Feast (Salmon, 1991); Return Single (Beaver Row Press, 1986); and Long Tongue (Beaver Row Press, 1982). Her prose work includes Clearing The Space: A Why of Writing (Salmon, 1996). Hartigan won the Mobil Prize for Playwriting for her play The Secret Game in 1995. In Other Worlds (2003) was commissioned and performed by Ohio University, USA, then performed at the Edinburgh Fringe Festival and Otago, Dunedin, New Zealand. Jersey Lilies was performed at the Samuel Beckett Theatre, Dublin 1996, where Anne acted with Robert Gordon in this two hander. La Corbiere was performed at the Project Theatre during the Dublin Theatre Festival 1989, and has since been performed in Beirut and by Solas Nua Theatre Company in Washington DC where it was the pick of the Fringe Festival.

TODD HEARON's two collections of poems are Strange Land and No Other Gods. He has received a PEN/New England "Discovery" Award; the Friends of Literature Prize from Poetry magazine and the Poetry Foundation; the Rumi Prize in Poetry; and the Campbell Corner Poetry Prize. Currently, he serves as Poet-in-Residence at Dartmouth College and the Frost Place and teaches in Exeter, New Hampshire, where he lives with his wife, the poet Maggie Dietz, and their twins, Lionel and Kempie.

MICHAEL HEFFERNAN's most recent books are *The Night-Watchman's Daughter* (Salmon Poetry, 2016), *Walking Distance* (Lost Horse Press, 2013), *The Breaking of the Day* (Salmon Poetry, 2012), and *At the Bureau of Divine Music* (Wayne State University Press, 2011). His awards include the Iowa Poetry Prize (1993), the Porter Prize for Literary Excellence (1998), two Pushcart Prizes (1998, 2001) and three fellowship grants from the National Endowment for the Arts, USA (1978, 1982, 1994). Since 1986 he has taught poetry in the Programs in Creative Writing and Translation at the University of Arkansas, Fayetteville. He lives with his wife Ann in Fayetteville.

AIDEEN HENRY lives in Galway and works as a writer and a physician. She was shortlisted for the 2009 Hennessy X.O. Literary Awards for poetry. Her first collection of poetry, *Hands Moving at the Speed of Falling Snow*, was published in 2010 by Salmon Poetry. *Slow Bruise* followed in 2015 (also with Salmon). She writes short fiction and her debut collection of short stories, *Hugging Thistles*, was published by Arlen House in 2013.

PATRICK HICKS is the author of ten books, including *The Commandant of Lubizec: A Novel of the Holocaust and Operation Reinhard* (Steerforth/Random House), *Adoptable* (Salmon Poetry) and *The Collector of Names* (Schaffner Press). His work has appeared in some of the most vital literary journals in America, including *Ploughshares, Glimmer Train, The Missouri Review, Prairie Schooner*, and many others. He has been nominated seven times for the Pushcart Prize, been a finalist for the High Plains Book Award, and also the Gival Press Novel Award. A former Visiting Fellow at Oxford, he has won the Glimmer Train Fiction Award as well as a number of grants, including ones from the Bush Artist Foundation and the National Endowment for the Humanities. His work with PBS's Over South Dakota was nominated for an Emmy. He is the Writer-in-Residence at Augustana College and also a faculty member at the low residency MFA program at Sierra Nevada College.

KEVIN HIGGINS facilitates poetry workshops at Galway Arts Centre and teaches creative writing at Galway Technical Institute. He is also Writer-in-Residence at Merlin Park Hospital and the poetry critic of the *Galway Advertiser*. He was a founding co-editor of *The Burning Bush* literary magazine and is co-organiser of over the edge literary events in Galway City. His first collection of poems *The Boy With No Face* was published by Salmon in February 2005 and was short-listed for the 2006 Strong Award. His second collection, *Time Gentlemen, Please*, was published in March 2008 by Salmon. His work also features in the generation defining anthology *Identity Parade — New British and Irish Poets* (ed roddy lumsden, Bloodaxe, 2010). *Frightening New Furniture*, his third collection of poems, was published in 2010 by Salmon Poetry. Kevin has read his work at most of the major literary festivals in Ireland, the USA, and Australia. *Mentioning The War*, a collection of his essays and reviews was published in April 2012 by Salmon. Kevin's poems have been translated into Greek, Spanish, Turkish, Italian, Japanese & Portuguese. *The Ghost In The Lobby*, his fourth collection of poetry, appeared from Salmon in 2014. *The Selected Satires of Kevin Higgins* was published by Nuascéalta in 2016.

MICHAEL D. HIGGINS is a politician, poet, sociologist, author and broadcaster. He is the ninth and current President of Ireland, in office since 11 November 2011. He previously served at almost every level of public life in Ireland, including as Ireland's first Minister for Arts, Culture and the Gaeltacht. Salmon published his first collection of poetry, *The Betrayal*, in 1990. Other collections are *The Season of Fire, An Arid Season* and *New and Selected Poems*.

RITA ANN HIGGINS was born in 1955 in Galway, Ireland. She divides her time between Galway City and Spiddal, County Galway. Her first five collections were published by Salmon: *Goddess on the Mervue Bus* (1986); *Witch in the Bushes* (1988); *Goddess and Witch* (1990); *Philomena's Revenge* (1992); and, *Higher Purchase* (1996). Bloodaxe Books published her next three collections: *Sunny Side Plucked* (1996); *An Awful Racket* (2001); and *Throw in the Vowels: New & Selected Poems* in May 2005 to mark her 50th birthday. *Hurting God: Part Essay, Part Rhyme* appeared from Salmon in 2010. Her plays include: *Face Licker Come Home* (Salmon 1991); *God of the Hatch Man* (1992), *Colie Lally Doesn't Live in a Bucket* (1993); and *Down All the Roundabouts* (1999). In 2004, she wrote a screenplay entitled *The Big Break*. In 2008 she wrote a play, *The Empty Frame*, inspired by Hanna Greally, and in 2008 a play for radio, *The Plastic Bag*. She has edited: *Out the Clara Road: The Offaly Anthology* in 1999; and *Word and Image: a collection of poems from Sunderland Women's*

Centre and Washington Bridge Centre (2000). She co-edited *FIZZ: Poetry of resistance and challenge*, an anthology written by young people, in 2004. She was Galway County's Writer-in-Residence in 1987, Writer-in-Residence at the National University of Ireland, Galway, in 1994-95, and Writer-in-Residence for Offaly County Council in 1998-99. She was Green Honors Professor at Texas Christian University in October 2000. She won the Peadar O'Donnell Award in 1989 and has received several Arts Council of Ireland bursaries. Her collection *Sunny Side Plucked* was a Poetry Book Society Recommendation. She was made an honorary fellow at Hong Kong Baptist University in November 2006.

JOHN HILDEBIDLE was a teacher for nearly forty years, from public secondary school, to Harvard, and the Massachusetts Institute of Technology (MIT) where he taught English, Irish, and American literature. He writes poetry and fiction. His third collection of poems *Defining Absence* was published by Salmon in 1999. It was followed by *Signs, Translations* in 2008 (also Salmon).

JENNIFER HORNE is a writer, editor, and teacher who explores identity and place through poetry, fiction, prose, and anthologies. She has taught classes and writing workshops in varied settings, from university Honors students to school children to women in prison. Her books include two poetry collections, *Little Wanderer* (Salmon, 2016) and *Bottle Tree*, two poetry chapbooks, *Miss Betty's School of Dance* and *Tineretului*, and a collection of short stories, *Tell the World You're a Wildflower*. The editor of a collection of poems and co-editor of two essay collections, she has received fellowships from the Alabama State Council on the Arts and the Seaside Institute in Florida. Raised in Arkansas and now based in Alabama, Horne has lived in Bucharest, Romania, and Oxford, England, has traveled widely in Europe, and is always pondering her next trip.

RON HOUCHIN writes from his home on the Ohio River across from his hometown, Huntington, West Virginia. He taught in public school for thirty years in southernmost Ohio. He has six books of poetry, most recently The Quiet Jars: New & Selected Poems (Salmon, 2013). His work has received notoriety, including Paterson Prize and Pushcart Prize nominations, as well as an Appalachian award for poetry Book-of-the-Year. He travels often to Ireland where his work frequently appears in *Poetry Ireland Review* and *The Stinging Fly*. His poems have been featured in a wide variety of U.S. venues, such as *Five Points, Birmingham Poetry Review, Valparaiso Poetry Review, Verse Daily, The New Orleans Review, Poetry Northwest, Puerto del Sol, The Southern Poetry Review, Hillbilly Solid* (Radio WMMT) and others. His poems have appeared in Irish and American anthologies: *Dogs Singing: A Tribute Anthology, Salmon: A Journey in Poetry, Motif I and II*, and *We All Live Downstream*. He reads and teaches in writing workshops on both sides of the Atlantic. Salmon published his first book in 1997.

BEN HOWARD is Emeritus Professor of English at Alfred University. For the past four decades, he has contributed poems, reviews, essays, and articles to leading journals in Ireland, England, and America. His numerous awards include the Milton Dorfman Award in Poetry, the Theodore Christian Hoepfner Award, and a fellowship from the National Endowment for the Arts. He is the author of ten books, most recently *The Backward Step: Essays on Zen Practice* (Whitlock, 2014) and *Firewood and Ashes - New and Selected Poems* (Salmon, 2015). Visit his website at www.howardbw.com and his blog at www.practiceofzen.com.

GERALD HULL comes from a 'mixed generation' Irish-American family in London and has lived in Ireland for many years, settling in Fivemiletown in Tyrone. He holds a Ph.D from the University of Wales and in recent years has been associated with the Pushkin Prize, Oliver Goldsmith and William Carleton International Summer Schools. He is widely published and, fitting for one whose poetry is fixated on the border counties, was guest editor for the acclaimed South-West edition of The Honest Ulsterman (HU). His first full collection, Falling into Monaghan, was published by Salmon in 1999.

For his entire professional career, LARRY JAFFE has been using his art to promote human rights. He was the poet-in-residence at the Autry Museum of Western Heritage, a featured poet in Chrysler's Spirit in the Words poetry program, co-founder of Poets for Peace (now Poets for Human Rights) and helped spearhead the United Nations Dialogue among Civilizations through Poetry project which incorporated hundreds of readings in hundreds of cities globally using the aesthetic power of poetry to bring understanding to the world. He was the recipient of the Saint Hill Art Festival's Lifetime of

Creativity Award, the first time given to a poet. He is most appreciative of Salmon Poetry for publishing his book *One Child Sold*.

FRED JOHNSTON was born in Belfast, Northern Ireland, in 1951 and educated there and Toronto, Canada. A journalist for some years, he worked in PR in Dublin in the early 'Seventies. He received a Hennessy Literary Award for Prose in 1972. With Neil Jordan and Peter Sheridan, he founded the Irish Writers' Co-operative (Co-Op Books) in the mid-Seventies. Two plays were performed at The Lantern Theatre, Dublin, where he also acted for a time. After a time in North Africa, he returned to Ireland, where he was awarded in succession the Sunday Independent Short Story and Poetry awards. Stories were both anthologised and later dramatised by BBC World Service and RTE radio. For many years he reviewed poetry, prose and theatre for, among others, *The Sunday Press, Hibernia, Books Ireland, Poetry Ireland, Studies*, and visual art for *The Sunday Times*. In 1986 he founded Galway's Cúirt poetry festival, now an international literature festival and later, The Western Writers' Centre, Galway. Three novels and two collections of short stories have been published and numerous collections of poetry. For a time he wrote and published poetry in French, with, among others, the French journals *Le Grognard, Hopala!, Verso*. In 2004 he was appointed writer in residence to the Princess Grace Irish Library at Monaco; in 2002 he had been awarded the Prix de l'Ambassade for his work on the poetry of Michel Martin. His translations of the poetry of Colette Wittorski are published by Lapwing Poetry. Recent work has appeared in *The Spectator, The New Statesman, STAND*, and widely elsewhere. Broadcast work has appeared, both prose and poetry, on RTE's Sunday Miscellany over the years. A musician, he has produced two solo albums and two with the group Parsons Hat. Recently he was a recipient of the Catherine and Patrick Kavanagh Bursary. He lives and works in Galway, Ireland.

JEAN KAVANAGH is an Irish poet living in Oslo, Norway. She studied Irish Folklore and English Literature in UCD, Dublin. She has been shortlisted twice, in 2010 and 2011, for Galway's Over The Edge New Writer of the Year, and in 2012 was shortlisted for the Patrick Kavanagh Poetry Award. Her work has been published in journals, showcase anthologies for the Galway Arts Centre, and in *Dogs Singing: A Tribute Anthology* (Salmon, 2011). *Other Places*, her debut collection, was published by Salmon Poetry in 2014, and was shortlisted for the Strong/Shine award.

JOHN KAVANAGH is from Sligo. *Blue Room*, his third collection from Salmon (2013), followed *Etchings* and *Half-Day Warriors*. He is a winner of the Listowel Writers' Week Poetry Award. He is also a playwright with five plays produced to date in Ireland and the US. His audio book The Life and Works of William Butler Yeats (Naxos Audio) won the Spoken Word Award in the UK.

COLM KEEGAN has read and performed his poetry at various festivals, including the Flat Lakes Festival, Electric Picnic and the Festival of World Cultures. He was the All Ireland Slam Poetry Champion in 2010. He also writes short stories and screenplays and has been shortlisted four times for the Hennessy New Irish Writing Award for both poetry and fiction. In 2008 he was shortlisted for the International Seán Ó Faoláin Short Story Competition. In 2011 he was nominated for the Absolut Fringe's 'Little Gem' Award for the play *Three Men Talking About Things They Kinda Know About* (co-written with Kalle Ryan and Stephen James Smith) which is touring 2012/2013. He is a poetry/arts reviewer and contributing poet for RTE Radio One's nightly arts show ARENA and co-founder of 'Nighthawks at the Cobalt'. He is co-founder and facilitator of Inklinks, a young writers club in Clondalkin and teaches creative writing in secondary schools across Ireland. He maintains a popular blog and his poetry performances are widely viewed on YouTube. His debut collection, *Don't Go There*, was published by Salmon. He will publish a second collection with Salmon in 2016.

PATRICK KEHOE was born in Enniscorthy, Co Wexford, Ireland in 1956. His first poems were published by the late James Liddy in broadsheets and issues of The Gorey Detail. Early poems were also published in the Irish Press. In recent times his work has appeared in Natural Bridge, Cyphers and The Scaldy Detail. Formerly a teacher, he has been working as a journalist in Dublin for the past 23 years. He is also a guitarist and songwriter. His debut collection, *Its Words You Want*, was published by Salmon in 2011. It was followed by a collection from Dedalus Press.

RITA KELLY was born in Galway in 1953. She has lived most of her life in the south east of Ireland with periods in New York, London and Germany. Her work has been widely published and translated as well as being placed on university courses in Ireland and abroad. She has won many awards. Her first literary award was adjudicated and granted by John B. Keane, of which she is very proud. Most recently she has been awarded a Patrick & Katherine Kavanagh Fellowship. She has had many Arts Council Bursaries. She holds an MA. Her work is thoughtful, rarely fashionable, sometimes challenging and evocative. *Further Thoughts in a Garden* was published by Salmon in 2013.

ANNE KENNEDY, poet, writer, photographer and broadcaster, came from Orcas Island, off the coast of Washington state, to live in Galway, Ireland in 1977. Her first book *Buck Mountain Poems*, published by Salmon in 1989, is based on her Orcas experiences. *The Dog Kubla Dreams My Life* was published in 1994. A keen documentor of history, in 1993 she contributed an oral history project to the Duke Ellington archive in the Smithsonian Museum of American History. Anne Kennedy died on 29th September 1998.

NOEL KING was born and lives in Tralee, Co Kerry. His poetry collections are published by Salmon: *Prophesying the Past* (2010), *The Stern Wave* (2013) and *Sons* (2015). He has edited more than fifty books of work by others and was poetry editor of *Revival Literary Journal* (Limerick Writers' Centre) in 2012/13. A short story collection, *The Key Signature & Other Stories,* will be published by Liberties Press in 2017.

PAUL KINGSNORTH's debut novel, *The Wake*, was longlisted for the Man Booker Prize in 2014, and his follow-up, *Beast*, is forthcoming from Faber and Faber. He is also the author of two non-fiction books. His debut poetry collection, *Kidland and other poems*, was published by Salmon in 2011. He lives in County Galway.

JACQUELINE KOLOSOV has two new young adult novels, and her memoir, *Motherhood, and the Places Between*, won the Mary Roberts Rhinehart Award and will be published in September 2016 by Stillhouse Press. She coedited *Family Resemblance: An Anthology and Exploration of 8 Hybrid Literary Genres* (Rose Metal, 2015), a finalist for Foreword's Indie Nonfiction Award. Her poetry, fiction, and nonfiction have recently appeared in *The Sewanee Review, The Southern Review, STAND, Prairie Schooner*, and *Bellevue Literary Review*. Find her at www.jacquelinekolosovreads.com

THOMAS KRAMPF's most recent book is *Selected Poems* published by Salmon Poetry in 2012. He has read his work in universities and other venues in the US and abroad, as well as on National Public Radio. He and his wife currently live in the foothills of the Allegheny Mountains in southwestern New York. They have three daughters and grandchildren.

JESSIE LENDENNIE was born in Arkansas, USA. After years of travel, she settled in Ireland in 1981. Her publications include a book-length prose poem *Daughter* (1988), reprinted as *Daughter and Other Poems* in 2001 and Walking Here (2011). She complied and edited: *Salmon: A Journey in Poetry, 1981-2007*; *Poetry: Reading it, Writing It, Publishing It* (2009); *Dogs Singing: A Tribute Anthology* (2010); and, *Even The Daybreak: 35 Years of Salmon Poetry* (2016). She is co-founder (1981) and Managing Director of Salmon Poetry. Her poems, essays and articles have been widely published and she has given numerous readings, lectures and writing courses in Ireland and abroad. She is currently working on a memoir.

JOSEPH LENNON is the Director of Irish Studies and associate professor of English at Villanova University. His book, *Irish Orientalism: A Literary and Intellectual History* won the Donald Murphy Prize from the American Conference for Irish Studies. Salmon Poetry published his first volume of poetry, *Fell Hunger*, in 2011. He has published in periodicals such as the *Times Literary Supplement, New Hibernia Review, Denver Quarterly*, and *Poetry Ireland Review*.

RAINA J. LEÓN is a Cave Canem graduate fellow, CantoMundo fellow, and member of the Carolina African American Writers Collective. Her collections of poetry include *Canticle of Idols, Boogeyman Dawn* (Salmon, 2013) and *sombra : (dis)locate* (Salmon, 2016). She is a founding editor of *The Acentos Review*, an online quarterly devoted to the promotion and publication of LatinX arts. She is an associate professor of education at Saint Mary's College of California.

JAMES LIDDY was born in Lr. Pembroke St., Dublin, in 1934. His parents hailed from the cities of Limerick and New York. He lived in Coolgreany, County Wexford, intermittently from 1941 to 2000. His books include *Blue Mountain* (Dolmen), *A Munster Song of Love and War* (White Rabbit), *Corca Bascinn* (Dolmen), *Baudelaire's Bar Flowers* (Capra/White Rabbit), *Collected Poems* (Creighton University), *Gold Set Dancing* (Salmon, 2000), *I Only Know that I Love Strength in My Friends and Greatness* (Arlen House), as well as memoirs *The Doctor's House* (2004) and *The Full Shilling* (2009), both from Salmon. For over 20 years, he lived in Milwaukee where he was a Professor in the English Department at the University of Wisconsin-Milwaukee and taught creative writing, and Irish and Beat literature. *James Liddy: A Critical Study*, by Brian Arkins, was published by Arlen House in 2001. James Liddy died at his home in the United States on Tuesday 4th November 2008 after a short illness.

CHRISTOPHER LOCKE is the Nonfiction Editor for *Slice* magazine in Brooklyn. His poems have appeared or are forthcoming in numerous publications, including *The North American Review*; *Verse Daily*; *Southwest Review*; *Poetry East*; *Arc Poetry Magazine*; *The Nervous Breakdown*; *32 Poems*; *The SHOp*; *West Branch*; *Rattle*; *The Literary Review*; *Ascent*; *The Sun*; *Connecticut Review*; *Upstreet*; *Agenda*, and on both National Public Radio in the US and Ireland's Radio One. Chris has five chapbooks of poetry and has received grants from the Massachusetts Cultural Council, New Hampshire Council on the Arts, and Fundacion Valparaiso (Spain). His first full-length collection of poems, *End of American Magic*, was released by Salmon Poetry in 2010. *Waiting for Grace & Other Poems* (Turning Point Books) and the collection of essays *Can I Say* (Kattywompus Press) were both released in 2013.

DAVE LORDAN is a writer, performer, editor, radio reviewer and researcher, and creativity facilitator. He is the first writer to win Ireland's three national prizes for young poets. He is a former holder of the Ireland Chair of Poetry Bursary Award, the Kavanagh Award, and the Strong Award. His collections of poetry are *The Boy in the Ring* (Salmon, 2007), *Invitation to a Sacrifice* (Salmon, 2010) and *Lost Tribe of the Wicklow Mountains* (Salmon, 2014). dlordan@hotmail.com. google him for all the scandal.

THOMAS LYDEN was born in 1949 in the village of Faulkeeragh in Clifden, County Galway, where generations of Lydens have lived. After finishing his schooling in London and working there for a few years he came back to Clifden to help his mother on the family farm. Even while busy with the pitchfork, the pen's work would always have been on his mind. Tom Lyden was deeply aware of the magic, mystery and power of the land of Connemara and in particular of Inishbofin, the home of his mother's O'Halloran family. He was a prominent member of the arts community in Clifden. As a founding member of Baskethouse, an arts collective of local and international writers and musicians, he organized weekly readings and events in the town. His passionate interest in music, nature and his intense observation of people were major influences in his writing. His poetry has been published in various magazines and anthologies both in Ireland and abroad. In recent years Thomas moved to Dublin, but always remained connected to his Connemara roots. He passed away on December 8th, 2015. A posthumous collection of poetry, Dancing on Top of a Broomstick (with illustrations by Ursula Klinger), was published by Salmon in 2016.

CAROLINE LYNCH was born in 1976 and grew up in Cork. She studied Law in UCC, taking part in student theatre productions. While in college, she was the inaugural winner of the Sean Dunne poetry competition. On completing her degree she studied acting and worked as a professional actor for a number of years. In 2001 she was short listed for the Seacat/Poetry Ireland award. She was granted an Arts Council Professional Development Award and obtained an MA in Writing from NUI, Galway. Her poems have appeared in *Poetry Ireland Review*, in an anthology of new writing (*The Incredible Hides in Every House*) edited by Nuala Ní Dhomhnaill, and in *Writers Seeking Lovers*, a collection from the MA in Writing. She won the Listowel Writers' Week poetry collection competition in 2007. That winning selection of poems was published in a slim volume entitled Lost in the Gaeltacht (Salmon, 2008).

PHIL LYNCH lives in Dublin and is fully engaged in reading and performing his work at poetry and spoken work events and festivals across the country and further afield. His poems have appeared in *Revival Literary Journal*, *Bare Hands Anthology*, *The Poetry Bus*, *Wordlegs*, *Silver Apples Magazine*, *Boyne Berries Series*, *Headstuff*, *Census 3*, *Outburst*, *Circle Time* and *Headspace*, amongst others. He has also been featured on national and local radio, including the Arena Arts Show and the Poetry Programme on RTE Radio 1. Phil is a Director of the LINGO Spoken Word Festival and a member of Dalkey Writers' Workshop. His first collection is *Hidden Treasures* (Salmon Poetry, 2016).

THOMAS LYNCH is the author of four collections of poems, three books of essays and a book of stories, *Apparition & Late Fictions. The Undertaking* won the American Book Award and was a finalist for the National Book Award. His work has appeared in *The Atlantic* and *Granta, The New Yorker* and *Esquire, Poetry* and *The Paris Review*, also *The Times* (of New York, Los Angelus, London and Ireland) and has been the subject of two documentary films, *Learning Gravity* by Cathal Black and PBS Frontline's *The Undertaking*. He lives in Milford, Michigan and Moveen, West Clare. Salmon published the Irish edition of *The Sin-Eater: A Breviary* (with photographs by Michael Lynch) in 2012.

CATHERINE PHIL MACCARTHY has published four collections of poetry and a novel. Her most recent collection, *The Invisible Threshold*, was published by Dedalus Press Dublin in 2012, and her first, *This Hour of the Tide* was published by Salmon Poetry in 1994. She is the recipient of The Lawrence O Shaughnessy Award in Poetry 2014 from the University of St Thomas, St Paul, Minnesota and a former editor of *Poetry Ireland Review*.

MARY MADEC is Director of Villanova University's Study Abroad Program in Ireland. She has a Ph.D in Linguistics from The University of Pennsylvania, U.S.A. She has published in Ireland, Britain and the USA, and in 2008 won The Hennessy XO Award for Emerging Poetry. Her first collection, *In Other Words*, was published by Salmon Poetry in 2010 and in 2012 she edited a book of poems *Jessica Casey & Other Works* (also from Salmon Poetry) from the award-winning community writing project Away With Words collective which she co-founded in 2008. Her second collection, Demeter Does Not Remember, was published by Salmon in 2014.

JOHN MACKENNA is the author of eighteen books – fiction, memoir and poetry. He has written several stage and radio plays. He teaches creative writing at NUI Maynooth and lives in Co. Carlow.

Born and raised in rural Arkansas, ED MADDEN is a professor of English at the University of South Carolina. He is the author of four books of poetry – including *Signals* (USC 2008), which won the 2007 South Carolina Poetry Book Prize; *Nest* (Salmon 2014); and most recently, *Ark*. His poems have appeared in *Poetry Ireland Review, Cyphers, Los Angeles Review, Crazyhorse*, and other journals, as well as in *Best New Poets 2007* and *The Book of Irish American Poetry*. He has published on Irish literature and culture in *Éire/Ireland, the Irish University Review*, and elsewhere. In 2015 he was named the poet laureate for the City of Columbia, South Carolina.

JOAN MCBREEN is from Sligo and now divides her time between Tuam and Renvyle, Connemara, Co. Galway. She has published four collections of poetry, the most recent being *Heather Island*. Her two anthologies are *The White Page-Twentieth Century Irish Women Poets* and The Watchful Heart–*A New Generation of Irish Poets–Poems and Essays*. In 2014 she produced a CD *The Mountain Ash in Connemara–Poems by Joan McBreen* with original music and traditional airs composed by Glen Austin and performed by the RTE Contempo String Quartet. In 2015 she brought out a broadside *The Mountain Ash*, a collaboration between the poet, visual graphic artist, Margaret Irwin West and printmaker Mary Plunkett. From Artisan House Publications, Letterfrack, Co. Galway it was launched at Clifden Arts Festival 2015. She is working on a new collection of poetry, *The Stone Jug.* Together with reading and lecture tours of the US, McBreen is closely associated with most of the major literary festivals in Ireland.

THOMAS MCCARTHY was born in Co. Waterford in 1954 and educated at UCC. His first book, *The First Convention,* was published by Dolmen Press in 1978, and was followed by eight further collections, including *The Sorrow Garden* and *The Last Geraldine Officer*, from Anvil Press Poetry. His *Pandemonium* will be published by Carcanet Press in 2016. He has won the Patrick Kavanagh Award, Alice Hunt Bartlett Prize and O'Shaughnessy Prize for Poetry, as well as the Annual Literary Award of the Ireland Funds. He is a member of Aosdana. He lives in Cork where he is a full-time writer.

JERI MCCORMICK, an American poet who lives in Madison, Wisconsin, has published two books with Salmon, most recently, *Marrowbone of Memory.* A recipient of poetry prizes and long-time teacher of creative writing, she has co-authored two books on writing and her work has appeared in many magazines and anthologies, including *The Book of Irish American Poetry from the 18th Century to the Present*

(Notre Dame Press); *Love Over 60: an Anthology of Women's Poems* (Mayapple Press); *75 Poems on Retirement* (U. of Iowa Press); *No, Achilles* (Waterwood Press); and *Salmon: A Journey in Poetry* (Salmon Poetry).

ROBERT MCDOWELL is the author of 15 books and 4 ebooks of poetry, creative non-fiction, fiction, translation and criticism from publishing houses such as Free Press/Simon & Schuster, Penguin Classics, University of Pittsburgh Press, Peterloo Poets (London) and New Directions, among others. His most recent book of poetry, *The World Next to This One*, appeared from Salmon Poetry. He is an international speaker, workshop leader focusing on gender enlightenment issues and women's rights and a former university professor. He co-founded Story Line Press, served as its editor and director for twenty-two years and selected and guided into print 300 volumes of poetry, books about poetry, fiction, non-fiction, drama and criticism.

HUGH MCFADDEN is a poet, critic, and literary editor. Born in Derry, he lives in Dublin. His poems have been published widely in literary magazines in Ireland and Britain. His collections are *City of Mirrors* (Beaver Row Press, 1985); *Pieces of Time* (Lapwing Press, 2004); *Selected Poems: Elegies and Epiphanies* (Lagan Press, 2005); and *Empire of Shadows* (Salmon Poetry, 2012). He is the executor of the literary estate of the writer John Jordan, and edited his collected poems and collected short stories, as well as *John Jordan: Selected Poems* (Dedalus Press, Dublin, 2008). He has reviewed for a variety of papers & journals, including *Hibernia*, *The Irish Independent*, *The Irish Press*, *The Irish Times*, *The Sunday Tribune* and *Books Ireland*.

AFRIC MCGLINCHEY is a Hennessy award-winning poet whose début poetry collection, *The lucky star of hidden things*, was published by Salmon Poetry in 2012, and later translated into Italian and published by L'Arcolaio. Nominated for the Pushcart and the Forward prizes, she has been a prize-winner in a number of competitions, and her work has been widely published and also translated into Irish, Spanish and Polish. Her second collection, *Ghost of the Fisher Cat*, also published by Salmon, was launched at the Cork International Poetry Festival in February 2016. She has been selected as one of Ireland's rising poets by *Poetry Ireland Review*. Afric lives in West Cork where she works as a freelance editor, reviewer and workshop facilitator. www.africmcglinchey.com

CECILIA MCGOVERN was born in County Mayo and has lived in Dublin all her adult life. Her poems have been published in *The Sunday Tribune* and in *Poetry Ireland Review* and her work features in anthologies of women's writing. She has twice been a prize-winner in Poetry Now, Dun Laoghaire International Poetry Festival. In 2007, she obtained an MA in Creative Writing from the UCD School of English, Drama and Film. Her collection, *Polishing The Evidence*, was published by Salmon in 1998.

STEPHANIE MCKENZIE has published three collections of poetry with Salmon: *Saviours in This Little Space for Now: Poems for Emily Carr and Vincent van Gogh* (2013); *Grace Must Wander* (2009); and, *Cutting My Mother's Hair* (2006), and a monograph, *Before the Country: Native Renaissance: Canadian Mythology*, with the University of Toronto Press (2007). She holds a Ph.D. in English literature from the University of Toronto. McKenzie was born and raised in British Columbia but lives on the opposite Canadian coast now in Corner Brook, Newfoundland. She teaches in the English Programme at Grenfell Campus, Memorial University, where she is an Associate Professor.

Born in Liverpool in 1959, JOHN MCKEOWN is an English/History honours graduate of John Moore's University and an alumnus of the city's seminal Dead Good Poets Society. He lived in Prague where he was a teacher and freelance journalist and part of the ex-pat literary scene in the 1990s, then moved to Ireland in 2000 becoming a columnist for the *Irish Examiner*, and arts feature writer for the *Irish Times*. He was theatre critic for the *Irish Daily Mail* from 2006 to 2008 and is currently reviewing theatre for the *Irish Independent* and raising his daughter Julia. He lives and writes in Monkstown, County Dublin. His poems have appeared in Orbis, The Eildon Tree, Dreamcatcher, Aerings, Earth Love, Envoi, Borderlines, The London Magazine, and Irish-based journals Cyphers, The Shop, and Southword. He has three collections of poetry in print: *Looking Toward Inis Oirr* (South Tipperary Arts, 2004), *Amour Improper* (Hub Editions, 2004), *Sea of Leaves* (Waterloo Press, 2009), with a fourth was published by Salmon Press in 2011.

ETHNA MCKIERNAN is author of three collections of poems, *Caravan*, *The One Who Swears You Can't Start Over*, and *Sky Thick with Fireflies*, the latter two published by Salmon Poetry. Widely published in anthologies and literary journals, she has twice received the Minnesota Arts Board Fellowship in literature. McKiernan earned her MFA from Warren Wilson College in 2004, and works as a homeless advocate for People Incorporated, St. Paul.

NICHOLAS MCLACHLAN was born in Dublin and now lives in west Kerry. His first collection of poetry *The Rain Barrel* was published by Salmon Poetry in 2015. He received the Patrick and Katherine Kavanagh Fellowship for 2016. His poems have appeared in a variety of journals, anthologies, broadsheets, artist catalogues and festschrifts; he was recently the featured poet in the winter 2015 edition of the *New Hibernia Review*. He also writes short fiction. His first story won the Martin Healy Short Story Award. Other stories have been published in *The Irish Times, Force 10* and the *Cork Literary Review*. For fifteen years he was director of Dingle Writing Courses, an organisation he founded with Abigail Joffe. He conducts workshops on poetry and the short story.

Born in Ottawa, Canada's glorious capital city, **rob mclennan** currently lives in Ottawa. The author of nearly thirty books of poetry, fiction and non-fiction, he won the John Newlove Poetry Award in 2010, the Council for the Arts in Ottawa Mid-Career Award in 2014, and was longlisted for the CBC Poetry Prize in 2012. His most recent titles include *notes and dispatches: essays* (Insomniac press, 2014), *The Uncertainty Principle: stories*, (Chaudiere Books, 2014) and the poetry collection *If suppose we are a fragment* (BuschekBooks, 2014). An editor and publisher, he runs above/ground press, Chaudiere Books, *The Garneau Review* (ottawater.com/garneaureview), *seventeen seconds: a journal of poetry and poetics* (ottawater.com/seventeenseconds), *Touch the Donkey* (touchthedonkey.blogspot.com) and the Ottawa poetry pdf annual *ottawater* (ottawater.com). He spent the 2007-8 academic year in Edmonton as writer-in-residence at the University of Alberta, and regularly posts reviews, essays, interviews and other notices at robmclennan.blogspot.com

TED MCNULTY was born in New York, of Irish parents from counties Cavan and Clare. A one-time news reporter and university lecturer, he began writing in his fifties. He spent the latter part of his life in Dublin with fellow poet Shiela O'Hagan. His two collections are *Rough Landings* (Salmon Poetry, 1992) and *On The Block* (Salmon Poetry, 1995). He won the Hennessey/Sunday Tribune Prize as New Irish Writer in 1991. He died in Dublin in September 1998 and is buried in Cavan.

DAVID MCLOGHLIN's publications are *Waiting for Saint Brendan and Other Poems* (Salmon Poetry, 2012) and *Sign Tongue*, which won the 2015 Goodmorning Menagerie Chapbook-in-Translation prize. His work has appeared in *Poetry Ireland Review, The Stinging Fly, Hayden's Ferry Review* and *Spoon River Poetry Review*. His second collection, *Santiago Sketches*, is forthcoming from Salmon. (www.davidmcloghlin.com)

DEVON MCNAMARA's poems, essays, interviews and reviews have appeared in *The Christian Science Monitor, The Hiram Poetry Review, The Laurel Review*, and *Wild Sweet Notes: Fifty Years of West Virginia Poetry*, among other publications. She has taught writing in schools, prisons, summer camps, and reform facilities in Appalachian and Midwestern states and originated the West Virginia Public Radio course "Women and Literature." Her poems have been performed in collaboration with dancers from The Dayton Ballet and The Dayton Contemporary Dance Company. She was the recipient of a YADDO fellowship. She is Professor of English, Irish Literature, and Creative Writing at West Virginia Wesleyan College. She is on the faculty of Wesleyan's MFA Creative Writing/Low Residency Program. Her collection *Driving* is published by Salmon in 2016.

MÁIGHRÉAD MEDBH was born in County Limerick. She has six published poetry collections and a prose work, *Savage Solitude: Reflections of a Reluctant Loner* (Dedalus, 2013). Since her first collection, *The Making of a Pagan*, in 1990, she has become widely known as a performance poet at home and abroad. Her work has appeared in many journals and anthologies, and has been translated into German and Galician. Máighréad has written three novels and a fantasy sequence for children. The novels are online as e-books. She has also written for radio, and publishes a blog on her website. The poem published here is from a verse fantasy, *Parvit of Agelast*, an extended ekphrasis, to be published by Arlen House in 2016. www.maighreadmedbh.ie

JOHN MENAGHAN, a prize-winning poet and playwright, has published four books with Salmon Poetry: *All the Money in the World* (1999), *She Alone* (2006), *What Vanishes* (2009) and *Here and Gone* (2014). A fifth book, *All the Things Your Mother Never Told You*, is forthcoming from Salmon. His short plays have to date received a total of six productions, and one of them – "A Rumor of Rain" – was published in *The Hollow & Other Plays* (2008). His poems have appeared in a wide variety of journals, including *The Hopkins Review, Ambit, Brilliant Corners, Poetry Ireland Review, Atlanta Review*, and *American Arts Quarterly*. He has been nominated for a Pushcart Prize each of the last four years. Menaghan teaches literature and creative writing at Loyola Marymount University in Los Angeles.

ÁINE MILLER is from Cork City. She was educated at University College Cork and at the University of Dublin, Trinity College, where she took the M.Phil (Creative Writing) in 1998. Her first collection *Goldfish in a Baby Bath* (Salmon 1994) won the Patrick Kavanagh Award. Her second collection was *Touchwood* (Salmon 2000). She has won many poetry prizes and her work features in several anthologies including *Dancing with Kitty Stobling* (The Lilliput Press 2004), *Volume* (Crawford Municipal Gallery, Cork 1997), *Out to Lunch* (Bank of Ireland Arts Centre, 2002), *Stream and Gliding Sun* (Wicklow County Council, 1998), *Jumping Off Shadows* (Cork University Press, 1995) and *The Field Day Anthology of Irish Writing V* (2002). She has given poetry workshops to teachers all over Ireland for the Pushkin Prizes and Co-Operation North. She lives in Dublin where she is currently teaching adults for the V.E.C.

KELLY MOFFETT is Associate Professor of English and Coordinator of Creative Writing at Northern Kentucky University. Her collection, *A Thousand Wings*, was published by Salmon Poetry and her earlier collections were published by Cinnamon Press and Dancing Girl Press. Her work has appeared in journals such as *Versal, Colorado Review, Cincinnati Review, Rattle*, and *Laurel Review*.

JUDITH MOK was born in Bergen in the Netherlands. She first published two novels with Meulenhoff and three books of poetry in Dutch. After moving to Dublin, her novel *Gael* was published by Telegram London and a book of poetry, *Gods of Babel,* by Salmon. She has written many pieces for radio and newspapers, which have appeared in the *Sunday Miscellany* books, edited by Marie Heaney. Her short stories have been shortlisted twice for the Francis Mc Manus award and her first novel *The Innocents at the Circus* for the Prix de l'Academie Francaise. Her work has appeared in anthologies and nationally and internationally in numerous literary Dutch, Irish, French, British and American magazines. Her translated erotic poems by Verlaine and Rimbaud appeared in the book *Obscene Poems by Verlaine and Rimbaud* with Vasalucci. Her next book *The State of Dark* will appear in 2017. Judith is a lyrical soprano and has travelled the world for years as a classical music soloist.

DOROTHY MOLLOY was born in Ballina, Co. Mayo in 1942. She studied languages at University College Dublin, after which she went to live in Madrid and Barcelona. During her time in Spain, she worked as a researcher, as a journalist and as an arts administrator. She also had considerable success as a painter, winning several prizes and exhibiting widely. After her return to Ireland in 1979, she continued painting but also began writing poetry. Her first collection, *Hare Soup*, was accepted by Faber and Faber, but Dorothy contracted cancer and died ten days before its publication. The papers she left after her death contained enough unpublished poems for two further books, which have been assembled by her husband, Andrew Carpenter. The first of these posthumous collections, *Gethsemane Day*, was published by Faber and Faber in 2007. The final collection of her work, *Long-distance Swimmer*, was published by Salmon in 2009.

PATRICIA MONAGHAN was Professor of Interdisciplinary Studies at De Paul University, Chicago. Her several Irish related works include, *Irish Spirit: Pagan, Celtic, Christian, Global*, an international collection of essays which she compiled and edited for Wolfhound Press in 2001. Her poetry collection *Dancing with Chaos* (Salmon, 2002) notably delights in the entanglements of the human and personal in poetry and science. Patricia was honored with a Pushcart Prize, the Paul Gruchow Nature Writing award, and the Friends of Literature award for poetry. She and her husband, Michael McDermott, founded The Black Earth Institute, a writers & artists think-tank whose current Fellows come from all over North America and Ireland, and she was vice-President of the Association for the Study of Women and Mythology as well as a lecturer for the Women's theological Institute. Patricia died on 11th November, 2012. Her poetry collection, *Sanctuary*, was published by Salmon in 2013.

NOEL MONAHAN has won numerous awards for his poetry and writing. His awards include The SeaCat National Poetry Award, organised by Poetry Ireland and The RTE P.J. O'Connor Award for drama. His poetry was prescribed text for Leaving Certificate English, 2011 & 2012. All six of his poetry collections to date have been published by Salmon: *Opposite Walls* (1991), *Snowfire* (1995), *Curse of The Birds* (2000), *The Funeral Game* (2004), *Curve Of The Moon* (2010), and *Where the Wind Sleeps: New & Selected Poems* (2014). A number of his poems have been translated into Italian, Russian, French and Romanian. "Celui Qui Porte Un Veau," a selection of French translations of Noel Monahan's work, was published by Alidades in 2014.

ALAN JUDE MOORE was born in Dublin in 1973. His work has been widely published in Ireland and abroad. He has published four collections with Salmon, most recently *Zinger* (2013). www.alanjudemoore.com

GEORGE MOORE's poetry collections include the forthcoming, *Saint Agnes Outside the Walls* (Future-Cycle 2016), *Children's Drawings of the Universe* (Salmon Poetry 2015), and *The Hermits of Dingle* (FutureCycle 2013). His poetry has appeared in *The Atlantic, North American Review, Poetry*, and recently in *Arc, Fiddlehead* and *Antigonish Review*, in Canada. After a career teaching at the University of Colorado, Boulder, he now lives with his wife on the south shore of Nova Scotia.

DANIEL THOMAS MORAN, former poet laureate of Suffolk County, NY is the author of seven collections of poetry, the most recent of which, *A Shed for Wood*, was published in 2014 by Salmon Poetry. He previous collection, *Looking for the Uncertain Past*, was published by Poetry Salzburg in Austria in 2006. His work has been published worldwide and two collections have been published in translation, one in Spanish and the other in Romanian. A collection in Albanian and a second collection in Romanian are expected in 2016. He is a retired Clinical Assistant Professor from Boston University's School of Dental Medicine, where he delivered the Commencement Address in 2011, and was recently appointed a Director on the Board of the New Hampshire Humanities Council. He and his wife Karen have lived on the Warner River in Webster, NH, USA since 2009.

PATRICK MORAN was born in Templetuohy, County Tipperary, where he still lives with his wife and family. He is a retired post-primary teacher. He has won the Gerard Manley Hopkins Poetry Prize; he has also been a winner at Listowel Writers' Week. In 1990, he was shortlisted for the Hennessy/Sunday Tribune Poetry Award. His poem, "Bulbs", won Poem for The Ploughing at the 2015 Ploughing Championships from a shortlist which included Patrick Kavanagh's "To the Man After the Harrow" & Seamus Heaney's "Digging" and "Follower". His work is featured in anthologies, including the inaugural *Forward Book of Poetry*, The *Stony Thursday Book*, as well as *The Best of Irish Poetry 2007* and *Best Irish Poetry 2010*. He is also repre-sented in *Windharp: Poems of Ireland Since 1916*. His work has been broadcast on the RTE radio programme, *Sunday Miscellany*. His collections of poetry are *The Stubble Fields* (Dedalus Press, 2001), *Green* (Salmon Poetry, 2008), and *Bearings* (Salmon, 2015).

A long-time Alaskan, JOHN MORGAN has published six books of poetry, most recently *Archives of the Air*, from Salmon. His work has appeared in *The New Yorker, Poetry, APR, The Paris Review, Prairie Schooner, The New Republic*, and many other journals.

TOM MORGAN was born in Belfast in 1943. His collections are *The Rat-Diviner* (Beaver Row Press, 1987); *Nan of the Falls Rd Curfew* (Beaver Row Press, 1990), which was nominated for the Irish Times/ Aer Lingus Awards; *In Queen Mary's Gardens* (Salmon, 1991); and *Ballintrillick in the Light of Ben Whiskin* (Lagan Press, 2006). He has collaborated with artists Patric Coogan, Brendan Ellis and Catherine McWilliams in joint poetry-painting exhibitions in Sligo, Belfast, Galway, Dublin and New York, and has worked with composer Frank Lyons for the Visconic Arts Festival in Belfast. He lives in Belfast and Ballintrillick, Co Sligo.

MARY MULLEN lived in County Galway for two decades. She now lives in Forest Grove, Oregon, USA. *Zephyr*, her first collection, was published by Salmon in 2010. Her second collection is in the oven.

PETE MULLINEAUX has published three collections: *Zen Traffic Lights* (Lapwing, 2005), *A Father's Day* (Salmon Poetry, 2008) and *Session* (Salmon, 2011). A fourth collection is forthcoming in 2016.

As a dramatist he has written several plays for the stage and Irish national radio (RTE). His 'Disconnect Song' was included on the Songs for Rossport CD released in 2015.

STEPHEN MURRAY was born in Ireland in 1974 and moved to London in 1975. His formative years were spent living with his mother and sister in Erin Pizzey's historic shelter for battered wives in West London. As a teenager, whilst living in a children's home, he was twice a runner-up in the W.H. Smith Young Writer of the Year Awards. In 2005 he was crowned Cúirt Grand Slam Champion. He has performed his work as guest reader at many of the world's most famous poetry venues. His first collection, *House of Bees*, was published by Salmon in 2011. It was followed in 2013 by *On Corkscrew Hill*, also with Salmon.

JOHN MURPHY's collection, *The Book of Water*, was published by Salmon Poetry in 2012. A second collection, *The Language Hospital*, is forthcoming from Salmon. He is the winner of the 2015 Stroke-stown International Poetry prize.

MARK A. MURPHY was born in 1969. He studied philosophy and poetry at university. He is currently looking for a publisher for his first stage play, *Lenny's Wake*, as well as working on several full length poetry manuscripts. His debut poetry collection, *Night-Watch Man and Muse*, was published by Salmon in 2013.

NUALA NÍ CHONCHÚIR was born in Dublin, she lives in East Galway. She has published four short story collections, the most recent *Mother America* appeared from New Island in 2012. Her third poetry collection *The Juno Charm* was published by Salmon Poetry in 2011 and Nuala's critically acclaimed second novel *The Closet of Savage Mementos* appeared April 2014, also from New Island; it was shortlisted for the Kerry Irish Novel of the Year Award 2015. Under the name Nuala O'Connor, Penguin USA, Penguin Canada and Sandstone (UK) published Nuala's third novel, *Miss Emily*, about the poet Emily Dickinson and her Irish maid, in summer 2015. Miss Emily was shortlisted for the Bord Gáis Energy Eason Book Club Novel of the Year 2015 www.nualanichonchuir.com

ÉILÍS NÍ DHUIBHNE was born in Dublin in 1954. Her novels are *The Bray House* (Dublin, Attic Press, 1990); *Singles* (Attic Press, 1992); *The Dancers Dancing* (Belfast, The Blackstaff Press, 1999/London Headline Review, 2001), which was shortlisted for the 2000 Orange Prize; and *Fox, Swallow, Scarecrow* (The Blackstaff Press, 2007); and *Dún an Airgid* (Dublin, Cois Life, 2008), which was awarded the Oireachtas Prize for Novel in Irish. She has published five story collections, including *Blood & Water* (The Attic Press, 1988); *Eating Women is Not Recommended* (The Attic Press); *The Inland Ice and other stories* (Blackstaff Press, 1997); *Pale Gold of Alaska And Other Stories* (Blackstaff Press 2000/London, Headline Review, 2001); and *The Shelter of Neighbours* (Blackstaff Press, 2012). Her novels in Irish are *Dúnmharú sa Daingean* (Dublin, Clo Cois Life, 2000), which was awarded the Oireachtas Prize for a Novel in Irish; and *Dordán* (Clo Cois Life, 2011). Her books for children include *The Uncommon Cormorant* (Dublin, Poolbeg Press, 1990). As Elizabeth O'Hara her books for children are *The Hiring Fair* (Dufour Editions, 1993) which was a Bisto Merit Award Winner in 1994; and *Hugo and the Sunshine Girl* (Learning Links, 2002). Editor of *Voices on the Wind*, a collection of Irish women's poetry, her play *Dún na mBan Trí Thine* was performed in the Peacock Theatre, Dublin, in 1994. She has also published a book of two plays, *Milseóg an tSamhraidh* (Baile Atha Cliath, Cois Life, 1997). A member of Aosdána, she lives in Wicklow.

JUDE NUTTER was born in North Yorkshire, England, and grew up near Hannover, in northern Germany. Her poems have appeared in numerous national and international journals and have received over 30 awards and grants. Her first book-length collection, *Pictures of the Afterlife* (Salmon Poetry, Ireland), winner of the Listowel Prize, was published in 2002. *The Curator of Silence* (University of Notre Dame Press), her second collection, won the Ernest Sandeen Prize from the University of Notre Dame and was awarded the 2007 Minnesota Book Award in poetry. A third collection, *I Wish I Had a Heart Like Yours, Walt Whitman* (University of Notre Dame Press), was awarded the 2010 Minnesota Book Award in poetry and voted Poetry Book of the Year by ForeWord Review in New York. In 2004-2005 she spent two months in Antarctica as part of the National Science Foundation's Writers and Artists Program.

JEAN O'BRIEN has had four collections published, all by Salmon, with the exception of *Dangerous Dresses* (Bradshaw Books 2005). Her last collection *Merman* was named after her poem that won the prestigious

Arvon International Poetry Award. She previously won the Fish International and has been shortlisted and placed many times in competitions, her most recent being the Forward Prize. She holds an M.Phil in Creative Writing from Trinity College, Dublin, and tutors in Creative Writing in places as diverse as prisons, schools, community groups, travellers' groups and the Irish Writers' Centre for the past 15 years. She was a Writer in Residence for Co. Laois. Her *New & Selected – Fish on a Bicycle* – appears from Salmon in Autumn 2016.

KERRIE O' BRIEN has been published in various Irish and UK literary journals. In February 2012 she was the first poet to read as part of the New Writers' Series in Shakespeare & Co., Paris. Her poem "Blossoms" was chosen as the winning entry in the Emerging Talent category of the 2011 iYeats Poetry Competition and her work was highly commended for the Over the Edge New Writer of The Year Competition 2011. She was the winner of the RTE Arena Flash Fiction Competition 2012 and Culture Ireland sponsored her to read in Los Angeles in June. She received an Arts Council Literature Bursary for her first official collection and two of her poems have appeared in *New Irish Writing* in *The Irish Independent*. She was one of the emerging writers chosen to read at the Cork Spring Poetry Festival 2013 as well as the Poetry Ireland Introductions Series 2013, Listowel Writers' Week 2013, Cuisle International Poetry Festival 2013 and The Bram Stoker Festival 2013. Her debut collection, *Illuminate*, was published by Salmon in 2016.

RUTH O'CALLAGHAN has seven collections of poetry, has been translated into six languages and is much anthologised. Invited to read throughout Asia, Europe, and the U.S.A., she was awarded a gold medal for poetry at the XXX WCP in Taiwan. The Arts Council of England sponsored her visit to Mongolia to collaborate with poets and this resulted in a book and a CD. A reviewer and interviewer her book, *Without Skin*, comprises interviews with 23 of the most eminent women poets throughout the world has been hailed as an 'important contribution to world literary history.' (Professor Brant, King's College London). An international competition adjudicator and editor she has also been a judge for the Koestler whose awards encourage prisoners to participate in the Arts. She hosts two poetry venues in London – the revenue from these events support three Cold Weather Shelters. She is also the poet for Strandlines, a community, multi-disciplinary project run under the auspices of Kings College, University of London. As mentor and workshop leader both in the U.K and abroad, she works with experienced poets to enable them to approach their poetry with a new perspective and with novice poets to achieve a first collection. Salmon published her collection, *An Unfinished Sufficiency*, in 2015.

MICHÉAL Ó CONGHAILE (born 1962) is an Irish-language writer who lives in Inverin, County Galway. He was born on the island of Inishtrevin in Conamara and was raised in an Irish-speaking community. In 1985 Ó Conghaile founded Irish-language publishing company Cló Iar-Chonnacht. It publishes books, music and spoken word albums. His own work includes short stories, a novel, drama, poetry and history. He has translated Martin McDonagh's plays *The Beauty Queen of Leenane* and *The Lonesome West*. Ó Conghaile's awards include The Butler Literary Award of the Irish American Cultural Institute (1997) and the 1997 Hennessy Literary Award for his short story "Athair".

CLAIRR O'CONNOR lives in Dublin. She has written two novels, four collections of poetry, numerous short stories. Her radio plays have been broadcast by BBC Radio 4, RTE Radio 1 and Radio Warsaw.

ULICK O'CONNOR is a biographer, poet and playwright. His books include biographies of Oliver St. John Gogarty, Brendan Behan and the much praised *Celtic Dawn*, a portrait of the Irish Literary Renaissance. He has written and acted in his own one man shows which have been staged in the Abbey Theatre Dublin and in Britain, Europe and the United States. His Irish Civil War play *Execution*, staged at the Abbey was described by the *Evening Standard* as "dynamite", and his one man play *Joyicity* by the *New York Times* as "supreme". His translations of Baudelaire's *Les Fleurs Du Mal* (1995) was hailed by a member of the Academie Francaise as "the best so far, a recreation of a new poem". His verse plays in the Noh form were published by Wolfhound Press in 1980. He has written four books of poetry (*Lifestyles*, Hamish Hamilton 1975, *All Things Counter*, Dedalus Press 1986, *One is Animate*, Beaver Row Press 1990, and *The Kiss, New and Selected Poems and Translations* published in 2008 by Salmon Poetry with an introduction by J.P. Donleavy. His *Diaries* were published in 2001 (John Murray London). *Word Magic*, a selection of his favourite poems (Currach Press 2005) was followed in 2007 by a second volume *Laugh At Gilded Butterflies* (The Liffey Press). *Words Alone* (2014), a CD box set, is a collection of his recitals, anecdotes and insights into the likes of James

Joyce, W.B. Yeats, Sean O'Casey, Patrick Kavanagh, Brendan Behan and others. Ulick O'Connor has been a champion boxer, held the Irish record in the pole vault and was a first class rugby player.

HUGH O'DONNELL has published three collections of poetry, the first of which, *Roman Pines at Berkeley,* was published by Salmon. The following collections, *Planting a Mouth* and *No Place Like it*, were published by Doghouse Books. His collection of reflections, *Songs for the Slow Lane*, was published by Columba Press in 2014.

MARY O'DONNELL's first three collections were published by Salmon, two of which were nominated for Irish Times Literature awards. Her most recent collection of poetry is *Those April Fevers* (Ark UK, 2015). She has also published four novels and two collections of short stories. Fiction and poetry have been widely published in journals and anthologies such as *Fiddlehead Review, The Seneca Review, The Prairie Schooner, Cyphers, Crannóg, Scéalta* (Telegram Books UK), *The London Magazine*, also in *The Mail on Sunday, the Financial Times* and *The Irish Times*. She was guest editor of the 2015 *Stony Thursday Book*. *Giving Shape to the Moment: the Art of Mary O'Donnell, Poet, Novelist, Short-story Writer,* (ed. María Elena Jaime de Pablos) will be published later this year. She is a member of Aosdana.

MARY O'DONOGHUE grew up in Co. Clare. She now lives in Tuscaloosa, Alabama and teaches at Babson College, Massachusetts. Her first collection of poems, *Tulle*, appeared from Salmon in 2001. She is also the author of *Among These Winters* (Dedalus Press, 2007) and *Before the House Burns* (Lilliput Press, 2010). Her short stories have appeared in *Dublin Review, Georgia Review, Stinging Fly, Guernica, Kenyon Review*, and *Granta*.

PEADAR O'DONOGHUE is the founder and co-editor of *Poetry Bus (PB)* literary magazine, an innovative journal of art, fiction and poetry, accompanied by a CD of the poets reading their work. He has had poems published in many publications including *Poetry Ireland Review, The SHOp, Abridged, Revival, The Irish Examiner*, and *The Burning Bush*. He has also published flash fiction in *Ink Sweat and Tears*. An accomplished photographer, Peadar's photos have been selected for a solo exhibition at The Signal Art Gallery, Bray and group exhibitions for Wicklow Arts Office and The Mermaid Arts Centre, Bray. They have been published in *The Stinging Fly* journal (and anthology) and *The SHOp*, including several front cover. They have also been published in *Magma* and *The Dubliner*. His debut collection, *Jewel*, was published in 2012, and his second collection, *The Death of Poetry*, is forthcoming from Salmon Poetry. He never sleeps, does his best work when he has nothing to lose, which fortunately/unfortunately is most of the time.

CIARAN O'DRISCOLL lives in Limerick, where for many years he was chairperson of Cuisle Limerick City International Poetry Festival. He is a member of Aosdána and has published six collections of poetry. He has also published a memoir, a novel and occasional criticism.

KATHLEEN O'DRISCOLL is from Galway. She is a renowned social activist, acclaimed writer and filmmaker. Her poetry collection is *Goodbye Joe* (Caledon Press). Her short story collection is *Ether* (Caledon Press). She has been published in the anthologies *Pillars of the House* (Wolfhound Press) and *The White Page* (Salmon). She has had short stories broadcast on RTE and she wrote and directed the short film *Berlin Blues*, which won first prize at the Cork Film Festival. She continues to work in film and to write poetry. Her collection, *Love Song,* was published in 2009 by the Marram Press (Galway).

EDWARD O'DWYER's poems are published in magazines and anthologies throughout the world, including *The Forward Book of Poetry* (2015). In 2010 he took part in Poetry Ireland's Introductions Series and edited the anthology, *Sextet* (Revival Press). He has been shortlisted for a Hennessy Award, the Desmond O'Grady Prize, the North West Words Prize, among others, and nominated for Pushcart, Forward and Best of the Web prizes. He represented Ireland in 2012 at Poesiefestival in Berlin for their European 'renshi' project. Salmon Poetry published his debut collection, *The Rain on Cruise's Street*, in summer 2014, a poem from which ("Poem for Someone of No Particular Importance") was committed to plaque by his national school to celebrate their fiftieth year anniversary in 2015. A follow-up collection is due in spring of 2017.

DESMOND O'GRADY was born in Limerick in 1935. He left Ireland during the 1950s to teach and write in Paris, Rome and America. While a Teaching Fellow at Harvard University, he took his M.A. and Ph.D. there in Celtic Languages and Literatures and Comparative Studies. He has also taught at the American University in Cairo and the University of Alexandria, Egypt. From the late 1950s to the mid-1970s, while teaching in Rome, he was a founder member of the European Community of Writers, European editor of The Transatlantic Review, and organised the Spoleto International Poetry Festival and played the Irish poet part in Federico Fellini's *La Dolce Vita*. His publications number nineteen collections of his own poems, including *The Road Taken: Poems 1956-1996* and *The Wandering Celt* and eleven collections of translated poetry, among them *Trawling Tradition 1954-1994, Selected Poems of C.P. Cavafy, The Song of Songs*, and in 2005, *Kurdish Poems of Love and Liberty*, in addition to prose memoirs of his literary acquaintances and friends. The publication of *On My Way* marks the 50th anniversary of his first published collection, *Chords and Orchestrations*. Desmond O'Grady was the 2004 recipient of the Patrick and Katherine Kavanagh Fellowship. He died on the 25th of August 2014 on the eve of his 79th birthday.

SHEILA O'HAGAN began writing in 1984 while studying at Birkbeck College, London University. In 1988 she won the Goldsmith Award for Poetry, and in 1990 returned to her native Dublin. In 1991 she won the Patrick Kavanagh Award and in 1992 the Hennessy/Sunday Tribune Award for New Irish Poet of the year. She has twice been awarded First Prize for Poetry at Listowel Writers' Week. She was the winner of the Strokestown International Prize for a single poem in 2000. Her short stories and poems have appeared in, among others, *The Adirondack Review, Atlanta Review, The Sunday Tribune, Syracuse Review* & *Working Papers in Irish Studies*. She has conducted literary workshops in Wormwood Scrubs Prison, UK, in Inter-City Schools, and for three terms in The Writers' Centre, Dublin. She was writer-in-residence for Kildare County Council from 1994 to 1996. In 1990 she conducted radio workshops for prisoners on 98FM. She was editor of the *Cork Literary Review* from 2005 to 2007. She also edited *Under Brigid's Cloak*, an anthology of Kildare writers, in 1994. Her three collections are *The Peacock's Eye* (1992), *The Troubled House* (1995) and *Along The Liffey: Poems and Short Stories* (2009), all published by Salmon.

NESSA O'MAHONY is a Dublin-born poet. She has published four books of poetry – *Bar Talk* (1999), *Trapping a Ghost* (2005), *In Sight of Home* (2009) and *Her Father's Daughter*, published by Salmon in September 2014. Novelist Joseph O'Connor described *In Sight of Home* as 'a moving, powerful and richly pleasurable read, audaciously imagined and achieved' whilst poet Tess Gallagher said of *Her Father's Daughter* that 'words are her witching sticks and she employs them with beautiful, engaging intent, the better to make present what has preceded and what approaches.' O'Mahony won the National Women's Poetry Competition in 1997 and was shortlisted for the Patrick Kavanagh Prize and Hennessy Literature Awards. She was awarded an Arts Council of Ireland literature bursary in 2004 and 2011. She lives in Rathfarnham, Dublin, with her husband, the videographer, Peter Salisbury.

MARY O'MALLEY was educated at University College, Galway. She spent many years living in Portugal before returning to Ireland in the late 1980s, and beginning a poetry career in 1990. Her work has been published in *Krino, Poetry Ireland Review, The Seneca Review, Atlanta Review, Da Braake Honde, Lictungen, The Lifelines Anthology* and the *Review of Irish American Studies*. She won the Hennessey Award in 1990 and the 13th annual Lawrence O'Shaughnessy Award in 2009. Her poetry collections are: *A Consideration of Silk* (Salmon, 1990), *Where the Rocks Float* (Salmon, 1993), *The Knife in the Wave* (Salmon, 1997), *Asylum Road* (Salmon, 2001), *The Boning Hall: New & Selected Poems* (Carcanet, 2002), *A Perfect V* (Carcanet, 2006) and *Valparaiso* (Carcanet, 2012). She is a member of Aosdána.

TOM O'MALLEY was the winner of the 1984 Patrick Kavanagh Award. His second poetry collection, *Journey Backward*, was published by Salmon in 1988. Much of O'Malley's poetry has derived from the landscape around Lough Mask, Co. Mayo.

PADRAIG O'MORAIN's poetry collection, *The Blue Guitar*, was published by Salmon Poetry in 2011. A collection of 20 poems, *You've Been Great*, won a Poetry Business Award in 2007 and was published by Smith Doorstop Books the following year. He writes a column for *The Irish Times* and is the author of several books on mindfulness. From Ladytown, Co Kildare, he lives in Dublin with his wife and two daughters. His website is www.padraigomorain.com.

IVY PAGE writes poetry, teaches at Plymouth State University, and plants flowers like the words in her poems. Her first poetry collection *Any Other Branch* was published by Salmon in 2013. It will be followed by *Elemental* in 2016 (also with Salmon). Her first textbook *Creative Writing Workshop* was published in 2014.

BARBARA PARKINSON is a poet, dramatist and scriptwriter from Donegal. Her poetry collection, *Any change for the Jugglers*, was published by Salmon in 1995. Her play *Legacy of a Saint* was performed by the Glencolumcille actors at the Edinburgh Fringe Festival in 1997. She is also a scriptwriter for Fair City on RTE television and has had two radio plays broadcast.

KARL PARKINSON is a writer and Creative writing teacher from Dublin. His work has appeared in the anthologies *New Planet Cabaret* (New Island) and *If ever you go: A map of Dublin in poetry and song* (Dedalus) and in the literary journals *The Stinging Fly, The Poetry Bus, Penduline* (as the featured Irish writer), *Can Can, The Pickled Body, The Bohemyth, The incubator, Revival Journal*, and *Wordlegs* amongst others. In 2013 Wurmpress published his debut poetry collection *Litany of the City and Other Poems*. He is an acclaimed performer of his work and has performed by invitation at festivals and venues in Ireland, the UK, America and Canada. His work has been broadcast on RTE 1's *Arena* Arts show many times. He is an editor with *Colony* arts webzine.

GWYN PARRY has been published widely in journals throughout the UK and Ireland. He was facilitator of the Dublin Writing Workshop for many years. He has three collections published — *Hurricane* (Poetry Wales), *Mynydd Parys* (Seren) and *Crossings* (Salmon). Gwyn performs his work regularly and is also vocalist/songwriter with his band Tacsi. Gwyn now lives in North Wales but retains strong connections with Ireland.

ANGELA PATTEN is author of three poetry collections, *In Praise of Usefulness*, Wind Ridge Books 2014, *Reliquaries*, Salmon Poetry, 2007, and *Still Listening*, Salmon Poetry 1999. A prose memoir, *High Tea at a Low Table: Stories from an Irish Childhood*, was published by Wind Ridge Books in 2013. A recipient of grants for poetry from the Vermont Arts Council and the Vermont Community Foundation, Patten's work has appeared in several anthologies, including *The White Page: An Bhileog Bhan: Twentieth Century Irish Women Poets*, and in many literary journals. Born and raised in Dublin, Ireland, she now lives in Burlington, Vermont, with her husband, poet Daniel Lusk, and teaches creative writing and literature at the University of Vermont.

PAUL PERRY was born in Dublin in 1972. His collections are *The Drowning of the Saints* (Salmon, 2003); *The Orchid Keeper* (Dedalus, 2006); *The Last Falcon and Small Ordinance* (Dedalus , 2010); and *Gunpowder Valentine: New and Selected Poems* (Dedalus, 2014). He has won the Hennessy New Irish Writer of the Year Award and The Listowel Prize for Poetry and has been a James Michener Fellow of Creative Writing at The University of Miami, and a Cambor Fellow of Poetry at The University of Houston. In 2002, he won the Listowel Prize for Poetry. He lives in Dublin.

Poet and visual artist ALLAN PETERSON earned degrees at the Rhode Island School of Design, Southern Illinois University, and the Claremont Graduate School. His books of poetry include *Anonymous Or* (2002); *All the Lavish in Common* (2005), winner of the Juniper Poetry Prize; *As Much As* (2011); and *Fragile Acts* (2012), which was nominated for a National Book Critics Circle Award. His chapbooks include *Assurances* (2011) and *Omnivore* (2009). Peterson's poetry is known for its wild logic and painterly effects. As a visual artist, Peterson has exhibited widely, including shows with the Minnesota Center for the Book Arts, the El Paso Museum of Art, and the New Orleans Academy of Art. His honors and awards include fellowships from the National Endowment for the Arts and the Florida Fine Arts Council, among others.

MARY PINARD teaches courses in literature and poetry in the Arts and Humanities Division at Babson College in Wellesley, MA. Her poems have appeared in a variety of literary journals, and she has written critical essays on poets, including Lorine Niedecker and Alice Oswald. *Portal*, her first collection of poems, was published by Salmon.

JO PITKIN is the author of *The Measure* (Finishing Line Press), *Cradle of the American Circus: Poems from Somers, New York* (The History Press), *Commonplace Invasions* (Salmon Poetry), and the forthcoming *Infidelity* (Salmon Poetry, 2017). She is also the editor of *Lost Orchard: Prose and Poetry from the Kirkland College Community* (State University of New York Press.) Her poems have appeared in such journals and anthologies as *The New York Review of Books, Little Star, Quarterly West, Salamander, Southern Humanities Review, Crab Orchard Review, Nimrod International Journal, A Slant of Light: Contemporary Women Writers of the Hudson Valley*, and *Raising Lilly Ledbetter: Women Poets Occupy the Workspace*. After working as an editor at Houghton Mifflin Company in Boston, Jo pursued a career as a freelance writer for educational publishers throughout the United States and is the author of more than forty books for kindergarten through high school students. She lives and works in New York's Hudson River Valley at the river's narrowest and deepest point.

FIONA PITT-KETHLEY is the author of more than twenty books of poetry or prose. She lives in Spain with her family and an adopted colony of feral cats. She is currently working on a prose book on the Sierra Minera, two poetry collections and a novel.

ANDREA POTOS is the author of *An Ink Like Early Twilight* and *We Lit the Lamps Ourselves*, both published by Salmon Poetry, *Yaya's Cloth* published by Iris Press, and three chapbooks. A new short-short entitled *Coffee in Greece* will be published by Anchor & Plume Press in 2016, and another full-length collection from Salmon Poetry in 2018. Andrea received two Outstanding Achievement Awards in Poetry from the Wisconsin Library Association, and the James Hearst Poetry Prize from the North American Review. She lives in Madison, Wisconsin.

DONNA L. POTTS is a professor of English and Chair of Creative Writing at Washington State University. Her book of poetry, *Waking Dreams*, was published by Salmon in 2012, and her books about poetry include *Howard Nemerov and Objective Idealism: The Influence of Owen Barfield* (1994), *Contemporary Irish Poetry and the Pastoral Tradition* (2011), and *This Landscape's Fierce Embrace: the Poetry of Francis Harvey* (2013). She is currently writing a book on campus rape for Rutgers University Press, as well as a book of ecocriticism, *The Wearing of the Deep Green: Contemporary Irish Writing and Ecology*, and a collection of poetry, *Turned Out*.

STEPHEN ROGER POWERS started writing poetry fifteen years ago to pass time in the middle of the night when he was too energized to sleep after coming off the stage in comedy clubs around the Midwest. He is the author of *The Follower's Tale* and *Hello, Stephen*, both published by Salmon Poetry. Other work has appeared in *32 Poems, Shenandoah, The Southern Poetry Anthology Volume V: Georgia*, and *Stone, River, Sky: An Anthology of Georgia Poems*. He hasn't done stand-up in a long time, but every once in a while he finds avenues for the performer he was born to be. He was an extra in *Joyful Noise* with Queen Latifah and Dolly Parton, and he can be seen if you know just where to look.

JAMES RAGAN is an internationally recognized poet, playwright, screenwriter, and essayist. Translated into 12 languages, he has authored 9 books of poetry including *In the Talking Hours, Womb-Weary, The Hunger Wall, Lusions, Selected Poetry, Too Long a Solitude, The World Shouldering I, To Sing Us Out of Silence*, and co-edited Yevgeny Yevtushenko's *Collected Poems*. He has read for 6 heads of state, the United Nations, and for audiences internationally. Honors include 3 Fulbright Professorships, 2 Honorary Doctorates, the Emerson Poetry Prize, 9 Pushcart Prize nominations, a Poetry Society of America Citation, and the Swan Foundation Humanitarian Award among others. Ragan's plays have been staged in the U.S, Russia, Greece, and China. For 25 years he was Director of the Professional Writing Program at the University of Southern California. He has a Ph.D. and is currently Distinguished Visiting Professor of Poetry at Charles University in Prague. He is the subject of the documentary "Flowers and Roots" (Arina Films, 2016).

STEVEN REESE is the author of *Enough Light to Steer By* (poems; Cleveland State University Press) and *American Dervish* (poems; Salmon Press), and translator of *Synergos: Selected Poems of Roberto Manzano* (Etruscan Press) and *Womanlands* (poems of Diana María Ivizate González, Verbum Press, Madrid). He teaches literature and creative writing at Youngstown State University in Ohio, and is a faculty member in the Northeast Ohio MFA program.

GER REIDY was born near Westport, Co. Mayo. He has won several national poetry competitions and has been the recipient of a number of bursaries and residencies sponsored by the Arts Council and Mayo County Council, most recently in 2011. His first collection, *Pictures from a Reservation*, was published by Dedalus Press. He has been published in many literary journals, both at home and abroad, and has read at numerous literary festivals, including the Cúirt Festival in Galway in 2010, where his second collection, *Drifting under the Moon*, was launched. His third collection, *Before Rain*, was launched in 2015.

BERTHA ROGERS is a poet, translator, and teaching artist whose poems have appeared in hundreds of literary journals and magazines and in the collections Sleeper, You Wake and Heart Turned Back (Salmon Poetry), and in several chapbooks. Her translation of the Anglo-Saxon epic Beowulf was published in 2001; and her translation of the Anglo-Saxon Riddle-Poems, Uncommon Creatures, *Singing Things*, is forthcoming.

MARK ROPER was born in England in 1951, and moved to Ireland in 1980. His poetry collections include *The Hen Ark* (Cornwall, Peterloo Poets 1990/Galway, Salmon Publishing, 1991), which won the 1992 Aldeburgh Prize for best first collection; *Catching The Light* (Belfast, Lagan Press, 1997); *The Home Fire* (Craigavad, Co. Down, Abbey Press 1998); *Whereabouts* (Peterloo/Abbey Press, 2005); *Even So: New & Selected Poems* (Dedalus Press, 2008); and *A Gather of Shadow* (The Dedalus Press, 2012). He was Editor of *Poetry Ireland Review* for 1999. He lives in Co. Kilkenny.

GABRIEL ROSENSTOCK born c.1949 in post-colonial Ireland. His latest title, *Antlered Stag of Dawn* (The Onslaught Press, Oxford, 2015) consists of haiku in Irish, English, Scots and Japanese. He blogs his heart out at http://roghaghabriel.blogspot.ie/

CAROL RUMENS's latest collection of poetry, *Animal People*, is published by Seren in 2016. A Fellow of the Royal Society of Literature, she has published short stories, a novel (*Plato Park*, Chatto, 1988), a trio of poetry lectures, *Self into Song* (Bloodaxe, 2007) and worked on occasional translations of Russian poetry with her late partner, Yuri Drobyshev. She teaches Creative Writing at Bangor University, Gwynedd, and contributes a popular weekly blog, "Poem of the Week," to *The Guardian* Books Online.

Born and raised in Portland, LEX RUNCIMAN has lived most of his life in Oregon's Willamette Valley. Holder of graduate degrees from the writing programs at the University of Montana and the University of Utah, he taught for eleven years at Oregon State University and is now Professor of English at Linfield College, where he has twice received the Edith Green Award for teaching excellence. His fifth book of poems, *One Hour That Morning & Other Poems* was published in 2014 by Salmon Poetry and won the Julie Olds and Thomas Hellie Award for Creative Achievement. A new and selected volume is due in 2017. Runciman is also the author of *Luck* (1981), *The Admirations* (1989) which won the Oregon Book Award, *Out of Town* (2004), and *Starting from Anywhere* (2009). His work has been featured on *Verse Daily* and in various anthologies including most recently *CutBank 40* and *Alive at the Center*, published by Ooligan Press. Individual poems have received the Kenneth O. Hanson Award and the Silcox Prize. He and Deborah Berry Runciman have been married more than forty years.

C. J. SAGE's poems appear nationally and internationally in publications such as *The Antioch Review, Black Warrior Review, Boston Review, Ploughshares, Shenandoah, The Threepenny Review*, et cetera. Her books are: *Let's Not Sleep* (poems), *AndWe The Creatures* (anthology), *Field Notes in Contemporary Literature* (textbook/anthology), *Odyssea* (poems), and *The San Simeon Zebras* (Salmon, 2010). After taking her M.F.A. in Creative Writing/Poetry, she taught poetry, writing, and literature for many years. A native of California, she now edits *The National Poetry Review* and Press. Sage resides in Rio Del Mar, California, a coastal town on the Monterey Bay.

AIMÉE SANDS is a MacDowell Colony Fellow and the author of *The Green-go Turn of Telling* (Salmon Poetry, 2012.) Poet Bruce Weigl praised this first collection of her poems, writing that "The elegant wedding of fresh intellect and lyric bravado distinguish Aimee Sands' new poems from much of our recent American poetry." Aimée's work has appeared in *FIELD, Poet Lore, Beloit Poetry Journal, Salamander, Measure* and other literary journals. She holds an MFA from Bennington College, and has co-directed the Brookline Poetry Series in Brookline, Massachusetts since 2001. She is also the producer/director of the independent documentary *What Makes Me White?* and has won numerous awards, including an Emmy, for her television and radio productions. She teaches at Bentley University, and leads the Word-Hoard Workshops, a series of poetry craft workshops and master classes.

JOHN W. SEXTON was born in 1958 and is the author of five previous poetry collections, the most recent of which was *The Offspring of the Moon* (Salmon Poetry, 2013). Under the ironic pseudonym of Sex W. Johnston he has recorded an album with legendary Stranglers frontman, Hugh Cornwell, entitled *Sons of Shiva*, which has been released on Track Records. He is a past nominee for The Hennessy Literary Award and his poem "The Green Owl" won the Listowel Poetry Prize 2007. In 2007 he was awarded a Patrick and Katherine Kavanagh Fellowship in Poetry.

TOM SEXTON's latest book is *A Ladder of Cranes*, University of Alaska Press, 2015. He's a former poet laureate of Alaska and lives in Anchorage with his wife, Sharyn, and their Irish Terrier, Murphy. Salmon Poetry published his *Autumn in the Alaska Range* in 2000.

LORNA SHAUGHNESSY was born in Belfast and lives in Co. Galway, Ireland. She has published three poetry collections with Salmon, *Torching the Brown River* and *Witness Trees* and *Anchored*, and her work was selected for the *Forward Book of Poetry*, 2009. Her poems have been published in *The Recorder, The North, La Jornada* (Mexico) and *Prometeo* (Colombia), as well as Irish journals such as *Poetry Ireland, The Shop* and *The Stinging Fly*. She is also a translator of Spanish and South American Poetry. Her most recent translation was of poetry by Galician writer Manuel Rivas, *The Disappearance of Snow* (Shearsman Press, 2012), which was shortlisted for the UK Poetry Society's 2013 Popescu Prize for translation. She lectures in Hispanic Studies and Creative Writing in NUI, Galway.

GLENN SHEA was born and has lived most of his life in Connecticut. He has worked in the library of a cancer clinic and in the French department of a foreign-language bookshop, washed dishes in the Scottish Highlands, gone to pilgrim's mass in Santiago, and eaten really good tex-mex in Chengdu. He has read his poems in local libraries and shops and venues in Dublin, Paris and Verona. He works with a group of illuminati in a huge used-book shop in Connecticut. *Find A Place That Could Pass For Home*, his first collection, was published by Salmon in 2010. His Book Notes may be read at www.bookbarnniantic.com.

NEIL SHEPARD's sixth book of poetry, *Hominid Up*, was published by Salmon Poetry in January 2015. His seventh book, *Vermont Exit Ramps II*, a full collection of poems and photographs, was published by Green Writers Press (Vermont) in October 2015. His five previous books include a chapbook and four full collections of poetry: *(T)ravel/Un(t)ravel* (Mid-List Press, 2011), *This Far from the Source* (Mid-List, 2006), *I'm Here Because I Lost My Way* (Mid-List, 1998), and *Scavenging the Country for a Heartbeat* (First Book Award, Mid-List Press, 1993). His poems appear online at *Poetry Daily, Verse Daily*, and *Poem-A-Day* (from the Academy of American Poets), as well as in several hundred literary magazines. He teaches in the low-residency MFA Writing Program at Wilkes University (PA) and is the Founding Editor of the literary magazine *Green Mountains Review*.

JANET SHEPPERSON was born in Edinburgh, educated at Aberdeen University and now lives in Belfast. She has worked as a trainee journalist, primary teacher, community service volunteer and creative writing facilitator. Her poetry has appeared in two pamphlets from Lapwing Press, in magazines and anthologies in Ireland, Scotland, Wales, England, Canada and the U.S, and in the Arts Council of Northern Ireland's Troubles Archive. Her two full collections are *The Aphrodite Stone* (Salmon Poetry, 1995) and *Eve Complains To God* (Lagan Press, 2004). She has published short stories widely, with two being shortlisted for Hennessy Awards. A novel, *Vinny's Wilderness*, is published by Liberties Press in 2016.

SCOT SIEGEL is the author of three full-length books and two chapbooks of poetry, most recently *The Constellation of Extinct Stars* (Salmon Poetry, 2016). He has been awarded fellowship-residencies with Playa at Summer Lake and has received awards and commendations from Nimrod International, Aesthetica (UK), the Oregon State Library, and the Oregon Poetry Association. Siegel lives in Oregon where he works as a town planner. More information is available at www.scotsiegel.com.

KEVIN SIMMONDS is a poet and musician originally from New Orleans. His books include *Bend to it* and *Mad for Meat* (Salmon, 2014 and 2011) and the anthology *Collective Brightness: LGBTIQ Poets on Faith, Religion & Spirituality*. He divides his time between San Francisco and Japan.

JAMES SIMMONS was born in Derry in 1933 and educated at Campbell College, Belfast, and at Leeds University. He taught in Northern Ireland and for three years in the sixties at Ahmadu Bellow University, Nigeria. On his return he lectured in drama and Anglo-Irish literature at the New University of Ulster, and founded and edited the literary periodical *The Honest Ulsterman*. His poetry collections include *Late But in Earnest*; *In the Wilderness and Other Poems* ; *Energy to Burn* ; *The Long Summer Still to Come* ; *West Strand Visions*; *Judy Garland and the Cold War*; *The Selected James Simmons*; *Constantly Singing*; *From the Irish*; *Poems, 1956-1986*; *Sex, Rectitude and Loneliness*; *Mainstream* (Salmon, 1995); and *The Company of Children* (Salmon, 1999). He published a critical study of *Sean O'Casey* (New York, St Martin's Press, 1983); and *Ten Irish Poets* (Cheadle (UK), Carcanet 1974). His recordings include *City and Eastern* (Belfast, NI Arts Council, 1971); *Love in the Post* (Coleraine, Poor Genius Records, 1975); *Resistance Cabaret*; and *The Rostrevor Sessions* (Rostrevor, Spring Records, 1987). In 1994 he moved to Falcarragh, in the Donegal Gaeltacht, where along with his wife Janice Fitzpatrick Simmons, Cathal Ó Searchaigh and others, he re-established the Poet's House/Teach na hÉigse. James died in 2001.

JANICE FITZPATRICK SIMMONS was born in Boston in 1954. Her collections are *Leaving America* (Lapwing, 1992); *Settler* (Salmon, 1995); *Starting at Purgatory* (Salmon, 1999); *The Bowspirit* (Lagan Press, 2005); and *Saint Michael in Peril of the Sea* (Salmon, 2009). A former Assistant Director of The Robert Frost Place in New Hampshire, with James Simmons she was co-founder and Director of The Poets' House/Teach na hÉigse, most latterly located in Falcarragh, County Donegal. She currently lives in Co. Cavan.

ROBIN SKELTON, a major figure in Britsh and Canadian literature, was born in Yorkshire in 1925 and lived in Victoria, British Columbia, until his death in 1997. He taught at the University of Victoria for almost 30 years; mentoring many of Canada's now-established writers. In the 1960s he became fascinated with Irish poetry and edited work by JM Synge and Jack B. Yeats, as well as *Six Irish Poets* (Oxford University Press, 1962) which includes work from John Montague, Richard Murphy and Austin Clarke. Robin Skelton published over 100 books in his remarkable career. *Samhain and other poems in Irish metres of the eighth to sixteenth centuries* was published by Salmon in 1994 and is part of a larger project in which Robin composed poetry in other Celtic verse forms. He died in August 1997.

KNUTE SKINNER lives in Clare. His collection *The Other Shoe* won the 2004-2005 Pavement Saw Chapbook Award. *Fifty Years: Poems 1957-2007*, from Salmon Poetry, contained new work collected along with work taken from 13 previous books. A memoir, *Help Me to a Getaway*, was published by Salmon in 2010. A limited edition of his poems, translated into Italian by Roberto Nassi, was published by Damocle Edizioni, Chioggia, Italy, in 2011. His latest book of poems, *Concerned Attentions*, was published by Salmon in 2013. www.knuteskinner.com

JO SLADE is a poet and painter. She is the author of six books of poetry including: a chapbook of poems *The Artist's Room* (Pighog Press, Brighton, England, 2010); *In Fields I Hear Them Sing* (Salmon, 1989); *The Vigilant One* (Salmon, 1994) which was nominated for the Irish Times/Aer Lingus Literature Prize; *Certain Octobers* (Editions Eireanna, Quimper France, 1997), a dual language English/French edition which received a publication bursary from the Centre du Livre, Paris, France; *City of Bridges* (Salmon, 2005); and, *The Painter's House* (Salmon, 2013), which was joint winner of the 2014 Michael Hartnett Poetry Award 2014.

LAURA LUNDGREN SMITH is a poet and playwright. Her plays *Sending Down the Sparrows, Digging Up the Boys*, and *The Shape of the Grave* are part of the Salmon Drama collection. In 2004, she was the recipient of an Arts Council of Ireland Commissions grant for playwriting. Laura lives in Fort Worth, Texas with her husband Ben and daughter India Samhaoir.

R. T. SMITH edits *Shenandoah* and serves as Writer-in-Residence at Washington and Lee University. He has previously been the visiting resident writer at VMI, Auburn, Converse College and Appalachian State University. His twenty books include fifteen collections of poetry, most recently *In the Night Orchard: New and Selected Poems*, and five books of short stories. He has received two Library of Virginia Book of the Year Awards and the Carole Weinstein Poetry Prize, as well as the Virginia Governor's Award for Achievement in the Arts. Smith lives on Timber Ridge in Rockbridge County, VA, with his wife, the novelist Sarah Kennedy, and their bluetick hound Gypsy, who does not write.

GERARD SMYTH has published eight collections of poetry, including, *A Song of Elsewhere* (Dedalus Press 2015), and *The Fullness of Time: New and Selected Poems* (Dedalus Press, 2010). He was the 2012 recipient of the O'Shaughnessy Poetry Award presented by the University of St Thomas in Minnesota.

JULIAN STANNARD is the author of several collections including *The Parrots of Villa Gruber Discover Lapis Lazuli* (Salmon. 2011) and *What were you thinking?* (CB Editions, 2016). He has published a study of Basil Bunting (Northcote, 2014) and co-edited *The Palm Beach Effect: Reflections on Michael Hofmann* (CB Editions, 2013). He is a Reader in English and Creative Writing at the University of Winchester (UK) and reviews for the *TLS*.

LAURA-GRAY STREET is the author of *Pigment and Fume* (Salmon Poetry, 2014) and co-editor with Ann Fisher-Wirth of *The Ecopoetry Anthology* (Trinity University Press, 2013). She has been the recipient of poetry prizes from *The Greensboro Review*, the Dana Awards, the Southern Women Writers Conference, *Isotope: A Journal of Literary Science and Nature Writing*, and *Terrain.org: A Journal of the Built and Natural Environments*. Her work has been published in *The Colorado Review, Poet Lore, Poetry Daily, Hawk & Handsaw, Many Mountains Moving, Gargoyle, ISLE, Shenandoah, Meridian, Blackbird, The Notre Dame Review*, and elsewhere; and supported by fellowships from the Virginia Commission for the Arts, the Virginia Center for the Creative Arts, and the Artist House at St. Mary's College in Maryland. Street holds an MA from the University of Virginia and an MFA from the Warren Wilson Program for Writers. She is an associate professor of English and directs the Creative Writing Program at Randolph College in Lynchburg, Virginia.

A. E. STRINGER is the author of three collections, most recently *Late Breaking*, Salmon, 2013. He taught writing and literature for 24 years at Marshall University in West Virginia, USA.

EITHNE STRONG was born in Limerick in 1925. Her poetry includes *Cirt Oibre* (Coiscéim, 1980); *Fuill agus Fallaí* (Coiscéim, 1983); *Aoife fe Ghlas* (Coiscéim, 1990); *An Sagart Pinc* (Coiscéim, 1990); *Poetry Quartos* (Dublin, Runa Press, 1943-45); *Songs of Living* (Runa Press, 1961); *Sarah in Passing* (Dublin, The Dolmen Press, 1974); *Flesh – The Greatest Sin* (Runa Press, 1980); *My Darling Neighbour* (Dublin, Beaver Row Press, 1985); *Let Live* (Salmon, 1990); *Spatial Nosing – New and Selected Poems* (Salmon, 1993); *Flesh – The Greatest Sin* (new edition, Dublin, The Attic Press, 1993); and *Nobel* (Coiscéim, 1998). Her short stories include the collection *Patterns* (Poolebeg, 1981). Her novels are *Degrees of Kindred* (Dublin, Tansey Books, 1979); and *The Love Riddle* (Dublin, The Attic Press, 1993). She won The Kilkenny Design Award for *Flesh – The Greatest Sin*, in 1991, and was a member of Aosdána. She is commemorated, with her husband the psychoanalyst and poet Rupert Strong, by the Eithne and Rubert Strong Award. She died in Dublin in 1999.

BREDA SULLIVAN was born and grew up in Athlone. Salmon published her three collections: *A Smell of Camphor, After the Ball* and *Sculpture in Black Ice*. *Streete and its People*, a local history in which she was involved, was awarded second prize in Listowel 2014. She is involved in the arts scene in Longford and Westmeath. Retired and widowed, she continues to enjoy life, family, friends, travel and theatre. Aqua aerobics and pilates help keep the arthritis under control. She lives in Streete, Co. Westmeath.

MATTHEW SWEENEY's most recent collection, *Inquisition Lane*, was published by Bloodaxe in October 2015. A previous collection, *Horse Music* (Bloodaxe, 2013), won the inaugural Piggott Poetry Prize.

TODD SWIFT is a British-Canadian poet and critic who lives in London with his Irish wife. He holds a PhD from UEA and taught for over ten years in academia, but is now focusing on running the indie press Eyewear Publishing, now in its 5th year. His nine trade poetry collections include *Seaway: New and Selected Poems* from Salmon. His poems have appeared in *Poetry* (Chicago); *The Guardian* (Saturday Review section); *Poetry London*; *Poetry Review*; *The Moth*, and many others. He turns 50 on April 8th, 2016.

ADAM TAVEL won the Permafrost Book Prize for *Plash & Levitation* (University of Alaska Press, 2015) and is also the author of the chapbook *Red Flag Up* (Kattywompus, 2013). Winner of the 2010 Robert Frost Award from the Robert Frost Foundation, Tavel's poems and reviews have appeared in *The Georgia Review, Beloit Poetry Journal, The Gettysburg Review, Indiana Review, Crab Orchard Review, Sycamore Review, West Branch*, and *The Journal*, among many others. Currently he is a professor of English at Wor-Wic Community College on Maryland's Eastern Shore and the reviews editor for *Plume*. His collection *The Fawn Abyss* appears from Salmon in 2016. You can find him online at http://adamtavel.com/.

ILSA THIELAN began writing when she was 7 years old and has written ever since. After studying literature and arts in Germany she made her home in Ireland. She joined the North Clare Writers' Workshop and her poems and stories appeared in their annual anthology. Her work was published in *Stet*, in "Women's Work", *The Burren Meitheal*, *Revival*, with the *North Clare Three Legged Stool Poets* as well as in Dogs Singing: A Tribute Anthology (Salmon). Her first collection of poetry *Night Horses* was published by Salmon in 2012. Her poetry and stories are borne out of her experience and observations in life, the natural environment of her Burren home, her travels, her relationship with people she meets, her love for animals and time she has spent in the Sahara, in the deserts of Arizona and New Mexico and in the wilderness of Northern Canada. Ilsa is also a nature photographer and weaver of tapestry.

RICHARD TILLINGHAST has published twelve books of poetry and four of creative nonfiction. Salmon published a chapbook of his, *A Quiet Pint in Kinvara*, in 1991, as well as *Today in the Café Trieste* in 1997. Richard lived in Kinvara, Co Galway, in 1990-91 and in Tipperary from 2005-2011. His *Selected Poems* came out from Dedalus in 2010, and in 2010 he was awarded a Guggenheim Foundation Fellowship in poetry in addition to a National Endowment for the Arts Fellowship in translation for *Dirty August*, his versions of poems by the Turkish poet, Edip Cansever, written in collaboration with his daughter, Julia Clare Tillinghast. His 2012 travel book, *An Armchair Traveller's History of Istanbul*, published by Haus in London, was nominated for the Royal Society of Literature's Ondaatje Prize. He currently divides his time between Sewanee, Tennessee, and the Big Island of Hawaii.

OLAF TYARANSEN was born in Dublin in 1971, but spent his formative years in Galway. His poetry collection *The Consequences of Slaughtering Butterflies* was published by Salmon in 1992. His bestselling memoir *The Story of O* was released in 2000, and he is the author of four other books. His journalism has appeared in numerous international publications including *Hot Press, Rolling Stone, Mojo, Penthouse* and *Time Out*. In 2013 he was named 'Journalist of the Year' at the Irish Magazine Awards. His twitter handle is @OlafTyaransen and his website is olaftyaransen.net.

JOHN UNRAU was born in Saskatoon and schooled in Alberta and Saskatchewan, Canada. He holds a B.A. from the University of Alberta and a doctorate from Oxford, which he attended as a Rhodes Scholar. From 1969-2006, he was a Professor of English at York University, where he is now a Senior Scholar. John's published works include two illustrated books on architecture: *Looking at Architecture with Ruskin* (Thames and Hudson, London, 1978), and *Ruskin and St. Mark's* (Thames and Hudson, London, 1984). *The Balancings of the Clouds: an illustrated biography and study of the watercolours of Mennonite artist Mary Klassen* (Windflower Publications, Winnipeg), was published in 1991. In his mid-40s, John began writing poetry and published his first collection of poems, *Iced Water*, with Salmon in 2000. He is a member of the League of Canadian Poets.

JEAN VALENTINE was the New York State Poet Laureate from 2008–2010. Her poetry collection, *Door in the Mountain: New and Collected Poems, 1965–2003*, was awarded the 2004 National Book Award for Poetry. Her most recent book, *Shirt In Heaven*, was published in 2015 by Copper Canyon Press. Before that, *Break the Glass* (Copper Canyon Press, 2010) was a finalist for the 2011 Pulitzer Prize for Poetry. Her first book, *Dream Barker*, won the Yale Series of Younger Poets competition in 1965. She has published poems widely in literary journals and magazines, including *The New Yorker*, and *Harper's Magazine*, and *The American Poetry Review*. Valentine was one of five poets including Charles Wright, Russell Edson, James Tate and Louise Gluck, whose work Lee Upton considered critically in The Muse of Abandonment: Origin, Identity, Mastery in Five American Poets (Bucknell University Press, 1998). She has held residencies from Yaddo, the MacDowell Colony, Ucross, and the Lannan foundation, among others. Salmon published her collection *The Under Voice* in 1995.

PETER VAN DE KAMP (1956) has published 18 books, including two collections of poetry with Salmon. His 19th, *Whodunnit in Dubliners*, is five years past its deadline due to his sole creation of real note (and that only through collaboration with his wife Caroline)—his daughters Saskia and Laura. With them, and with his dog Poppy, he lives in Tralee, where he teaches Creative Writing and muses about mortality (his own) while listening to classical music (not his own).

EAMONN WALL's recent books include *Junction City: New and Selected Poems* (Salmon 2015) and *Writing the Irish West: Ecologies and Traditions* (Notre Dame 2011). He edited two volumes of James Liddy's prose for Arlen House/Syracuse: *On American Literature and Diasporas* and *On Irish Literature and Identities*, both published in 2013. A native of Co. Wexford, Eamonn Wall lives in Missouri where he is employed by the University of Missouri-St. Louis.

MICHÈLE VASSAL is from Barcelonnette, a small town in the French Alps. he moved to Ireland, aged seventeen, to learn English and stayed there for thirty years. Her collection, *Sandgames* (Salmon 2000), received first prize at Listowel Writers' Week and some of her poems were short-listed for the Hennessy/Sunday Tribune Awards. She has been widely published internationally, in both French and English. Her second collection, *A Taste for Hemlock*, was published by Salmon in 2011. Michèle currently lives and writes in France.

DRUCILLA WALL's book of poetry is *The Geese at the Gates*, published by Salmon Poetry in 2011. Her co-edited collection, *Thinking Continental: Essays and Poems of Place*, is forthcoming in 2017 from University of Nebraska Press. Poems and essays appear in various literary and scholarly journals, and are anthologized in such books as *Red Lamp Black Piano: The Caca Milis Cabaret Anthology*, *The People Who Stayed: Southeastern Indian Writing After Removal*; and *True West: Authenticity and the American West*. She teaches American and Native American Literatures, and Poetry Writing at the University of Missouri-St. Louis. Her Ph.D. in English is from the University of Nebraska.

EMILY WALL is a poet and an Associate Professor of English at the University of Alaska Southeast in Juneau, Alaska. She has been published in a wide variety of literary journals in the US and Canada. In 2013 a poem of hers was chosen in a statewide contest to be placed in Totem Bight State Park in Ketchikan, Alaska. She has also had a poem chosen for the Best Indi Lit of New England 2013-2015. Her second book of poems, *Liveaboard*, was published in 2012; her first book, *Freshly Rooted*, came out in 2007. Both books were published by Salmon Poetry. Emily lives with her family on a beach in Douglas, Alaska.

WILLIAM WALL is the author of three collections of poetry, the most recent, *Ghost Estate*, from Salmon; four novels and two collections of fiction. His most recent book is *Hearing Voice/Seeing Things* (Doire Press, 2016). He translates from Italian.

GORDON WALMSLEY was born in New Orleans, in 1949. He was educated at Princeton University and Tulane Law School. He has lived in Denmark for a number of years where he is a member of Danish Writers of Poetry and Fiction and editor and founder of The Copenhagen Review (www.copenhagenreview.com). He has published six poetry collections, most recently *Echoes of a River, Poems of New Orleans and Beyond* (Salmon, 2011). He has translated other poets' work from Danish, Norwegian, Swedish, German and French, including that of Tomas Tranströmer, Inger Christensen, and Katarina Frostenson, among others. In 2004, he compiled and edited *Fire and Ice – Nine Poets From Scandinavia and the North* (Salmon). www.gordonwalmsleywriter.com

JOHN WALSH was born in Derry and now lives in Connemara. His first poetry collection *Johnny tell Them* was published by Guildhall Press (Derry) in October 2006. In 2007 he received a Publication Award from Galway County Council to publish his second collection *Love's Enterprise Zone* (Doire Press, Connemara). Salmon Poetry published his third and latest collection *Chopping Wood with T.S. Eliot* in 2010. His poems and fiction have been published in Ireland, the UK, Austria and the USA. He has read and performed his poems and fiction at events in Ireland, the UK, Germany, Sweden and the USA. A Publication Award from Galway County Council led to his debut short story collection *Border Lines* in April 2012. He is now co-director and commissioning editor at Doire Press, which he co-founded with his American partner, Lisa Frank. More at www.johnwalshpoet.com or www.doirepress.com

YUN WANG grew up in rural southwest China. She is the author of the poetry books *The Book of Totality* (Salmon Poetry, 2015), and *The Book of Jade* (Winner of the 15th Nicholas Roerich Poetry Prize, Story Line Press, 2002), and a poetry chapbook, *The Carp* (Bull Thistle Press, 1994). Wang's poems have been published in numerous literary journals, including *The Kenyon Review, Cimarron Review,*

Salamander Magazine, Green Mountains Review, and *International Quarterly*. Wang works as a cosmologist at the California Institute of Technology.

IAN WATSON was born in Greenisland, Co. Antrim and now lives in Bremen, North-West Germany. Since the seventies, he has been writing and publishing poems, articles and reviews in anthologies and magazines in Ireland, Britain, Germany, Austria and the United States. *Kurzpass-Spiel*, a German-language collection of poems and micro-prose on football, was published in 2011 by Kellner, and *Riverbank City — A Bremen Canvas*, a volume of English-language poems about his second home, came out with Blaupause Books in 2013. Some of his poems have been translated into German by Jürgen Dierking for both print and radio performance. He has, in turn, translated Heinrich Böll, Arne Rautenberg and Hans Meier into English and poems by Harry Clifton into German. His non-fiction includes *Song and Democratic Culture* (Croom Helm/St. Martin's Press, New York 1983), the bilingual *Alive and Kicking: Fußball zwischen England und Deutschland* (Argument Verlag, Berlin 1994; co-edited with Diethelm Knauf and Jürgen Dragowski) and two teaching texts: *War and Peace: Voices from the Battlefield* (Klett, Stuttgart 1995); and *Riverbank City: Teaching Material — Ideas, exercises and projects for poetry and local history in English language learning* (Blaupause Books, Hamburg 2014). He has worked freelance for radio and in 1999, with Marcus Behrens, he made the documentary *Cool to be Celtic* (62 Min.) on Irish popular music for the Franco-German television channel arte. In 1994 he founded newleaf Press and *newleaf* magazine, which he edited with Simon Makhali and Julia Boll. He is vice-chairman of the Virtual Literature House in Bremen.

MIKE WATTS was one of the original members of the Galway Writers' Workshop. A qualified mental health practitioner and family therapist, he produced his PhD thesis under the supervision of Prof. Agnes Higgins of School of Nursing and Midwifery, TCD. He has now retired from the position of national co-ordinator of GROW in Ireland, a position he held for seventeen years.

ESTHA WEINER's newest poetry collection is *In the Weather of the World* (Salmon Poetry, 2013). She is author of *The Mistress Manuscript* (Book Works, 2009) and *Transfiguration Begins At Home* (Tiger Bark Press, 2009); and co-editor/contributor to *Blues for Bill: A Tribute to William Matthews* (Akron Poetry Series, University of Akron Press, 2005.) Her poems have appeared in numerous anthologies and magazines, including *The New Republic* and *Barrow Street*. Nominated for a 2008 Pushcart Prize, she was a 2005 winner of a Paterson Poetry Prize, and a 2008 Visiting Scholar at The Shakespeare Institute, Stratford, England. Estha is founding director of Sarah Lawrence College NY Alumnae Writers Nights, Marymount Writers Nights, and a Speaker on Shakespeare for The New York Council For The Humanities. She is a Professor in the English Dept. at City College of NY, and serves on has served on the Poetry/Writing faculties of The Frost Place, The Hudson Valley Writers Center, Stonecoast Writers Conference, Poets and Writers, Poets House, and The Writers Voice. She also serves on the Advisory Board of Slapering Hol Press, Hudson Valley Writers Center. In her previous life, Estha was an actor and worked for BBC Radio.

GARY J. WHITEHEAD's first collection of poems, *The Velocity of Dust*, was published by Salmon in 2004. His most recent book, *A Glossary of Chickens*, was published by Princeton University Press in 2013. His writing awards include, among others, a New York Foundation for the Arts Fellowship, the Pearl Hogrefe Fellowship at Iowa State University, and the PEN Northwest Margery Davis Boyden Wilderness Writing Residency Award. He has also conducted residencies at Blue Mountain Center, Mesa Refuge, Marble House Project, and the Heinrich Boll Cottage. His poems have appeared widely in the U.S. and abroad, most notably in *The New Yorker*, and he has been a featured poet at the Geraldine R. Dodge Poetry Festival and the Princeton Poetry Festival. He teaches English and creative writing at Tenafly High School in New Jersey and lives in New York's Hudson Valley.

SABINE WICHERT was born in Graudenz, West Prussia (now Grudziadz, Poland) and grew up and was educated in West Germany. She spent more than 35 years in the School of History at Queen's University Belfast where she was a senior lecturer and scholar of 20th-century British foreign policy and had a special interest in the visual arts. She was a member of the Arts Council of Northern Ireland from the mid-1980s to 1994 and a member of the Board of Annaghmakerrig appointed by both Arts Councils in Ireland. She was the author of two collections of poetry, both from Salmon, *Tin Drum Country* (1994) and *Sharing Darwin* (1999), and the academic text *Northern Ireland since 1945* (1991). She also edited *From the United*

Irishmen to Twentieth-century Unionism: Essays in Honour of A.T. Q. Stewart (2004), a Festschrift for the Irish historian Anthony Terence Quincey Stewart, who died in 2010. After visiting Belfast as a tourist, she fell in love with the city and settled there. Ms Wichert died on 8 September, 2014.

TERENCE WINCH's most recent books are *This Way Out* (Hanging Loose Press, 2014), *Lit from Below* (Salmon Poetry, 2013), and *Falling Out of Bed in a Room with No Floor* (Hanging Loose, 2011). His work has appeared in more than 40 anthologies and in such journals as *The Paris Review, The New Republic,* and *American Poetry Review.* He is a regular blogger for the Best American Poetry site. Winch has received various awards and honors, including an American Book Award, an NEA grant, and a Gertrude Stein Award for Innovative Writing. Born in the Bronx to immigrant parents, he has lived in the Washington, DC, area for many years. Also a songwriter and button-accordionist, he has played traditional Irish music all his life. See www.terencewinch.com.

SANDRA ANN WINTERS is an American poet, and frequent visitor to Ireland. She owns a home in Millstreet, County Cork, where she regularly spends time reading and writing. From 1986 to her retirement in 2010, she served as a lecturer of English and Irish literature at Guilford College in Greensboro, NC. She is author of the collection *The Place Where I Left You* (Salmon, 2014) and a chapbook, *Calving Under the Moon* (Finishing Line Press, 2013). Her poems have won a variety of awards. "Death of Alaska" won the 2011 Gregory O'Donoghue International Poetry Competition. The editors of the North Carolina Literary Review nominated "Water Signs" for the 2011 Pushcart Prize. "Talking to Okra" won first place in the 2012 Carteret Writers 21st Annual Writing Contest. Her poems have been finalists in the 2012 Randall Jarrell Poetry Competition, the 2011 Press 53 Open Poetry Award, the 2010 Rita Dove Poetry Award, and the 2010 Inkwell Journal poetry contest. She received an Honorable Mention in the 2012 Deane Ritch Lomax Poetry Competition. Sandra Ann Winters' poems have appeared in the *Cork Literary Review, Southword, the North Carolina Literary Review,* and others.

JOSEPH P. WOOD is the author of four books and five chapbooks of poetry, which include *Fold of the Map* (Salmon), *You,* and *Broken Cage.*

ADAM WYETH is a poet, playwright and essayist. Born in Sussex in 1978, he has lived in Ireland since 2000. His poetry has won and been commended in many international competitions, including The Bridport Poetry Prize, The Arvon Poetry Prize and The Ballymaloe Poetry Prize. His work appears in several anthologies including The Forward Prize Anthology (2012 Faber), The Best of Irish Poetry (Southword 2010) and The Arvon 25th Anniversary Anthology. Wyeth's critically acclaimed collection, Silent Music was Highly Commended by the Forward Poetry Prize. Wyeth's second book The Hidden World of Poetry: Unravelling Celtic Mythology in Contemporary Irish Poetry was published by Salmon in 2013. The book contains poems from Ireland's leading poets followed by sharp essays that unpack each poem and explore its Celtic mythological references. Wyeth's debut play Hang Up, produced by Broken Crow, has been staged at many festivals, including the Electric Picnic and the Galway Theatre Festival. It was adapted into a film in 2014 and premiered at Cork Film festival. His third play, Lifedeath was showcased at the Triskel Arts Centre mini-festival of new work in December 2013 and was named by the Irish Examiner as the play of the festival. 'An Evening of Adam Wyeth' took place in Berlin, 2015, showcasing three of Wyeth's plays. His second collection is forthcoming with Salmon 2016. Wyeth runs ongoing, international poetry and creative writing courses at adamwyeth.com and Fish publishing offering one to one tutorials and editing services.

The only girl in a large Mormon family, ANN ZELL was born and raised on a potato farm in Idaho. After years of schooling, mothering, casual jobs and radical politics at street level, she began writing seriously in her early fifties during a stint as a medical secretary in the Royal Victoria Hospital, Belfast. She lived in New York and London before settling in West Belfast in 1980. Her work has been published in many publications, including, *Virago New Poets, The Atlanta Review, Word of Mouth* (Blackstaff), and *Poetry Ireland Review.* Her first full collection, *Weathering,* was published by Salmon in 1998.

Bibliography of Salmon Poetry Titles 1985-2016

1985	*Gonella*	Eva Bourke

1986	*We Came Out Again to See the Stars*	Michael Egan
	Goddess on the Mervue Bus	Rita Ann Higgins
	Monkeys in the Superstructure	Peadar O'Donnell

1987	*Gog & Magog*	Ciaran O'Driscoll

1988	*Song at the Edge of the World*	Fred Johnston
	Daughter	Jessie Lendennie
	The Night Parrot	Clarinda Harriss-Lott
	Learning to Spell Zucchini	Knute Skinner

1989	*The Hour of Pan/ama*	Nuala Archer
	Litany of the Pig	Eva Bourke
	The Goose Herd	Roz Cowman
	Striking Water	Paul Genega
	Buck Mountain Poems	Anne Kennedy
	The Salmon Guide to Poetry Publishing in Ireland	Jessie Lendennie
	When You Need Time	Clairr O'Connor
	In Fields I Hear Them Sing	Jo Slade

1990	*Walking the Marches*	Sam Burnside
	Oar	Moya Cannon
	The Ordinary House of Love	Theo Dorgan
	The Betrayal	Michael D. Higgins
	Goddess & Witch	Rita Ann Higgins
	Roman Pines at Berkeley	Hugh O'Donnell
	Reading the Sunflowers in September	Mary O'Donnell
	A Consideration of Silk	Mary O'Malley
	Ireland's Musical Instrument Makers	Joyce Pye
	The Hen Ark	Mark Roper
	Let Live	Eithne Strong

1991	*Strange Bedfellows*	Pat Boran
	Abigail Brown	Heather Brett
	Moving into the Space Cleared by Our Mothers	Mary Dorcey
	Up She Flew	Michael Gorman
	Now is a Moveable Feast	Anne Le Marguand Hartigan
	Face Licker Come Home	Rita Ann Higgins
	Etchings	John Kavanagh
	The Salmon Guide to Creative Writing in Ireland	Jessie Lendennie & Patrick Hickson
	Opposite Walls	Noel Monahan
	In Queen Mary's Gardens	Tom Morgan
	Tipperary	Desmond O'Grady

	The Bears & Other Poems	Knute Skinner
	A Quiet Pint in Kinvara	Richard Tillinghast
1992	*The Hour of Pan / Amá*	Nuala Archer
	Oasis in a Sea of Dust	Vicki Crowley
	Columbus Rides Again	Gerard Donovan
	Philomena's Revenge	Rita Ann Higgins
	Rough Landings	Ted McNulty
	The World Faces Johnny Tripod	John Millett
	The Peacock's Eye	Sheila O'Hagan
	There is Something	Kate Thompson
	Consequences of Slaughtering Butterflies	Olaf Tyaransen
1993	*Silence and the Blue Night*	Angela Greene
	Immortal Sins	Anne Le Marquand Hartigan
	A Smell of Camphor	Breda Sullivan
1994	*Above the Waves Calligraphy*	Patricia Burke Brogan
	Eclipsed	Patricia Burke Brogan
	The Back Road to Arcadia	Michael Heffernan
	This Hour of the Tide	Catherine Phil MacCarthy
	Goldfish in a Baby Bowl	Áine Miller
	Echoes of Memory	John O'Donohue
	What Trudy Knows & Other Poems	Knute Skinner
	Samhain and Other Poems	Robin Skelton
	The Vigilant One	Jo Slade
	Dyckmann--200th Street	Eamonn Wall
1995	*Kings & Bicycles*	Gerard Donovan
	The River that Carries Me	Mary Dorcey
	Rosa Mundi	Theo Dorgan
	A Walled Garden in Moylough	Joan McBreen
	On the Block	Ted McNulty
	Snowfire	Noel Monahan
	The Troubled House	Sheila O'Hagan
	Any Change for the Jugglers	Barbara Parkinson
	The Aphrodite Stone	Janet Shepperson
	Settler	Janice Fitzpatrick Simmons
	Mainstream	James Simmons
	The Under Voice	Jean Valentine
	Tin Drum Country	Sabine Wichert
1996	*The Old in Rapallo*	Rory Brennan
	The New Pornography	Patrick Chapman
	Clearing the Space: A Why of Writing	Anne Le Marquand Hartigan
	Higher Purchase	Rita Ann Higgins
	Selected Poems 1950-1995	Adrienne Rich
	The Cold Irish Earth	Knute Skinner
1997	*Verbum et Verbum*	Mícheál Fanning
	Midcentury	Ben Howard
	Death and the River	Ron Houchin

	True North	Fred Johnston
	The Shadow Keeper	Jean O'Brien
	The Knife in the Wave	Mary O'Malley
	Certain Octobers	Jo Slade
	Today in the Café Trieste	Richard Tillinghast
	Iron Mountain Road	Eamonn Wall
1998	*The White Beach: New & Selected Poems 1960-1998*	Leland Bardwell
	Wednesday: Selected Poems 1966-1997	Marvin Bell
	When It Came Time	Jeri McCormick
	Unlegendary Heroes	Mary O'Donnell
	Journey Backward	Tom O'Malley
	Crossings	Gwyn Parry
	After the Ball	Breda Sullivan
	Weathering	Ann Zell
1999	*The Portable Creative Writing Workshop*	Pat Boran
	The Puzzle-Heart	Louise C. Callaghan
	Story Hunger	Jerah Chadwick
	A Curb in Eden	Joseph Enzweiler
	Kerry On My Mind	Gabriel Fitzmaurice
	The Interior Act	Frank Golden
	Another Part of the Island	Michael Heffernan
	Defining Absence	John Hildebidle
	Falling into Monaghan	Gerard Hull
	Half-Day Warriors	John Kavanagh
	The White Page / An Bhileog Bhán: 20th Century Irish Women Poets	Joan McBreen
	Tenant	Máighréad Medbh
	All the Money in the World	John Menaghan
	Still Listening	Angela Patten
	Starting at Purgatory	Janice Fitzpatrick Simmons
	The Company of Children	James Simmons
	Split the Lark	R.T Smith
	Notes	Peter Van de Kamp
	Terebinthos	Gordon Walmsley
	Sharing Darwin	Sabine Wichert
2000	*The Getting of Vellum*	Catherine Byron
	The LightHouse	Gerard Donovan
	The Salmon Carol Ann Duffy	Carol Ann Duffy
	The Last Regatta	Maurice Harmon
	Gold Set Dancing	James Liddy
	Little River: New & Selected Poems	Linda McCarriston
	Touchwood	Áine Miller
	Curse of The Birds	Noel Monahan
	Autumn in the Alaska Range	Tom Sexton
	Iced Water	John Unrau
	Sandgames	Michèle Vassal
	The Crosses	Eamonn Wall

2007	*Ancestor Worship*	Michael S. Begnal
	That Morning Will Come: New & Selected	Seamus Cashman
	Breaking Hearts & Traffic Lights	Patrick Chapman
	Twenty-One Sonnets	Gabriel Fitzmaurice
	Anatomy of a Love Affair	Mélanie Francès
	The Sky Road	Mark Granier
	Poems to My Wife and Other Women	Thomas Krampf
	The Boy in the Ring	Dave Lordan
	Digging Up the Boys	Laura Lundgren Smith
	Freshly Rooted	Emily Wall
2008	*Ground Forces*	Paul Allen
	Object Found	Gustáv Báger
	Conflicted Light	J.P. Dancing Bear
	Catastrophic Chords	Marck L. Beggs
	Thornfield: Poems by the Thornfield Poets	Andrew Carpenter, editor
	Catching the Light: Views & Interviews	Gerald Dawe
	Big Pink Umbrella	Susan Millar DuMars
	Tethered to the Earth	Tyler Farrell
	In Daily Accord	Frank Golden
	The Mischievous Boy and other poems	Maurice Harmon
	To Keep the Light Burning	Anne Le Marquand Hartigan
	The Odor of Sanctity	Michael Heffernan
	Finding the Gossamer	Patrick Hicks
	Time Gentlemen, Please	Kevin Higgins
	Signs Translations	John Hildebidle
	Lost in the Gaeltacht	Caroline Lynch
	Polishing the Evidence	Cecilia McGovern
	Lost Republics	Alan Jude Moore
	Green	Patrick Moran
	A Father's Day	Pete Mullineaux
	The Kiss: New & Selected Poems	Ulick O'Connor
	Torching the Brown River	Lorna Shaughnessy
	Seaway: New & Selected Poems	Todd Swift
	In Train	Peter van de Kamp
	A Tour of Your Country	Eamonn Wall
2009	*The Essential Guide to Flight*	Celeste Augé
	Truckers' Moll	Rosemary Canavan
	Falling Body	David Cavanagh
	Long Division	Andrea Cohen
	Are you ready?	John Corless
	Cohort	Philip Fried
	Downstate	David Gardiner
	Standing in the Pizzicato Rain	Georgina Eddison
	At Grattan Road	Gerard Hanberry
	Museum Crows	Ron Houchin
	Leaf, Sunlight, Asphalt	Ben Howard
	Poetry: Reading it, Writing it, Publishing it	Jessie Lendennie
	The Full Shilling	James Liddy

Index by Author

ABOUT SALMON POETRY

Salmon Poetry, taking its name from the Salmon of Knowledge in Celtic mythology, was established in 1981 as an alternative voice in Irish literature. *The Salmon*, a journal of poetry and prose was a flagship for writers in the west of Ireland, and Salmon's first books, *Gonella* by Eva Bourke and *Goddess on the Mervue Bus* by Rita Ann Higgins broke new ground for women poets. Since then almost 500 volumes of poetry have been produced, and Salmon has become one of the most important publishers in the Irish literary world. By specialising in the promotion of new poets, particularly women poets, Salmon has enriched Irish literary publishing. In recent years Salmon has developed a cross-cultural, international literary dialogue... "broadening the parameter of Irish literature by opening up to other cultures and by urging new perspectives on established traditions. That enviable balance of focus and ranginess is a rare and instructive achievement" ('Opening up to Other Cultures', *Poetry Ireland Review* 54, Kathleen McCracken. Originally based in Galway city, Salmon moved to County Clare in 1995. The day to day running of Salmon is undertaken by founder & editor Jessie Lendennie and designer & book production manager Siobhán Hutson, who has worked with Salmon since 1991.

Salmon Poetry has contributed enormously to making poetry a popular and regular shopping commodity.   BOOKS IRELAND

As a major publisher of poetry, Salmon has nurtured the talents of both new and emerging poets and its publications have been consistently exciting and varied.
SEAMUS HOSEY, RTE Radio

Salmon has brought out collections by some of the most stimulating and innovative of writers and has worked particularly hard to develop an international list and to profile Irish poets abroad.

AILBHE SMYTH
Director of Women's Studies, University College, Dublin

Salmon's unique profile grows from the diversity of the work it publishes... most notably, Salmon is distinguished by the number of women on its list.
PATRICIA B. HABERSTROH, Irish Literary Supplement

Salmon Poetry has, as no other Irish publisher, crossed the borders of nation, gender, age and class.

VICTOR LUFTIG
Yale University, "Salmon Publishing: A Model for Ireland's Future"

ABOUT THE EDITOR

JESSIE LENDENNIE was born in Arkansas, USA. After years of travel, she settled in Ireland in 1981. Her publications include a book-length prose poem *Daughter* (1988), reprinted as *Daughter and Other Poems* in 2001 and *Walking Here* (2011). She complied and edited: *Salmon: A Journey in Poetry, 1981-2007*; *Poetry: Reading it, Writing It, Publishing It* (2009); *Dogs Singing: A Tribute Anthology* (2010); and, *Even The Daybreak: 35 Years of Salmon Poetry* (2016). She is co-founder (1981) and Managing Director of Salmon Poetry. Her poems, essays and articles have been widely published and she has given numerous readings, lectures and writing courses in Ireland and abroad, including Yale University; Rutgers University; The Irish Embassy, Washington D.C; The University of Alaska, Fairbanks and Anchorage; MIT, Boston; The Loft, Minneapolis, MN; Café Teatre, Copenhagen, Denmark; the University of Arkansas, Fayetteville; The Irish American Cultural Centre, Chicago and The Bowery Poetry Club, New York City. She is currently working on a memoir.